Dewey's Ethical Thought

Dewey's Ethical Thought

Jennifer Welchman

CORNELL UNIVERSITY PRESS · ITHACA AND LONDON

First published 1995 by Cornell University Press.

Library of Congress Cataloging-in-Publication Data

Welchman, Jennifer.
    Dewey's ethical thought / Jennifer Welchman.
        p.   cm.
    ISBN 0-8014-2729-0 (alk. paper)
    1. Dewey, John, 1859-1952.   2. Ethics.   3. Pragmatism.   I. Title.
    B945.D4W45   1995
    171'.2—dc20   94-40873

Printed in the United States of America

⊗ The paper in this book meets the minimum requirements
of the American National Standard for Information Sciences—
Permanence of Paper for Printed Library Materials, ANSI Z39.48-1984.

Contents

Acknowledgments

I am grateful for the help and advice I have received, along the way, from friends, colleagues, former professors, and family. Chief among these are J. B. Schneewind and Susan Wolf, my advisers on the project from which this book originated, and Andrew J. Reck and John J. McDermott, whose suggestions for expansion and revision of the original manuscript I have tried to follow. Ralph Sleeper, J. E. Tiles, Dennis Biggie, and my husband, Robert Smith, read and provided comments on earlier versions of portions of the text.

This book is dedicated to Elly Toop.

J. W.

A Note on Abbreviations

All references to the published papers, reviews, addresses, and books of John Dewey are to the following collections of his works and employ the abbreviations listed:

EW   *The Early Works: 1882–1898.* 5 vols. Edited by Jo Ann Boydston. Carbondale: Southern Illinois University Press, 1967–1972.

MW   *The Middle Works: 1899–1924.* 15 vols. Edited by Jo Ann Boydston. Carbondale: Southern Illinois University Press, 1976–1983.

LW   *The Later Works: 1925–1953.* 16 vols. Edited by Jo Ann Boydston. Carbondale: Southern Illinois University Press, 1981–1991.

Introduction

In his foreword to the 1930 Modern Library edition of *Human Nature and Conduct*, Dewey wrote: "In the eighteenth century, the word Morals was used in English literature with a meaning of broad sweep. It included all the subjects of distinctly humane import, all of the social disciplines as far as they are intimately connected with the life of man and as they bear upon the interests of humanity. . . . Were it not for one consideration, [this] volume might be said to be an essay in continuing the tradition of David Hume."[1] To Anglo-American moral philosophers trained during or after the Second World War, these remarks summed up precisely what was wrong with Dewey's ethics. Dewey had never learned to abandon the eighteenth-century empiricist belief that ethical theory could be raised to the status of a natural science. Like Hume, Dewey believed that ethics was a practical science of community organization, specifically of the engineering of cooperation under conditions of moderate scarcity and limited generosity, for enhancing human flourishing. And like Hume again, Dewey believed that solutions to the problems of promoting social cooperation were to be found in the study of human nature. Dewey refused to follow the 'linguistic turn' taken by twentieth-century English-language philosophy. And he refused to accept the view that, as a young R. M. Hare put it, moral philosophy was nothing but "the logical study of the language of morals."[2] Contemporary ethical philosophy's retreat from the study of human nature and social life into the analysis and formalization of common-sense moral ideas or intuitions was only beginning in 1922, when the first edition of *Human Nature and Conduct* appeared. But already Dewey was almost bitter in his condemnation of the trend, arguing: "The neglect of sciences that deal specifically with facts of the natural and social environment leads to a side-tracking of moral forces into an unreal privacy of an unreal self. . . . It is impossible to say how much of the unnecessary slavery of the world is due to the conception that moral issues can be

1. John Dewey, foreword to the Modern Library edition, *Human Nature and Conduct*, MW 14:228.
2. R. M. Hare, *The Language of Morals* (Oxford: Oxford University Press, [1952] 1964), p. i.

settled within conscience or human sentiment apart from consistent study of facts and application of specific knowledge in industry, law and politics."[3]

Dewey imagined that his one significant divergence from Hume's approach to morality was the rejection of Hume's atomistic individualism in favor of a more Hegelian understanding of the relation of individuals to their societies. His analytically trained critics thought otherwise. If Dewey was proposing to construct a natural science of ethics, then he must be violating Hume's dictum that you cannot derive an 'ought' from an 'is.' Normative conclusions about conduct and character cannot be derived from purely descriptive premises. Psychology, sociology, and the other social sciences upon which Dewey proposed to base ethical inquiry yield purely descriptive conclusions. Thus not only was Dewey's conception of moral philosophy hopelessly outdated; it rested upon a fallacy.

Dewey would have begged to differ. His naturalistic ethics was not committed to the possibility of deriving evaluative conclusions from purely descriptive premises. Dewey never held that this was possible, nor did he consider it necessary. All that is necessary, according to Dewey, is to reject the simplistic characterization of scientific inquiry as 'purely descriptive.' It is not true that scientific investigation neither constructs nor yields evaluative statements. Scientific investigation is something people do, an activity governed by its own rules of procedure. It is a project of constructing descriptions, predictions, and explanations in accordance with those rules: rules governing what shall count as evidence for the correctness of a prediction, how disputes about descriptions should be resolved, which explanations should be adopted and acted upon, and so forth. Thus scientists can, on the basis of those rules, not only derive descriptions of the components of some complex phenomenon from their data; they can also derive prescriptions about what they ought to believe about the phenomenon and about how they ought to behave with regard to it in future.

A natural science of ethics will necessarily adopt analogous methodological (i.e., normative) principles. Thus it will be the case that from their investigations of what people naturally do want, approve, disapprove, think right or wrong or obligatory, ethical theorists can formulate general descriptions and predictions regarding these phenomena. Moreover, as we shall see, they can also generate prescriptions about what

3. *Human Nature and Conduct*, MW 14:10.

they ought to believe regarding the phenomena of wanting, approving, disapproving, and being obliged, and about how they ought to conduct themselves with regard to these phenomena in future.

Such a theory of ethics could in fact tell us what we ought to believe about our own and others' conduct and what sorts of reasons for action we ought to consider compelling—provided, of course, that we first accepted its procedural rules. Lacking such a commitment to the practice of rational, scientific inquiry into morals, we would have no obligation to accept its conclusions as justified. Additionally, the adequacy of our conclusions would be conditional upon the correctness of the information about human nature, desire, and dispositions with which we have to work. What at one moment may be a rationally acceptable and scientifically warranted conclusion may in the next moment prove just the reverse. Moral truth, like scientific truth, would be a matter of degree.

Dewey's moral philosophy, in particular his thesis that the methods of the natural sciences could fruitfully be applied to ethics, generated widespread interest (if not agreement) in the English-speaking philosophical community. The success of his moral, logical, and epistemological theories in the first decades of this century established Dewey as preeminent among living American philosophers. He enjoyed a national reputation and prestige almost unimaginable to American philosophers today. But by the time of his death in 1952, his philosophy had gone into an eclipse.

Dewey's loss of popularity and influence in Anglo-American thought stemmed from several sources. One was his failure to adopt the language and techniques of the newly developed mathematical logic pioneered by Gottlob Frege, Bertrand Russell, and A. N. Whitehead. In comparison with the newer logic, Dewey's own language and techniques soon came to seem hopelessly imprecise. A second was his refusal, noted above, to follow contemporary philosophy's linguistic turn. While younger Anglo-American philosophers were looking to the nature and function of linguistic systems to explicate the nature of meaning, Dewey persisted in looking to the behavior that gives rise to meaning and the functions of that behavior in sustaining an agent in a social environment. A third was a combined effect of the first and second: Dewey's work became increasingly incomprehensible to students of the newer logic, epistemology, and theory of language. As a result, his reasons for believing that the impossibility of deriving an 'ought' from an 'is' does not mean that a natural science of conduct is impossible or that the notion of ethical experimentation is incoherent likewise became increasingly incomprehensible.

After the Second World War, Dewey's work began to look isolated from the mainstream of twentieth-century philosophy and, eventually, irrelevant to its development. In histories of twentieth-century philosophy written after his death, Dewey's instrumentalism, and the related theories of his fellow pragmatists William James and Charles S. Peirce, began to be relegated to footnotes or treated as a survival of fundamentally nineteenth-century doctrines.[4]

Very recently, the status of Dewey's philosophy has begun to change. Much of the credit must be given to Richard Rorty's *Philosophy and the Mirror of Nature* in which Rorty persuasively argued that Dewey's major works anticipated important criticisms now widely advanced against the analytic tradition in contemporary philosophy to which the work of Frege, Russell, and the Vienna Circle had given rise.[5] Independent of Rorty's efforts, a simultaneous revival of interest in pragmatic theories of truth has developed in the areas of philosophy of science and epistemology. Together these sources have worked to produce a reevaluation of Dewey's role in twentieth-century philosophy, evidenced by the thin but steady stream of articles, papers, and monographs on Dewey's epistemology and metaphysics which has since appeared.

To date, Dewey's moral philosophy has not experienced the same revival of interest. This is doubly regrettable. First, neglect of Dewey's work in this area hampers our understanding of the development of his instrumentalist epistemology and naturalistic metaphysics. Important transitions in his thinking in these areas were often preceded and colored by shifts in his ethics. Second, recent interest in naturalizing ethics has encouraged a reexamination of past theories as possible sources for future inquiry. If Dewey's ethics continues to be neglected, the opportunity to exploit what is arguably the most original, systematic naturalistic moral theory produced in this century will be missed.

Critical scrutiny of Dewey's ethics has unfortunately been hindered by the (at times) very considerable difficulty of understanding what

4. This has particularly been true of histories by English philosophers. Some ignore pragmatist ethics entirely. See, e.g., G. J. Warnock, *Contemporary Moral Philosophy* (New York: St. Martin's Press, 1967); W. D. Hudson, *A Century of Moral Philosophy* (New York: St. Martin's Press, 1980). Others treat it as merely of historical importance to the work of other American philosophers. See, e.g., Mary Warnock, *Ethics since 1900*, 2nd ed. (London: Oxford University Press, 1978). Some American histories have imitated the British examples. See, e.g., George C. Kerner, *The Revolution in Ethics* (New York: Oxford University Press, 1966).

5. Richard Rorty, *Philosophy and the Mirror of Nature* (Princeton: Princeton University Press, 1979).

Dewey is trying to say. First, Dewey's prose is notoriously poor.[6] Second, Dewey and the modern reader are often 'divided by a common language.' Dewey began his career in 1884 as an absolute idealist who by his own account "drifted away from Hegelianism in the next fifteen years: the term 'drifting' [expressing] the slow, and for a long time, imperceptible character of the movement."[7] In those fifteen years, Dewey published his first two books on moral philosophy and helped found the famous Chicago school of functionalist psychology out of which important elements of his instrumentalism emerged. These texts are written in a style now unfamiliar, using a technical vocabulary so obsolete as to be at times unrecognizable as such.[8] But they cannot safely be ignored. These publications are crucial to our understanding of Dewey's mature moral philosophy, for it was in this period that Dewey developed the conceptions of scientific and moral judgment on which his later naturalist ethical theory was based.

Of all the impediments to understanding Dewey's transition from absolute idealism to pragmatism, possibly the greatest is the common failure to recognize the accomplishment Dewey's mature conception of scientific inquiry actually was. Although it has been noted that Dewey's interest in science played an important role in the development of his philosophy generally, and during his fifteen-year 'drift' specifically, it has too often been assumed that this role was merely destructive, that Dewey's faith in natural science gradually dissolved his belief in absolute idealism. What has not always been grasped is that the conceptions

6. Reading Dewey is always a strenuous affair—as one reader has put it, like "swimming through oatmeal" (Thomas Alexander, *John Dewey's Theory of Art, Experience, and Nature: The Horizons of Feeling* [Albany: State University of New York Press, 1987], p. xii). More famous is Justice Oliver Wendell Holmes's remark in reference to *Experience and Nature*: "So methought God would have spoken had he been inarticulate but keenly desirous to tell you how it was" (Mark DeWolf Howe, ed., *Holmes-Pollock Letters: The Correspondence of Mr. Justice Holmes and Sir Frederick Pollock, 1874–1932* [Cambridge: Harvard University Press, 1941], 2:287, quoted in Robert B. Westbrook, *John Dewey and American Democracy* [Ithaca: Cornell University Press, 1991], p. 341).

7. John Dewey, "From Absolutism to Experimentalism," *LW* 5:154.

8. To give just one example: it is not uncommon to find Dewey in the 1880s and early 1890s arguing the importance of making ethics, psychology, and/or philosophy 'experimental,' encouraging some to believe that he was already advocating the use of scientific procedures of experimentation in this period. Among absolute idealists, however, the term 'experimental' was often used as a metaphysically neutral synonym for 'empirical' (William James's avoidance of the label 'empiricist' in favor of 'pragmatist' and 'radical empiricist' arose from the same need to avoid empiricism's 'materialist' linkages). Consequently, it is more likely that Dewey was suggesting that philosophers of mind and morals pay close attention to human *experience* in these early texts than advocating what we now call 'experimentation.'

of 'science' and 'scientific method' often attributed to Dewey in the 1880s and the early 1890s are anachronisms: the products of his struggles to reform absolute idealism rather than their causes. To the young John Dewey, as we shall see, neo-Hegelian philosophy *was* science. The special physical sciences, for all their impressive technological offshoots, were to him simply defective realizations of the systematic understanding of the world which was Science. Because the understanding that his neo-Hegelian philosophy sought to achieve was the complete realization of the system of relations which organizes the universe and its constituents, and because, by contrast, the special sciences generated only fragmentary information about the universe, Dewey concluded that philosophy was not only a science—it was the ultimate science.

Such a conception of science was hardly likely to have undermined Dewey's faith in idealism. In fact, it did not. His allegiance to idealism was eroded by the contradictions Dewey could not resolve between its absolutist metaphysics and its functionalist accounts of logic, mind, and morality. William James's persuasive demonstration in *The Principles of Psychology* that functionalist accounts of mind, knowledge, and morals could be defended without appeal to an idealist metaphysics, bolstered by the influence of his colleagues at the University of Chicago, seems gradually to have convinced Dewey that he did not need idealism to save him from mechanistic materialism.[9] He was thus freed to reconsider his conceptions of science, philosophy, facts, and values.

After reworking these conceptions to his own satisfaction, Dewey not infrequently operated as if they were transparent to his audience. In order to make sense of his pragmatic writings, one must frequently go back to the publications of his 'transitional' period for explanations. This is especially true of his post-idealist moral philosophy. It is thus essential that Dewey's early work be read if his subsequent attempts to construct and defend a pragmatic 'science' of ethics are to be understood or fairly evaluated. A final determination of whether Dewey's ethical theory is of philosophical as well as historic interest cannot be made until it can once more be comprehended.

My own opinion is that Dewey's moral philosophy is of philosophical interest and that his work is a source that proponents of naturalistic ethics would do well to investigate. Indeed, it may even prove that his work is of greatest value for what now seems its most hopelessly out-

9. William James, *The Principles of Psychology*, 3 vols. (Cambridge: Harvard University Press, 1981).

dated feature: his attempts to elevate ethics to the status of a natural science. That Dewey should have been interested in making ethics scientific is readily understandable given the historical context of his career. He entered the profession at a time when the academic discipline of philosophy was under threat, its claim to the mental and moral sciences disputed by the emerging human and social sciences of psychology, physiology, anthropology, and sociology. Philosophers concerned to defend their discipline were obliged to find ways of reconciling science and philosophy, either by demonstrating the existence of a subject matter for philosophy beyond the ken of physical science or by demonstrating the scientific legitimacy of philosophical theorizing.

Today, philosophers are not similarly called upon to justify their inclusion in institutions of higher learning. A knowledge of philosophical classics has come to be accepted as one of the hallmarks of a well-rounded education. Unfortunately, like other such hallmarks—classical languages, for example—philosophy is commonly thought to serve little or no other purpose. The relevance to contemporary life of philosophical theorizing is widely regarded as questionable at best. Of course, the study of philosophy is credited with sharpening the critical skills that must be brought to bear on our moral and social problems, but the same can be said of any number of other disciplines. Besides acquaintance with its peculiar literature, it is unclear whether philosophy has a unique contribution to make to contemporary life and culture that could be called upon to justify its continuance.

Richard Rorty sees this outcome of philosophy's struggle to maintain its position in the modern university as desirable and credits Dewey in part with its accomplishment. He writes:

> Dewey thought that if he could break down this notion, if scientific inquiry could be seen as adapting and coping rather than copying [reality], the continuity between science, morals, and art would become apparent. . . .
>
> Finally we might move . . . to the realization that philosophers' criticisms of culture are not more "scientific," more "fundamental," or more "deep" than those of labor leaders, literary critics, retired statesmen, or sculptors. . . . Philosophers could be seen as people who work with the history of philosophy and the contemporary effects of those ideas called 'philosophic' upon the rest of the culture—the remnants of past attempts to describe the "generic traits of existence."[10]

10. Richard Rorty, "Dewey's Metaphysics," in *New Studies in the Philosophy of John Dewey*, ed. Steven M. Cahn (Hanover: University Press of New England, 1977), pp. 70–71.

Yet as Rorty himself notes, "Dewey sometimes described philosophy as the criticism of culture, but he was never quite content to think of himself as a kibitzer or a therapist or an intellectual historian."[11] Dewey did indeed hope that the dissolution of sharp distinctions between knowing and doing, between science, art, and morals, would transform the role of the philosopher. But he would have been profoundly disappointed to learn that the effect of his efforts was to support contemporary Anglo-American philosophy's retreat from the world into intellectual history and cultural kibitzing. To Dewey, questions about the design of the institutions and practices of public and private life, systems of distributing benefits and burdens, codes of criminal justice, and the like are as 'objective' as are questions about the design of buildings and bridges, their internal distributions of stresses and supports, the interactions of their materials and the surrounding environment. We recognize that to make decisions about the design and construction of buildings and bridges without first scientifically examining sites, materials, and the relative merits of given structures for the purposes intended is liable to lead to disaster. Dewey wanted people to recognize that the same is true of the decisions we make about the design and construction of social institutions. If disasters are to be avoided, Dewey thought, some group must serve as brinksmen, operating at the margin between social scientists and the communities they serve, as, for example, research engineers do between materials scientists and the communities they serve. This role he thought philosophers uniquely qualified to play.

Philosophy, as Dewey wanted it practiced, would be a more interdisciplinary affair than it now is. Moral philosophers, for instance, would probably have to be acquainted with at least the rudiments of sociology, demography, economics, and psychology, to be the effective participants in the formation of social policies that Dewey envisioned. They would require more and deeper knowledge of the world than they have recently been expected to possess. It is hard to see how this could be a bad thing. But even if we reject Dewey's solution to the question of what role moral philosophers should try to play in an era shaped by experimental science and the technological revolutions that have followed in its wake, the question remains. I believe Dewey's work offers us valuable material for the construction of our own responses.

I am not in a position to prove my belief that Dewey's ethical theory is

11. Ibid., p. 46.

of philosophic as well as historical interest. The only evidence that can be offered to show that a theory is of philosophical interest is that philosophers do take an interest in and use that theory. My opinion would be better stated as a prediction: could philosophers, especially those interested in naturalizing ethics, readily understand Dewey's moral philosophy, they would find it of philosophic interest. This book is an attempt to bring about a necessary condition for my prediction coming true.

The book is divided into two parts. Part I covers the development of Dewey's moral philosophy from 1884 through 1894, the year in which his last idealist ethical treatise was published. Part II examines Dewey's instrumentalist theory of judgment and the pragmatic ethics he based upon it through the publication of *Human Nature and Conduct* in 1922. Though this work does not represent the end of the evolution of his thinking either about the nature of value or about the social and political implications of his conceptions of human values, Dewey was to remain unwaveringly committed to the essentials of the ethical theory he had worked out by 1922. Thus *Human Nature and Conduct* marks the end of an important phase in the development of his thought.

In Chapters 1 and 2, I examine the sources and nature of Dewey's early conceptions of philosophy, science, and values, relating them to the views of contemporary idealists such as T. H. Green, F. H. Bradley, and G. S. Morris, on whose texts Dewey drew and with whom his earliest important philosophical disputes were conducted. In Chapters 3 and 4, I discuss Dewey's first two ethics texts (1891, 1894). In each he sought to collapse the popular distinction between natural scientific and philosophic approaches to human life through the application of Hegelian conceptions of both. In the process, Dewey made radical revisions to his idealist metaphysics, theory of mind, and epistemology but did not abandon his belief that consciousness is both universal and the material of the universe. In Chapter 5, I argue that collaboration with experimental psychologists at the University of Chicago in 1894–1903 led to a crucial reformulation of Dewey's conception of science, which undermined his remaining commitments to absolute idealism by making the postulation of a universal consciousness unnecessary for the explanation of human knowledge of the world. By 1902, Dewey had abandoned his earlier idealist notions for instrumentalism and had begun to construct new arguments for reconciling science and ethics. In Chapter 6, I explicate and defend the reconciliation Dewey achieved through the use of his new instrumentalist moral epistemology in his first, and arguably most important, pragmatic ethical treatise, the 1908 *Ethics* (coauthored with J. H. Tufts). In Chapter 7, I look at Dewey's responses to his contemporaries' worries about his ethical theory. In particular, I examine whether its fundamental principles were, as Dewey claimed, consistent with a liberal, egalitarian social philosophy.

Part I   Idealism: 1884–1894

⊰1⊱ Origins of Dewey's Idealism

It is more or less of a commonplace to speak of the crisis which has been caused by the progress of the natural sciences in the past few centuries. . . . This effect of modern science has, it is notorious, set the main problems for modern philosophy. How is science to be accepted and yet the realm of values to be conserved? This question forms the philosophical version of the popular conflict of science and religion.

The Quest for Certainty

J ohn Dewey's historical sketch of Western philosophy, *The Quest for Certainty*, like most philosophers' histories of their own discipline, is more revealing about the sources, interests, and idées fixes of its author than of the discipline of which he writes.[1] And so it has been natural to suspect that the "crisis" Dewey describes as the driving force behind the development of modern Western philosophy was probably the driving force in Dewey's own development—in particular, the development of his pragmatic, value-friendly conceptions of science, knowledge, and judgment.

The circumstances of Dewey's own philosophical training seem to confirm that suspicion. When Dewey arrived at Johns Hopkins University to take up his graduate studies in 1882, a 'crisis' in the direction of the Department of Philosophy already existed. G. S. Morris, a theistic idealist, and G. Stanley Hall, a Darwinian empiricist, were both holders of half-year appointments in philosophy and thus in competition for the same philosophy chair through the period Dewey was in attendance (1882–84).[2] Whether Dewey liked it or not, the crisis between science

1. See John Dewey, *The Quest for Certainty* (1929), LW 4.
2. A third member of the department, C. S. Peirce, had also been in competition but was disqualified from serious consideration on grounds of character. See, e.g., Hugh Hawkins, *Pioneer: A History of the Johns Hopkins University, 1874–1889* (Ithaca: Cornell University Press, 1960), pp. 195–97.

and values was thrust upon him from the outset of his professional career.

Because Dewey enthusiastically endorsed both the theistic form of absolute idealism professed by Morris and the 'new psychology' (physiological psychology) imported from Germany by Hall, his early philosophy has widely been read as an unhappy attempt to merge Hall's scientism with Morris's theistic idealism. This project Dewey is supposed to have abandoned in the mid-1890s, when the impossibility of success had at last sunk in. So, for example, in his biography, *Young John Dewey*, Neil Coughlan interprets Dewey in the 1880s as "torn between Morris and Hall, between his loyalties and his nascent ambitions," torn because as Coughlan sees it, "science for [Dewey] was Hall's experimental psychology, and theistic philosophy was Morris's Hegelianism. Bringing the one into a genuinely sustaining relationship with the other looked to be impossible."[3] In this respect at least, Coughlan is in agreement with Dewey's earlier biographers George Dykhuizen and Morton G. White.[4] Dykhuizen sees Dewey's graduate and early postgraduate philosophy as strained by the respective pulls of "Neo-Hegelianism and the new psychology," and "the problem of bringing the two together—a problem that was to engage his very best efforts over the next few years."[5] And White specifically identifies two of Dewey's 1884 articles as evidence of the respective pulls of Morris and Hall: "Kant and Philosophic Method" and "The New Psychology."[6] White remarks, "The first was an expression of his idealism, the second an eloquent appraisal of the latest developments in psychology. The first testified his allegiance to Morris, while the second aligned him with Hall."[7] But although the competition between Hall and Morris did in a sense enact a wider "crisis" in contemporary philosophy, it is unlikely that Dewey would have experienced the crisis as personal or as a choice between science and religious or moral values. His crisis was professional: had scientific progress rendered his chosen career obsolete?

Because Anglo-American neo-Hegelianism is typically recalled, if recalled at all, primarily for its defense of theistic metaphysics and Chris-

3. Neil Coughlan, *Young John Dewey* (Chicago: University of Chicago Press, 1975), p. 49.

4. See George Dykhuizen, *The Life and Mind of John Dewey* (Carbondale: Southern Illinois University Press, 1973), and Morton G. White, *The Origin of Dewey's Instrumentalism* (New York: Octagon, 1964).

5. Dykhuizen, *Life and Mind of John Dewey*, p. 38.

6. See John Dewey, "Kant and Philosophic Method," *EW* 1:34–47; and "The New Psychology," *EW* 1:48–60.

7. White, *Origin of Dewey's Instrumentalism*, p. 34.

tian virtues, it is often assumed that to the university's president, Daniel Coit Gilman, and board of trustees Morris would have represented "Religion" in competition with Hall as the representative of "Science." But in fact, neo-Hegelianism was not simply Christian apologia; it was a philosophical program offering radical analyses of epistemology, theory of mind, morals, aesthetics, and metaphysics. Furthermore, Morris himself was not simply a theist, and his philosophical works are no more limited to Christian apologetics than Hall's were free of them. If the choice Morris and Hall represented for Gilman had been between Science and Religion, Hall would not have been given the chair. No university president in the 1880s could afford to choose 'science' over 'religion,' least of all Gilman, who needed to placate a local community still scandalized by T. H. Huxley's address at the university's founding. Hall could not have been a serious candidate if Gilman had not been personally assured that Hall was both friendly to religion and willing to defend theistic interpretations of mind and morals against 'materialist' and agnostic attacks.[8]

Hall himself described the competition as having been between two varieties of philosophy, "my more experimental type" versus Morris's "history of philosophy."[9] But it would probably be more correct to describe the situation as a competition between science and philosophy. Since the university's need for instruction in both 'facts' and 'values' could be provided for simultaneously by Hall (who held a degree in divinity), 'philosophy' was a luxury Gilman could do without.[10]

For Dewey, then, the crisis the competition represented was professional: inductive science (girded by religion) was threatening to render the discipline of philosophy extinct. As he remarks in *The Quest for Certainty*, "as long as the view obtained that nature itself is truly known by the same rational method [as philosophy employs]. . . . [t]here was no break between philosophy and genuine science—or what was conceived to be such. In fact, there was not even a distinction; there were simply various branches of philosophy, metaphysical, logical, natural,

---

8. See Hawkins, *Pioneer*, chap. 11. On the need to find a candidate for the philosophy chair of sufficient orthodoxy to quell local concerns over Huxley's appearance, see p. 189 n. 9.

9. Ibid., p. 201.

10. Hall had evidently given assurances to Gilman on his willingness to cultivate a rapprochement with religion and its local representatives. See Dorothy Ross, *G. Stanley Hall: The Psychologist as Prophet* (Chicago: University of Chicago Press, 1972), chap. 8, and Hawkins, *Pioneer*, pp. 194 and 202.

moral, etc., in a descending scale of demonstrative certainty."[11] But by the 1880s, there had not only been a 'break'; there had been a permanent rupture. Inanimate nature had long since been ceded to the inductive sciences. The rapid progress of chemistry and the biological sciences in the nineteenth century suggested that philosophy's remaining territory—the mental and moral sciences—ought to be ceded as well. Whether philosophy could or should continue to exist as an independent discipline was thus a matter of dispute.

Since Dewey was not personally interested in making a career in either inductive psychology or anthropology, he would have had little reason to expect that his nascent career ambitions would be well served by promoting Hall's vision of philosophy or reconciling it with Morris's in his own philosophical work. He would instead have had good professional reasons for siding with Morris and against Hall, even had he not found Morris's idealist philosophy appealing. Gratitude or personal loyalty to Hall himself might nevertheless have given Dewey reason to attempt the merger attributed to him—if, in fact, he ever felt any. There is no evidence that he did. Neither his own 1930 autobiographical essay, "From Absolutism to Experimentalism," nor his daughter Jane's "Biography of John Dewey," drawn from Dewey's notes,[12] supports the suggestion that he felt indebted to Hall personally or philosophically.

The only grounds for supposing that Hall did exert a continuing influence on Dewey's philosophy of the 1880s and 1890s, an influence distorting and ultimately undermining his faith in absolute idealism, appears to be Dewey's enthusiasm for the new physiological psychology. His knowledge of the new German psychological research was due to Hall. Nevertheless, Dewey's continuing interest in the subject could reasonably be attributed to the influence of Hall only if such an interest could not have been sustained by the neo-Hegelian approach to human psychology Dewey had learned from Morris and if Dewey's views on the nature or significance of the new psychology were substantially similar to Hall's. Neither appears to be the case.

First, absolute idealism was not inherently antithetical to physiological research into human mental life. What absolute idealists, Morris among them, opposed was the thesis that *all* psychological phenomena are reducible to physical phenomena and the implication that a nonem-

11. *Quest for Certainty, LW* 4:22.
12. See John Dewey, "From Absolutism to Experimentalism" (1930), *LW* 5:147–60, and Jane Dewey, "Biography of John Dewey," in *The Philosophy of John Dewey*, ed. Paul Arthur Schlipp (Evanston: Northwestern University Press, 1939), pp. 3–45.

pirical, philosophical 'science' of mind or morals has no unique contribution to make to these subjects. This opposition Dewey shared well into the 1890s. Second, Dewey's view of the nature and significance of physiological investigations of mind does not resemble Hall's. As we shall see, Dewey's conceptions of science, scientific method, and scientific psychology were vehemently opposed to Hall's. Dewey's reconciliation of philosophical and physiological sciences of mind and morals in the 1880s and early 1890s owed more to Morris than to Hall, and more to Hegel than to either.

BACKGROUND OF DEWEY'S IDEALISM

Dewey's adoption of neo-Hegelianism as a graduate student is often explained in psychobiographical terms. The approach is invited by Dewey's own description of his encounter with Hegelian thought as "an immense release, a liberation" from "divisions and separations that were . . . a heritage of New England culture, divisions by way of isolation of self from the world, of soul from body, of nature from God." Hegelian thought appealed to Dewey because it "supplied a demand for unification that was doubtless an intense emotional craving, and yet was a hunger only an intellectualized subject-matter could satisfy." But it would be a mistake to imagine that the attraction of neo-Hegelianism was purely emotional. As Dewey further remarks, Anglo-American absolute idealism was "the vital and constructive [movement] in philosophy"[13] in the latter half of the nineteenth century, one that could justifiably claim to be working on the cutting edge.

   The crisis of confidence in philosophy that played itself out so theatrically at Johns Hopkins University in the early 1880s was by no means a provincial matter. Nineteenth-century fascination with inductive science and its offshoots created an insatiable demand for books, journals, lectures, and instruction in the physical sciences in this period. Demand for philosophical treatments of the same topics did not rise in proportion. In colleges and universities throughout the English-speaking world, there was increasing pressure on academic institutions to shift resources from the 'unscientific' disciplines such as philosophy to the rapidly expanding body of 'scientific' disciplines. The crisis for philosophy was particularly acute in the universities and colleges of the United States, where philosophy had never been firmly established in the cur-

13. "From Absolutism to Experimentalism," pp. 153, 152.

riculum and the most desirable credential any philosopher could have was still a degree in divinity. As British idealist T. H. Green ruefully remarked, in an atmosphere of such hostility to traditional philosophy, "with such opinion in the air all around him, it must be with much misgiving that one who has no prophetic utterance to offer in regard to conduct, but who still believes in the necessity of a philosophy of morals which no adaptation of natural science can supply, undertakes to make good his position."[14]

Of the prevailing schools of thought, only absolute idealism was interested in or capable of mounting a creditable case for the continuing viability of philosophy as a vehicle of inquiry. The alternatives—empiricism and intuitionism—lacked the will, the credibility, or both. For example, positivism and (Spencerian) evolutionary empiricism each argued for the reconstitution of philosophy as the theory of science and scientific reasoning and for the abandonment of speculative and other traditional branches of philosophy that exceeded the boundaries of epistemology of science. Other empiricists of a more skeptical bent had no use for even this attenuated conception of philosophy. Hall was probably speaking in jest when he once described philosophical epistemologists as suffering from a "morbid neurosis" so severe that "these so-called epistemological vagaries [are] in some forms hardly less than the physiological equivalents of self-abuse."[15] But what he said, others, equally impatient with philosophers' inability to achieve consensus, must certainly have been thinking.

Intuitionists, usually but not exclusively allied to the school of 'Scottish' philosophy, were more favorably inclined toward the retention of philosophy as the chief exponent of the mental and moral sciences. But the critical attacks of more skeptical empiricists against intuitionist theories of knowledge and morals, bolstered by the implications of Darwinism, had left this school largely discredited in philosophically minded circles by the second half of the nineteenth century.

Thus the field was left clear for absolute idealism to promote and defend its conception of philosophy as the only viable game in town. It was no accident that absolute idealism's abrupt rise to prominence among Anglo-American philosophers in the second half of the nineteenth century coincided with the growing threat to philosophy's posi-•

---

14. T. H. Green, *Prolegomena to Ethics*, 3d ed., ed. A. C. Bradley (Oxford: Clarendon Press, 1890), p. 3. The first edition appeared in 1883.

15. Ross, *G. Stanley Hall*, p. 254. Hall's incomprehension of Josiah Royce's anger over the remark suggests that Hall was speaking at least partly in jest.

tion within academia. Nor was it an accident that absolute idealism began its equally abrupt fall from favor after the turn of the century just as philosophy's status as a discipline was becoming secure once more. To Dewey and his contemporaries, absolute idealism's appeal was not only emotional but also intellectual and professional: it offered a coherent body of theory and research together with a persuasive case for believing that philosophical research could make original contributions to the mental and moral sciences without collapsing into a branch of the natural sciences.

To understand the conceptions of philosophy, science, and value that were to drive Dewey's philosophical development, we must first understand the conceptions from which he started, conceptions supplied by his mentor, Morris, and other idealist sources. In theory, Anglo-American absolute idealism, like most philosophical movements, was unified by its members' commitment to a shared set of principles and conceptions. In practice, absolute idealism, like most philosophical movements, was unified by its members' commitment to the overthrow of the shared principles and conceptions of rival schools of thought. Absolute idealism was unusual only in the degree of the practical consensus it achieved. Whatever the personal views of a given idealist about the nature of the absolute mind, the human mind, or the physical universe, he or she was bound to attack substantially the same empiricist and materialist doctrines and in substantially the same ways as other idealists.

Absolute idealism's most vehement attacks focused on the empiricist contentions that (1) all knowledge is empirical and thus accessible by the means and methods of the natural sciences and (2) the mental and moral sciences must each be empirical natural sciences. So, for example, in Morris's 1882 defense of philosophy, "Philosophy and Its Specific Problems," the stalking horse is an unnamed German author said to contend that it should be "the task of a new generation to study philosophy not simply with the aid of the physical sciences, but through and in them alone—in short, to resolve philosophy into physical science."[16] In case we should suppose the view typical of German thought, Morris hastily assures us of its true origin and his proper target: "the wisdom of Britain's philosophic sages . . . from the time of Francis Bacon down to this day" (209), that is, those contemporary positivists and evolutionary empiricists who claimed Bacon as their patron saint and inspiration.

16. G. S. Morris, "Philosophy and Its Specific Problems," *Princeton Review* N.S. 9 (1882):208.

The preferred response to such charges was invariably to construct reductio ad absurdums upon the premises of empiricist epistemological arguments. Morris's paper again provides a typical example. He begins his rebuttal by accepting for the sake of argument that (1) "all science is physical science" and (2) all physical science is "of sensible phenomena and of nothing else. Its legitimate and only concern is to ascertain precisely what the phenomena are, and to point out the rules of their coexistence in space and of their sequence in time" (210, 211). He then argues that the two premises and their implications are contradictory. The unqualified claim that all science, all *knowing*, takes the form of inductive, physical science, is neither a claim about sensible phenomena nor confirmable by induction from empirical data available to us. In other words, an empiricist can know that all knowledge is knowledge of and about sensible phenomena only if some knowledge is not. Thus the empiricist account of knowledge is incoherent.

Nonskeptical forms of empiricism, especially evolutionism, peculiarly lent themselves to this sort of burlesquing. Morris and his fellow idealists took full advantage. In reply to evolutionists' assertions that empirical science proves the determination of human nature by natural forces, Morris happily pointed out that the conclusion was incompatible with the premises from which it was derived:

> Hume . . . but anticipated the now universal voice of physical science. . . . which honestly and honorably confesses the limitations of its true province, when it restricts this province to the field of sensible phenomena and . . . professes to find no reality of power or "force," but only phenomena of motion. For it force is an "abstraction," a convenient, and perhaps practically necessary "auxiliary," or working "idea," but not an object of scientific knowledge, not a scientific reality. It is not an object of sensible observation, it is not a "phenomenon," and if it makes its way into the armory of scientific ideas, it is . . . an interloper there.[17]

As far as Morris was concerned, the only consistent form of empiricism was Humean skepticism, a conclusion in which he delighted because he considered Hume's skeptical conclusions paradoxical and evidently absurd. He writes:

> The "empirical philosopher" first determines that all our knowledge or experience is strictly of a sensible nature. This means . . . that all that I know is

17. G. S. Morris, *British Thought and Thinkers* (Chicago: S. C. Griggs, 1880), p. 350.

rigorously confined to the consciousness of my own individual mental states or "feelings." The immediate inference then is that I have no knowledge, properly speaking, of the "external world" which my consciousness is popularly supposed to represent, nor of myself as a knowing agent. . . . I and the external world are, if we really exist at all, "*meta*-physical" entities. . . . The "belief" in our existence is indeed inexpugnable [*sic*], but it is wholly unaccountable, mysterious.[18]

Because he thought it ridiculous to think that we do not and cannot know that we and the world exist, Morris insists that our experience of the world is not wholly sensible.

Morris's conclusion invites the questions by what means our nonempirical experience is gained and whether and how philosophy can make sense of that experience in a way physical science cannot. The absolute idealist response is that we must reconsider our received notions of how ordinary 'perception' actually works. According to empiricist interpretations, 'perception' is a state of consciousness that arises from the collision of impenetrable, material objects. The content of a particular state of consciousness is determined by the 'impression' made upon the percipient's sense organs and nervous system by the colliding external object. As the object that gives rise to a state of consciousness internal to the percipient's mind is not itself internal to or immediately present to the percipient, the percipient can only guess as to the nature of the cause of its perceptions. Thus skepticism is the necessary conclusion of the interpretation of perception as a *mechanical* interaction.

But why assume the interaction is mechanical? Since this assumption cannot be used to explain how it is that we know we and the world exist, a new conception is needed. Specifically, we need a conception that can allow for the immediate presence of the objects of perception to the perceiving mind. As Morris put it, "the immediate lesson of the science of knowledge is that all true consciousness is self-consciousness, all knowledge self-knowledge, all experience self-experience. But then in order to recognize the substantive, objective truth of this, we have to revise and enlarge the individualistic conception of 'self.' "[19] In other words, if the world and the percipient are internal and immediately present to the percipient's mind or self, the percipient must be conceived as containing the universe within itself—an enlargement indeed!

According to absolute idealism, there is nothing absurd or unrealistic

18. Morris, "Philosophy and Its Specific Problems," p. 213.
19. Ibid., p. 227.

about readjusting our notions of ourselves in this way. The world and ourselves remain what they are. All that changes is the relation between them. We give up conceiving of the relation that perception establishes between its 'subject' and 'object' as a mechanical interaction of mutually exclusive entities and substitute a conception of an organic relation between the functionally distinct but mutually interdependent components of a single entity. Morris gives the following illustration. A naturalist can determine the identity both of an animal and of its environment from the examination of a single bone. Now the bone is in one sense a discrete component of the creature to which it belonged, functionally distinct from, and mechanically interacting with, the other bones and organs of their common owner. Yet at the same time, the bone and the other organs are all 'one flesh,' all constituents of one organism. The bone's identity, its character and characteristics, are determined by the whole of which it is a part. At the same time, the identity of the whole creature, its character and characteristics, is likewise determined (in part) by its possession of that particular bone. The relation of each to the other is 'internal' to or constitutive of each. Thus their relationship is different in kind from the 'external' and nonconstitutive relations that obtain between mechanically interacting bodies.

If we conceive of the subject and object of perception as organically related, then subject and object must be 'of one flesh,' mutually constitutive components of a larger whole. Continuing with his example of the bone, Morris writes:

> Now suppose the bone restored to its original place in the whole and living organism, and then endowed with the capacity of consciousness. . . . [T]he bone will be the immediate, empirical subject of consciousness, and the rest of the organism will be the direct or empirical object. Can we, now, suppose the subject to have true and complete consciousness of itself, unless this consciousness include the consciousness . . . of the whole organic structure which is implied in and revealed in itself? Can the "subject" bone have real consciousness of itself, unless it see itself, not merely . . . in itself, *qua* individual, but in its other, its so-called object, which, while numerically other than, is yet ideally and organically one with . . . the individual bone?[20]

A conscious bone might be conscious of itself and of its surroundings in either of two ways. It might be conscious of the physical/mechanical interactions occurring between itself and the surrounding organs as

20. Ibid., pp. 225–26.

each performs its own distinguishing function. Of course, if this were the bone's sole source of information about its surroundings, it would have to be skeptical of its capacity to know what its surroundings were or even whether they existed. But the bone has another means of acquaintance with its own external form and surroundings: the examination of its own consciousness. The bone's nature is one with the nature of the whole of which it is part, so that if the bone determines that it is, for example, certain of its own consciousness, reality, and material existence, then the same must be true of the whole in which it participates. The whole too must possess consciousness, reality, and material existence.

Since human percipients appear to know or be acquainted directly with truths about themselves and their external world that sensible perception could not provide, idealists argued that the logical conclusion was that human perception is not merely sensible. And if it is not merely sensible, then the conclusion that human beings are organically rather than merely mechanically related to their world is not wholly unreasonable. In Morris's words: "We must regard self as not only individual, but also universal or participating in—organically one with—the universal."[21] We find the stuff of the universe given or immediately present within us because we are of that stuff. Whatever is essentially true of it is, therefore, true of us, and vice versa.

Empiricists generally conceded that empirical methods of investigation were incapable of establishing the existence of the very subject matter to which those methods were intended to apply: matter and force. As their idealist rivals saw it, empiricists were also obliged to concede that their methods were incapable of establishing what must be established if inductive reasoning is to be fruitfully applied: that matter and force behave uniformly through changes in time or space. Philosophy thus complements the inductive physical sciences by providing the analysis and justification of the fundamental presuppositions physical scientists necessarily make. Specifically, philosophical inquiry explains how it is we do know that there is a real material world outside our minds, containing real forces, by appeal to the organic relations underlying the merely mechanical or chemical relations scientists study. Philosophy provides the intellectual underpinnings that allow physical science to get on with its own particular work.

The same relation obtains between philosophic and scientific method

21. Ibid., p. 227.

with regard to mental and moral phenomena. The organic relations that give rise to the mental and moral phenomena of our experience also give rise to physical, empirically observable phenomena. And to the extent that mechanical or other physical interactions play a role in mental and moral life and action, there is a role for empirical methods of inquiry. But that role is far more circumscribed than empirical psychologists have imagined.

To make their case, idealists employed critical strategies similar to those sketched above. A typical rebuttal of contemporary forms of psychophysical reductionism opened by granting, for the sake of argument, some reasonably representative set of premises supporting the conclusion that minds are merely material organs. For example, it might be granted for the sake of argument that human beings had evolved from lower animals; that there exist mental processes of the association of ideas analogous to physical processes of combination and disintegration; and even that what we call the mind might be nothing more than the collection of all the intellectual processes occurring to an individual at a given moment. F. H. Bradley followed this procedure to devastating effect in his first book, *Ethical Studies*.

To illustrate, Bradley invites the reader to picture the mind's relation to the body as analogous to the relation of a ripple's wispy crest of foam to the ripple. The picture looks plausible enough, he points out, up to the moment we try to incorporate the phenomenon of self-consciousness. He writes:

> We can see the stream is a flux, and that the wisp which plays on it has really no more of permanence than the stream; but how that wisp is ever to think about these things, and to delude itself into the belief, and to publish the theory, that it can not help thinking of itself as one being, and that yet after all it is nothing but a wisp—to see how this is seems really impossible. The only way to represent it is to picture a delusion, which is nothing but a delusion, and which, after belief that it is *not* a delusion, has at length found out that it really *is* a delusion. And . . . this is the conclusion to which 'inductive' psychology, if we carry it out, seems necessarily to lead.[22]

The absurdity of the 'mind' of empirical psychologists is, as far as Bradley was concerned, sufficient proof of the errors of their claims.

The point Bradley and other idealists were trying to make, in raising

22. F. H. Bradley, *Ethical Studies*, 2d ed. (Oxford: Clarendon Press, 1927), p. 39. The first edition appeared in 1876.

objections like the one above, was that the empirical psychologists' inability to directly observe the self whose phenomenal manifestations they describe does not entail the conclusion that the self is nothing other than its manifestations. As Morris put it:

> British empirical psychology, deriving its model of method from physical "inductive" science, naturally arrives by it at results analogous to those reached by physical science. It furnishes a more or less admirable description of the field of conscious phenomena, with their rules of coexistence and sequence. But it does not go behind them, objectively or subjectively. Naturally, as physical science finds no "force" among the subjects of its analytical observation, so empirical psychology "hits upon" no "power" among conscious phenomena.[23]

That we cannot observe gravity or causal processes directly does not lead us to conclude that they do not exist. It is only by postulating the existence of forces and causes that a coherent theory of the natural world can be formed. Likewise, only on the postulate that a nonnatural principle exists in the human mind, self-consciousness, is it possible to make sense of human mental life. This active principle is the explanation of the unity and continuity of mental life as we know it.

Both are justified by our own immediate awareness. We know that force exists and operates in the world because acquaintance with the existence and operation of a force (volition) is given in our own internal experience. So we are not just making use of a convenient fiction when we attribute events we observe in the external world to the action of causal forces. Similarly, in conceiving of ourselves as more than mere collections of physically generated phenomena—as 'spiritual' as well as material beings—we are not just making use of a convenient fiction. Nor do we do so when we attribute spirit or consciousness to the universal whole of which we are members. As explanations of our own behavior make reference to the force of our volitions supervening upon the merely physical forces operating upon our bodies, so also may our explanations of events in the universe make reference to an analogous force underlying and directing the physical forces whose operations scientists record. Thus empirical methods of inquiry are inadequate to comprehend the whole of human nature, either as an individual conscious subject of experience or as part of a greater, universal conscious-

23. Morris, *British Thought and Thinkers*, pp. 253–54.

ness. Morris spoke clearly, if bluntly, for his fellow idealists when he wrote:

> We are justified in insisting, in special behalf of British philosophy, that the
> *coup de grace* be at last administered to the idea that has so long had all the
> power of a superstition, that so-called empirical, phenomenally descriptive,
> sensational, or physiological psychology, or that physical science, be its high-
> est law evolution or gravitation, is, *as such,* either philosophy or any specific
> part of philosophy, or has any competence whatever to answer, even nega-
> tively, philosophical questions.[24]

But it would be a mistake to conclude that Morris, Green, Bradley, or their colleagues were all actually opposed to empirical, physiological psychology. On the contrary, they were willing to tolerate and even applaud the new psychology provided it remembered its limitations and its place. Nor were they in general opposed to the application of evolutionary theory to the study of human nature. They simply insisted that over and above the physical forces driving the natural selection of characteristics in such species as *Homo sapiens,* there must be another, nonphysical force or influence whose operations supervene upon the merely physical. That purely physical forces operating on randomly generated variations in inheritance could have resulted in a being like man was incredible to them—in the most literal sense. It had required the conscious volition of generations of human beings supervening upon natural selection to create the physical variations in domesticated species that Darwin had cited as evidence of evolution. They presumed the same must have been true of the gradual development of the human form. Some conscious volition must have lain behind the so-called spontaneous variations on which natural selection worked: a consciousness determined that the world should develop organisms capable of sharing its consciousness. So, for example, Green could recommend the study of the merely natural processes involved in the modification of species for the "purpose of improving man's estate," and then go on to remark:

> That countless generations should have passed during which a transmitted
> organism was progressively modified by reaction on its surroundings, by
> struggle for existence, or otherwise, till its functions became such that an
> eternal consciousness could realize or reproduce itself through them—this

24. Ibid., p. 387.

might add to the wonder with which the consideration of what we do and are must always fill us. . . . If such be discovered to be the case, the discovery cannot affect the analysis of knowledge—of what is implied in there being a world to be known and in our knowing it,—on which we found our theory of the action of a free or self-conditioned and eternal mind in man.[25]

That evolution operated, prior to the existence of human consciousness, to produce a biological form adequate to the needs of that consciousness was viewed as evidence by neo-Hegelians that consciousness is an essential feature of the universe as a whole and not a unique attribute of the human species or its immediate ancestors.

Moreover, inductive physical science is no more sufficient for the comprehension of moral phenomena than it is for the comprehension of mental phenomena. Empirical investigation can give us much valuable information about what in fact people believe, how in fact they behave. But as Green noted, "it has generally been expected of a moralist, however, that he should explain not only how men do act, but how they should act."[26]

From the observation and inductive generalization of human behavior, the only valid conclusions we can draw are descriptive. No amount of purely empirical investigation can justify a moral principle or settle a moral question. So if we propose to reconstruct morality on a purely scientific basis, we will be forced to interpret all moral principles, opinions, and debates as expressions of arbitrary tastes, without any scientifically meaningful foundation. Green correctly predicted that "when this consequence is found to follow logically from the conception of man as in his moral attributes a subject of natural science, it may lead to a reconsideration of a doctrine which would otherwise have been taken for granted as the most important outcome of modern enlightenment."[27] As naturalistic ethical theories came to be seen as fallaciously deriving normative conclusions from descriptive premises, nonnaturalistic alternatives took on a new appeal.

By these and other devices, neo-Hegelians sought to establish a partition between philosophy and science, paralleling the metaphysical divide between what is and what is not yet real. Absolute idealism held that the world is an organism evolving through embryonic stages toward an end state of infinite and perfect self-realization. Thus their

25. Green, *Prolegomena to Ethics*, pp. 87–88.
26. Ibid., p. 9.
27. Ibid., pp. 10–11.

philosophical program in all its branches focused on the issue of "becoming": for example, the becoming of the world as we know it, the becoming of consciousness in that world, and the becoming of individual and social character through social and historical processes. In every case, the objective is ultimately to grasp the process itself—the method or design according to which the absolute's self-determined evolution is occurring. Thus what as a matter of fact happens to be true of the phenomena of any particular state of the world at any particular time was, relatively speaking, a triviality they were happy to leave to observation (physical science) to record.

Following Hegel, the method favored for isolating and abstracting the absolute's underlying design or method of construction was logical analysis of the most fundamental categories and concepts implied or given in our conscious experience. As we are finite beings, the merest fragments of the absolute's all-inclusive consciousness, our minds are not able to grasp in full the design in which we participate. That we are able to do so in part was supposed to be evident from our ability to perceive ourselves as objects as well as subjects of experience. The phenomenon of viewing oneself and others from an impersonal, objective point of view, it was thought, would be impossible if we were truly limited to one, personal perspective. Since objectivity does not seem to be beyond us, this capacity stands in need of explanation. Absolute idealism explained it as a capacity to partially reproduce the absolute's objective point of view within our own subjective consciousness.

We are nearest to grasping the absolute's thought when we reproduce its impartial, impersonal standpoint in our consciousnesses. And we seem most purely to achieve and maintain this condition when we are engaged in logical analysis and proof. Green holds:

> The consciousness which varies from moment to moment, which is in succession, and of which each successive state depends on a series of 'external and internal' events. . . . consists in what may properly be called phenomena . . . media for the realisation of an eternal consciousness, but which are not this consciousness. On the other hand, it is this latter consciousness, as so far realised in or communicated to us . . . that constitutes our knowledge, with the relations, characteristic of knowledge, into which time does not enter, which are not in becoming but are once and for all what they are.[28]

28. Ibid., pp. 72–73.

Temporal relations cannot enter into the absolute's consciousness, because, for the absolute, time does not exist. Temporal relations are internal to the absolute, beginning with the beginning of its evolution, ending with the realization of its objective. Just as temporal relations in the purely physical world are now supposed to have begun with the Big Bang and to hold only between changes of state occurring within the universe since that event and not to the universe as a whole, so absolute idealists reasoned that temporal relations could not apply to the absolute as a whole or inform its view of itself. Logical operations are operations into which time does not enter. Thus we more accurately reproduce the absolute's objective understanding when we engage in logical modes of inquiry.

NEO-HEGELIAN ETHICAL THEORY

Although the idealist movement was certainly committed to rebutting any epistemology that rendered values subjective, arbitrary, or unreal, construction of an ethical theory consistent with idealist epistemology and metaphysics represented a serious problem. Its solution demanded a radical departure from contemporary naturalistic or intuitional ethical theories.

The problem was that ethics is practical. It deals with the evaluation of past and future actions. Temporal relations are inexpungible from its subject matter. So it would seem that none of our ethical thinking could be an accurate reproduction of the absolute's objective evaluations. Not only could the absolute never be in doubt about what objectively it should do; it could not even conceive of its acts as to be done or having been done. Since its perception of itself does not involve time, it must perceive all its activity as simultaneously occurring phenomena of its self-realization.

The solution adopted was to recast the central question of ethical life, 'what ought I to do?' as 'am I what I ought to be?'(Although the absolute could never be in doubt about the answer to the latter question, the latter could at least be meaningful to it, whereas the former could not.) The job of the moralist was likewise recast. When Green said moralists were expected to tell men how they ought to act, he was reporting a fact, not making a recommendation. His recommendation was that moralists confine themselves to understanding what men ought to *be*. By these means, idealists endeavored to transform ethics from a practi-

cal 'art' into a purely analytic or 'logical' mode of inquiry from which
temporal relations could be excluded. By their rejection of normative
ethics in favor of what we would now call 'metaethics,' idealist ethical
theorists laid the groundwork for the analytic moralists who were to
succeed them.

At the same time, this move left idealists with a problem. A case for
recasting ethics as an analytic, theoretical inquiry, rather than a practical
art, made on metaphysical grounds would carry weight with the metaphysically minded. But in the latter half of the nineteenth century, the
metaphysically minded were decreasing in numbers. Anglo-American
neo-Hegelians needed a more immediately appealing case for reorient-
ing contemporary ethical thought. They got it from F. H. Bradley's *Ethical Studies*. Since Bradley's work was to play an important role in the
development of Dewey's early ethics, I will review his arguments in
some detail.

Bradley recognized that in an era of enthusiasm for the inductive sciences, neo-Hegelian idealism was likely to seem "a bad metaphysical
dream, a stale old story . . . which cannot hold its own against the logic
of facts."[29] *Ethical Studies* was written to rebut that impression and to
turn it against the rival doctrines of utilitarianism and Kantianism.
Bradley aimed to show that on the one hand, neo-Hegelian ethics alone
was truly defensible in terms of the data of our ordinary experience and,
on the other, that Kantianism and utilitarianism were the 'bad metaphysical dreams' to be avoided.

In his review of the book, Henry Sidgwick criticized Bradley's style of
composition as "vehemently propagandist" and Bradley himself for
having used "all the rhetorical resources at his command—more perhaps than the canons of good taste would permit—to bring his audience
to the acceptance of a set of doctrines, chiefly derived from Hegel."
Bradley's criticisms of his opponents were condemned as "rather superficial and sometimes even unintelligent," owing to a lack "of patient
effort of intellectual sympathy which Mr. Bradley has never learned to
make."[30] Sidgwick did not exaggerate. *Ethical Studies* is unabashedly vi-
tuperative in its criticism of doctrines Bradley rejects. It defends vigor-
ously, even melodramatically, the claims of Hegelian moral theory. It is
by far the most 'Hegelian' of Bradley's several books, in both inspiration
and content. But though partisan in his analyses, Bradley was neither

29. Bradley, *Ethical Studies*, p. 163.
30. Henry Sidgwick, review of *Ethical Studies*, by F. H. Bradley, *Mind* 1 (1876):545.

unfair in his criticisms of opponents nor unwilling to subject his own views to criticism. If his criticisms of classical hedonism were not original, they were comprehensive and destructive. Though his criticisms of Kant rely upon a Hegelian reading of Kant not now accepted, they are not toothless. Despite Sidgwick's low opinion, Bradley's text was widely read for its critical analyses well into this century.

By contrast with Sidgwick's own painstaking, meticulous exegesis of common-sense morality, *Methods of Ethics*, Bradley's *Ethical Studies* is superficial and sometimes obscure. But it is never unintelligent or wholly unpersuasive. Its central thesis is that the object of morality is "self-realization"—that is, the realization of all one's latent, potential personhood. And because 'personhood' is a social product rather than a property or quality of individual human beings, self-realization is at once humanity's private and public summum bonum. Absolute idealists held that 'personal identity' was not the property of an individual but the product of social practices and institutions. Thus *Ethical Studies* argues that there can be no absolute, universal principles of moral action. Although there is only one moral end, the end that reproduces the absolute's impersonal, objective purposes, the social institutions and practices that are the essential means to human self-realization are relative to times and places. Consequently, moral practical reasoning about the means one may adopt toward the realization of one's end cannot be a form of discursive reasoning from absolute principles to particular cases. Theoretical moral analysis cannot generate universally applicable rules or principles of conduct.

That self-realization is our end, Bradley treats as a self-evident truth. Though we can argue about how to interpret 'self-realization,' the ultimate aim of every act is to produce an effect of some kind in the agent. Value attaches to acts and objects only when and because they have such effects.[31] So Bradley baldly asserts: "In desire what we want, so far as we want it, is ourselves in some form, or is some state of ourselves; and that our wanting anything else would be psychologically inexplicable" (*Ethical Studies*, p. 68).

According to Bradley, a common philosophical failing is the habit of reflecting on human experience "not to find the facts, but to prove our theories at the expense of them" (2). Since neither Kantians nor utilitarians deny that the object of human action is to promote certain states

31. Certainly few contemporary moralists have held that acts or objects can have value independent of effects upon some conscious self (G. E. Moore being a rare and thus notable twentieth-century exception).

of or within ourselves, this is not a fact they can be accused of overlooking. What Bradley does claim they overlook are the further facts that
when we act, we act for the *whole* self and that the 'whole' for which we
act is not simple but complex.

First, it is necessarily the whole rather than a part of the self that we
act for, because it is impossible for us to induce one sort of internal
state—say, sensual pleasure—without inducing changes of state
throughout the whole of the self. This is borne out, Bradley argues, by
ordinary practical reason: in ordinary life our desires to bring about one
sort of change of state within ourselves is always qualified by the
thought of the other, perhaps less desirable, consequences we will also
endure. Second, the whole for which we act is not a simple quality,
property, or state of ourselves but a complex of several incommensurable constituents. This is again, according to Bradley, borne out by our
ordinary moral experience. Common-sense morality advises us always
to consider our desires in terms of our long-term goals. Common-sense
morality does this, he thinks, because whatever the desire in question, it
is not the only desire we have ever had or are ever likely to have. Usually, our willingness to satisfy a given desire is qualified by the thought
that the satisfaction will come at the price of delaying or sacrificing other
desires or interests.

Both Mill and Kant had, of course, built some complexity into their
moral ideals: Mill, a complex of qualitatively distinct pleasures; Kant, a
complex of pleasure and purity. But neither, according to Bradley, was
willing or able to accommodate theoretically the true scope of our ultimate ends. Each assumes at the outset of his inquiry that people can
only desire some particular finite set of ends that are in principle obtain-
able, the content of which is predetermined by their antecedent assumptions about human moral psychology. Instead of accepting all desires as
equally real facts of moral life to be explained, each acknowledges as
genuine only those desires or objectives that are consistent with his psychological assumptions. If the plain man reports that he has had a desire
the investigator thinks no one could have, the plain man's observation
will be treated as an illusion. Bradley argues that Mill and Kant were
guilty of trimming their facts to fit their theories in this fashion.

Bradley retorts, "We have no right first to find out just what we happen to be and to have, and then to contract our wants to that limit. We
can not do it if we would, and morality calls to us that, if we try to do it,
we are false to ourselves" (74). The facts of moral life do not support the
postulation that our desires are finite in number or bear any relation to
the possibility of their being satisfied by human effort. Anyone can de-

sire any and every thing of which he or she can however vaguely conceive. An ethics mindful of actual moral experience must recognize that the end of human action is infinite, that the object of self-realization is to realize ourselves as persons of infinite powers and capacities. Or as Bradley puts it, " 'Realize yourself' does not mean merely 'Be a whole' but 'Be an infinite whole' " (74).

Leaving aside, for the moment, the question of how one realizes oneself as an infinite whole, let us continue with Bradley's indictment of utilitarian and Kantian moral methodologies. Each school stands accused of allowing its own metaphysics of mind to blur its vision of the nature of moral life. The distortions produced are still more glaring, Bradley argues, when we consider the nature of moral practical reasoning.

On either the utilitarian or Kantian approach, moral practical judgments are (or should be) conclusions of discursive reasoning from universal principles. Utilitarianism holds that the rightness or wrongness of acts is a function of their consequences. A practical judgment that 'this act is right' is supposed to be a conclusion derived from a major premise, 'acts that maximize pleasurable consequences are right,' and a minor premise or premises about the probable pleasantness of this act and any alternatives. On the Kantian interpretation, practical judgment operates on a different major premise, but the general form is the same. 'This act is right' is supposed to be a conclusion derived from a major premise, the Categorical Imperative, and minor premises establishing that the motive for the act is consistent with the Categorical Imperative.

Bradley replies that this is nonsense. Ordinary people do not arrive at their moral practical judgments by way of explicit discursive reasoning from principles. They report instead that they *perceive* acts *as* wrong or right. Bradley remarks:

> In practical morality no doubt we *may* reflect on our principles, but I think it is not too much to say that we never do so, except where we have come upon a difficulty of particular application. If anyone thinks that a man's *ordinary* judgment, 'this is right or wrong,' comes from the having a rule *before* the mind and bringing the particular case under it, he may be right; and I can not try to show that he is wrong. I can only leave it to the reader to judge for himself. We say we 'see' and we 'feel' in these cases, not we 'conclude.' (194)

And common-sense morality is unapologetic on the point. Bradley notes: "There is a general belief that the having a reason for all your actions is pedantic and absurd. . . . [and] sometimes very dangerous. Not only the woman but the man who 'deliberates' may be 'lost' " (195).

Now presumably, he would agree that some practical judgments, such as nonmoral practical judgments, do involve explicit discursive reasoning: for example, 'if you want to catch the next train to Boston, you must leave the house by noon.' So he cannot mean that no practical judgments are conclusions of discursive reasoning. His point is rather that we take a false step when we try to assimilate moral practical judgments to nonmoral practical judgments. We must suppose that a moral practical judgment is a conditional judgment to the effect that 'if you want to be moral, this is the right act to do.' Such a judgment would involve reasoning from theoretical moral principles defining the nature of morality and the properties of action relevant to moral judgments. But this, Bradley insists, is not what ordinary people mean when they say that an act is right. They do not mean that they have determined that given certain fundamental principles of action, the act is right. All they mean is that they *perceive* that the act is right. If this is correct, then ordinary moral judgments more closely resemble observation statements (in Bradley's terms, "judgments of perception") than they do nonmoral practical judgments.

The ordinary person's ordinary judgment that 'this act is right' is as immediate as the judgments that 'this is a tree' or 'that log is aflame.' On Bradley's account, such immediate judgments, though not discursively formed, nevertheless "start from and rest on a certain basis" (194). For example, one's ability to judge that 'this is a tree' depends upon (has as its basis) one's possessing procedures for classifying one's experience into various categories and kinds. It is important to note that the relation of these procedures to the particular identifications made with them is not a relation of justification. For example, if someone misapplies the procedures for identifying perceptions as perceptions of 'trees,' and so mistakenly refers to a cow as a 'tree,' one would not call her mistake a mistake of judgment. One would not assume that a judgment had been made. One would assume that she misunderstood the rules for classifying her perceptions. She *misapplied* a concept but did not *reason* incorrectly from it.

What Bradley calls judgments of perception, we would call 'observations' or 'observation statements.' Observations are precisely what Bradley argues a moral judgment like 'this act is right' reports. Consequently, he argues that we should give up the idea that ordinary moral practical judgments depend upon or require the justification of theoretical moral principles. An observation that the sun rises over the eastern horizon, for example, does not depend upon or require the justification of any particular theory of the constitution of the solar system. It is the theory of the solar system that depends upon and requires the justification of such observations. The relation of moral practical judgments to theoretical moral principles is analogous. Moral practical judgments justify, rather than require the justification of, theoretical moral principles. Kantian and utilitarian ethical theorists ignored this fundamental truth, to the detriment of their own inquiries. As Bradley sees it, the methodological errors these schools commit condemn their respective theories as dogmatic and unscientific woolgathering.

What Bradley believes we observe when we perceive an act as right or wrong is a relation between ourselves and the act. Right acts are those whose performance would tend to promote our self-realization. Wrong acts are those whose performance would tend to the reverse. A consequence of this view is that there may be less moral disagreement in the world than one might imagine. For example, if one person calls an act 'right' while another calls it 'wrong,' it does not follow that they disagree. Their different observations may simply be the result of different points of view, so that "A is struck by one aspect of the case, B by another" (195). Or it may be that they each correctly observe the different potential the act has for their own personal self-realizations. To understand precisely what this means, however, we must now determine in what sense the object of human desire is *infinite* self-realization and how it can be achieved by the performance of *finite* acts.

To be 'infinite' is to be boundless in some sense, but not necessarily the same sense in every case. For example, Bradley holds, mathematics' conception of infinity as limitlessness or indeterminateness of extension or number, though appropriate to the abstract entities with which mathematics deals, is inappropriate to real concrete beings like ourselves. Everything real is particular. No real particular is 'limitless' or indeterminate in number or extension. So Bradley argues that the difference between infinite and finite particulars cannot be that the latter are determinate and the former are not. The difference lies instead in the nature and origin of the determinateness in each case. Finite things are determined by objects and forces external to them. An infinite thing must then be a thing that is not externally but rather internally determined, neither molded nor shaped by things external to itself. If this is correct, then the object of desire, to realize one's self as an infinite whole, is a desire to be self-determined, or as Dewey and other idealists sometimes put it, to be 'free.'

The fundamental problem of human life and conduct is, for Bradley,

"How can I be extended so as to take in my external relations? Goethe has said, 'Be a whole *or* join a whole', but to that we must answer, 'You can not be a whole, *unless* you join a whole'" (79). To join a whole is to become part of a greater self, all of whose relations are internal. Take a softball team, for example. To join a team is to commit one's self to a common goal and to take on an identity determined by the role one performs within the team. The players' identities or roles—catcher, shortstop, and so forth—are not determined by external forces but are internal to the game and its purpose. Realization of that purpose, moreover, requires "team spirit," the mutual sublimation of personal ego for the sake of the group's common goal. Likewise, an individual who joins a society with its many complex group activities and shares the society's ends joins a 'whole' and, in effect, becomes part of a greater self whose differentiation into particular personal roles is internally determined.

One might object that Bradley is reading too much into collective action. Surely, the members of any group were already persons when they joined. Moreover, each joined in furtherance of particular personal ends. Their identities are not substantially altered by their membership in the group even during the periods of their participation in the group's activities. The so-called group spirit is an illusion. To suggest otherwise is simply metaphysical nonsense.

In Essay V, "My Station and Its Duties," Bradley argues that the conception of personal identity employed in this objection is a 'dogma' imported from the objector's preconceived metaphysical notions. The facts of human life, he says, "lead us in another direction. To the assertion, then, that selves are 'individual' in the sense of exclusive of other selves, we oppose the (equally justified) assertion, that this is a mere fancy. We say that, out of theory, no such individual men exist" (166). It is Bradley's contention that the idealist theory of the nonexclusivity of personal identity can alone claim the justification of being a generalization from observation and consistent with common sense.

Bradley argues that (1) common-sense views of human development, moral training, and moral responsibility all operate on the implicit hypothesis that individual selves are really internally individuated components of a common social self and (2) our experience supports this hypothesis. His argument is unnecessarily confusing at times, because he uses the term 'individual' in two distinct senses throughout. To avoid misunderstanding, in what follows I use the term 'person' rather than 'individual' where Bradley means by the term 'individuated self.' I follow Bradley's usage of 'individual' when it has the more ordinary sense of 'particular' or 'single.'

Human beings are (or are housed in) particular, impenetrable organic bodies and so are mutually exclusive physical entities. But in addition, human beings can be persons. Personality is not a property of the human organism but a function, or rather a complex of functions, that human properties can be used to perform. To be a person is to be able to perform these functions in accordance with certain general criteria. Bradley does not specify exactly what the criteria are, but his examples suggest that they include competence in at least one language, an ability to reason logically, the capacity to recognize social rules and exercise rights. He argues that it is not sufficient to be a person that one is biologically human. Humanity is not even a necessary condition of personality, since nonhumans (e.g., God, angels, the absolute) are also thought capable of personality. That personality is a matter of function, not material, is implicit in the different behavior ordinary people think appropriate toward humans who behave as persons and those who from youth or incapacity do not. To be recognized and treated as a person, one must demonstrate one's ability to act as other persons do and in accordance with the socially instituted rules others observe. Personality is thus no more a private property or possession than language.

To the objection that exclusive personal identity predates one's becoming a person, Bradley replies that the contention is incoherent. One cannot be a 'person' prior to learning and performing the functions that comprise personality. Moreover, it cannot even be said that personality is something a prepersonal self chooses to acquire. Long before an infant has any sense of himself as an entity separate from his world, the community around him has already habituated him to performances of person-defining activities (spoken to him, played with him, etc.). By the time the child is sufficiently self-conscious to be in a position to make such a choice, he can no longer think of himself except as a *person*, and that in the terms his social group has established. Bradley writes: "The soul within him is saturated, is filled, is qualified by, it has assimilated, has got its substance, has built itself up from, it *is* one and the same life with the universal life, and if he turns against this he turns against himself" (172). In any case, the very idea of a nonpersonal self choosing to become a person is incoherent. Only a person has the capacity to make such a choice or understand what it means.

Before becoming a person, everyone has a body exclusively one's own, but it is the use of one's body to realize personality that makes one a person and the sort of person one is. Were one to try to strip from one's self all the person-constituting functions one performs in the same ways and to the same ends others do, in the romantic hope of finding one's true personal identity underneath, what would one find? Not one's true personality but no personality at all.

Returning to the problem of self-realization, Bradley argues that self-realization cannot be a purely private achievement, possession, or even goal for persons. All persons are persons only because they belong to a greater whole (society) and participate in a common endeavor (the realization of personality). What distinguishes particular persons are the contributions they make to the common social project. The realization of that project exceeds the capacities of any one person to achieve, hence the division of labor of realizing the various functions of personality among members of social groups. Every social group apportions the essential functions among various mutually supporting social roles, or in Bradley's terms, social stations. What sort of person one is, one's individual realization of personality, is given by one's choice and performance of particular roles. Or as Bradley put it, "what he has to do depends on what his place is, what his function is, and that all comes from his station in the [social] organism" (173).

On this understanding of the nature of persons and their relations to one another, Bradley holds, we can at last understand the role of morality in pursuit of the object of desire. The object of desire is realization of one's self as a whole by realizing oneself as a member of one self-determining whole. This necessarily involves desiring and willing that the internal relations of the whole be as fully realized as possible by each member, including oneself: that necessary 'stations' be established and the duties of each be attended to. Or in other words, implicit in the object of desire is the desire that those relations we call *moral*, signified by rights and duties, be recognized and fulfilled by persons. Realizing oneself as a person involves the realization of moral relations between one's self and others.

What in particular are persons morally obligated to do? Whatever acts are integral to the stations they undertake. If I am a citizen, parent, friend, employee, what I am obliged to do is whatever is essential to being a citizen, parent, friend, or employee, as these stations are currently defined. To the degree that I meet the duties of my stations, I am as I ought to be. If I do not meet those duties, or do so in a consciously piecemeal, desultory fashion, I am not as I ought to be. I transform my relations to the surrounding community into external relations. Were I simply to leave my community and live and act in physical exile, the actions would be merely amoral. But if I remain within the sphere of the group so as to benefit from the common achievement of personal life without undertaking roles essential to the maintenance of that way of life, I am a parasite on society, weakening its internal unity and coherence of purpose.

Because one's individual personality is the complex of one's stations, whose definitions are generally understood, people can usually observe the rightness or wrongness of one another's acts and personality directly. One can often tell at a glance whether an act is consistent with an agent's role and thus whether the agent is meeting or trying to meet the duties that he is bound to attempt to fulfill. In fact, we can see that no one quite fulfills all the duties of his stations to the fullest possible extent. No one is all what he ought to be or ever does all that he ought. But so long as we are conscientious about our duties, our conduct and character are morally good.

The stress on observation and experience up to this point in Bradley's argument gives the impression that after all morality might be a matter for natural scientific investigation. If it is a fact that we do invariably desire and act for our self-realization, then morality consists primarily in the discovery and execution of the means by which this object can best be accomplished. Surely, morality and self-realization would benefit from more explicitly scientific, empirical methods of inquiry. Bradley's reply is that neither morality nor self-realization can be studied in the way we study the physical world, because neither operates as physical phenomena do. First, the world of moral stations, relations, rights, and duties is not the sort of coherent system the physical world is. Unlike the physical world, the moral world is an incoherent patchwork that cannot be reduced to a single complete and consistent order of things and events by scientific induction or any other rational means. Second, morality cannot be reduced to an applied science of realization-engineering, because morality is neither sufficient for nor always conducive to our self-realization.

Induction from observation of the moral world will not yield a consistent set of generalizations on which predictions or explanations of the future can be constructed, because the phenomena are never consistent. Bradley writes:

A man cannot take his morality simply from the moral world . . . for many reasons. (a) That moral world, being in a state of historical development, is not and can not be self-consistent; and the man must thus stand before and above inconsistencies, and reflect on them. . . . With this co-operates (b) what may be called cosmopolitan morality. Men nowadays know to some extent what is thought right and wrong in other communities now, and . . . at other times; and this leads to a notion of goodness not of any particular time and country. (204)

No one living through the enormous social changes brought about by the industrial revolution could doubt that social institutions and practices evolve over time or that between relatively stable periods there occur 'transitional forms' in which vestiges of prior social arrangements coexist with the new and incompatible forms that eventually replace them. Moreover, because even stable periods are only relatively so, every social arrangement is to some degree transitional and inconsistent in its internal arrangements. Thus observation of the workings of a society's constituent stations will necessarily lead to inconsistent generalizations about both what stations are really essential to that society and what the duties of those stations really are.

Knowledge of the different social arrangements, past and present, complicates the situation further. If we try to explicate trends in our own society by analogy to others, we simply multiply our observations and likewise the inconsistencies in our data. Thus conscientious moral agents find they must go beyond the data available to them, to create their own hypotheses about (1) what stations really are essential to their own society, (2) which are essential to any and all societies' progress toward self-realization, and (3) what exactly the duties of those stations are. Once the agent forms (and acts) upon such hypotheses, she abandons the scientific outlook, according to Bradley, for creative speculation. The agent's hypotheses are *ideals* constructed in the absence of evidence to support them. Every conscientious agent who forms and acts upon the basis of ideals indulges in what Bradley calls a leap of faith, a leap that takes the agent beyond observation and scientific reasoning.

This is not the sort of leap a scientific investigator makes when he tentatively adopts a hypothesis in advance of experimentation to confirm or disconfirm it. The hypotheses or ideals upon which conscientious moral agents act are not hypotheses about what people in fact do. They are hypotheses about what people should do for their own self-realization. Nor can these hypothetical prescriptions be generated from or confirmed by scientific or even philosophical investigation. Bradley holds that the job of the moral theorist, scientific or philosophical, is to "understand morals which exist, not to make them or give directions for making them" (193). Observation of current social roles tells us what people are obligated to do under current arrangements. It does not provide grounds for saying how the inconsistencies should be remedied. Self-realization is more art than science and relies more heavily on imagination and inspiration than observation and induction. As for the second problem, Bradley argues that it is manifestly not the case that moral realization is self-realization. Indeed, the more conscientious agents are in fulfilling the duties of their stations, the more likely they are to find that their other capacities are frustrated and ignored. Not all our capacities for personhood are capacities for social action. Creativity, discovery, and invention, for example, are not inherently social. Bradley remarks:

> The making myself better does not always directly involve relation to others. The production of truth and beauty (together with what is called 'culture') may be recognized as a duty; and it will be hard to reduce it in all cases to a duty of any station that I can see. If we like to say that these duties to myself are duties to humanity, that perhaps is true; but we must remember that humanity is not a visible community. If you mean by it only past, present, and future human beings, then you can not show that in all cases my culture is of use . . . to any one but myself. Unless you are prepared to restrict science and fine art to what is useful, i.e., to common arts and 'accomplishments,' you can not hope to 'verify' such an assertion. (205)

Realization of ourselves as the best, most fully self-determined persons we can be may demand the development of talents not used in our various stations in life. The development of such talents is often incompatible with the performance of our social duties.

Conscientious agents must again resort to idealization to bridge the gaps or conflicts that arise between their personal and their moral self-realizations. In such cases, not only do agents have to form ideals of what their roles are under the existing social order or what roles should exist as constituents of that order; they have to form ideals about the moral relations that compose that order. They solve their dilemmas, in other words, by forming and acting upon hypothetical ideals about what moral relations ought to exist and what those relations entail, so that their moral and personal realizations may be rendered coherent. But in so doing, they add to the incoherence of the moral world.

The theory that humanity's summum bonum is self-realization through collective social action, and that one's realization as a moral being lies in doing the duties of one's station, differs significantly from other moral theories. It does not provide the kind of principles or premises that tell us what we should do in particular cases. It cannot even tell us to do the duties of our stations in all cases. Bradley himself believed that the presumption should always be in favor of existing over ideal social arrangements. He declares: "Common morality [is] both the cradle and protecting nurse of its aspiring offspring, and, if we ever forget that, we lie open to the charge of ingratitude and baseness. Some neglect is unavoidable; but open and direct outrage on the standing moral institutions which make society and human life what it is, can be justified . . . only on the plea of overpowering moral necessity" (227).

There are and probably never will be absolute or universal rules of evidence that could determine when a moral necessity is sufficiently overpowering to justify abandoning an old family custom, a rule of etiquette, or a political institution. Judgments about the preferability of an ideal to the real are, like moral practical judgments, more intuitive than discursive. They 'rest upon and proceed from' the basis of ordinary morality and its institutions and practices, but are neither deduced nor induced from it. This ultimately is the point of Bradley's critical analysis of the limitations of the morality of 'my station and its duties.' Bradley is not advocating the abandonment of a self-realization ethics in favor of a more complete, consistent, and instructive 'science' of ethics, empirical or philosophical. He is advocating the abandonment of the centuries-old struggle to construct a 'science' of ethics that can tell us what we ought to do.

In his concluding remarks to *Ethical Studies*, Bradley argues that the gaps between our moral and full personal realization can be reconciled only by faith that there is more contributing to our realization than we can see—that we are part of an organic whole larger and more potent than humanity. This he considers an essentially religious attitude to the world and our ultimate destiny. Bradley's pessimism about the practical value of a philosophical ethical inquiry for the improvement of the social institutions and practices that now hinder our realization was greater than that felt by some of his idealist colleagues.[32] But in his pessimism about the practical value of attempting to construct an empirical, natural science of ethics, he spoke for many.

Morris's views were in keeping with those of the British neo-He-

---

32. Green came very close, however. In *Prolegomena to Ethics*, he writes, "One is sometimes, indeed, tempted to think that Moral Philosophy is only needed to remedy the evils which it has itself caused" (339).

gelians, whose work he regularly introduced to students at Johns Hopkins University and subsequently at the University of Michigan. To Morris, there was a solid partition between philosophy and physical science which neither could usefully step over. Not surprisingly, he was willing and actually enthusiastic about working at Johns Hopkins with Hall, whose research Morris saw as a complement and aid to his own.[33] But as we shall see, the young John Dewey rejected the rapprochement his mentor and British idealist sources had so painstakingly constructed between philosophy and physical science in favor of more radically Hegelian conceptions. In his early papers, Dewey sought to turn the tables on those who meant to collapse philosophy into physical science by collapsing physical science into philosophy instead.

33. Hawkins, *Pioneer*, p. 200.

⊰{2}⊱ Dewey's Early Idealism

Since science has made the trouble, the cure ought to be found in an examination of the nature of knowledge, of the conditions which make science possible. If the conditions of the possibility of knowledge can be shown to be of an ideal and rational character, then, so it has been thought, the loss of an idealist cosmology in physics can be readily borne. The physical world can be surrendered to matter and mechanism, since we are assured that matter and mechanism have their foundation in immaterial mind. Such has been the characteristic course of modern spiritualistic philosophies since the time of Kant.

The Quest for Certainty

D ewey worked toward a doctorate in philosophy at Johns Hopkins University in the midst of a debate about whether and how the discipline of philosophy should be retained in a modern research university. His initial response was to reject G. Stanley Hall's scientism in favor of G. S. Morris's idealist conception of philosophy. In the three papers Dewey wrote and published during his graduate years, "Knowledge and the Relativity of Feeling" (1883), "Kant and Philosophic Method" (1884), and "The New Psychology" (1884), he presented contemporary neo-Hegelian interpretations of empiricism and Kantianism, derived from his studies of T. H Green, Edward Caird, Bernard Bosanquet, F. H. Bradley, and of course Morris.[1]

Dewey rapidly became disenchanted, however, with the conciliatory tone mainstream idealism adopted toward the physical sciences, in particular its willingness to surrender to the physical sciences a department of knowledge once exclusively its own. To do so, he would argue, was wrong on two counts. First, it was to construct an artificial dualism in

1. See John Dewey, "Knowledge and the Relativity of Feeling," *EW* 1:19–33; "Kant and Philosophic Method," *EW* 1:34–47; and "The New Psychology," *EW* 1:48–60.

knowledge where none actually existed. Second, it was to misrepresent the relation between philosophy and the physical sciences as a relation between peers. In an 1886 series of articles published in the British journal *Mind*, Dewey argued against mainstream idealism's partitioning of knowledge and in favor of the reassertion of philosophy's claim to the title of queen of the sciences. A year later, he put his principles into practice through the publication of *Psychology*, a textbook that set empirical psychology firmly in its place by presenting it as propadeutic to idealist philosophy of mind.

DEWEY'S INITIAL RESPONSE

In "Knowledge and the Relativity of Feeling," Dewey tries his hand at generating absurd conclusions from central tenets of empiricism: for example, that all knowledge originates with sensation and that all sensation or 'feeling' is relative to its subject. He complains that according to the first, "we must know only our feelings," and according to the second, "we must know the relation of our feelings to an object; this the feelings cannot give, except by transcending their relativity" (*EW* 1:23). Dewey does not deny that sensation is relative to the state or condition of the subject. On the contrary, he insists upon it in order to make the point (more than once) that "the theory of the Relativity of feeling . . . is so far from proving the subjectivity of our knowledge that it is impossible, except upon a theory which assumes that we do have objective knowledge" (*EW* 1:29).

In "Kant and Philosophic Method," a paper believed to be a short version of his doctoral dissertation,[2] Dewey demonstrates his mastery of the neo-Hegelian rejoinder to Kant's critique of reason and its scope. Here Dewey commends Kant for having recognized that the mind is something more than the collection of associating ideas and feelings that empiricism imagined it to be. Kant had demonstrated that the mind was a source of synthetic activity, constructing the phenomenal world with its relations—temporal, spatial, causal—out of a meaningless mass of unorganized raw material. Kant's 'method' of getting at the nature and extent of humanity's capacity for knowledge, however, was limited to determining the fundamental, rational categories of organization implied in it. The distinction between the real and the merely apparent is to be determined by reference to Kant's categories. But, Dewey continues,

2. See Dykhuizen, *Life and Mind of John Dewey*, pp. 36–37.

Kant's method is unable to deliver on its promises. As Kant himself points out, we have no reason to believe that the categories our minds impose upon our experience necessarily reflect real relations in the objective world. So Kant's method turns out to be nothing but a method for distinguishing between coherent and incoherent human experience, rather than between the real and the merely apparent.

Dewey identifies the assumption of an essentially empiricist picture of human experience, in which human percipients respond passively to the impacts of external sources of stimulation, as Kant's undoing. Why, Dewey asks, should we assume there are such objects? Surely, it is simpler, and therefore more reasonable, to postulate that the subject-object relationship is itself a category imposed by the mind on its experience. If so, Kant's method is not the end but only the beginning of philosophical progress toward a perfected method of human determination of reality: Hegelian Logic. "Logic in the Hegelian use," Dewey says, "is just that criterion of truth which we thought at first to find in Kant's Transcendental Logic—it is an account of the concepts or categories of Reason which constitute experience, internal and external, subjective and objective, and an account of them as a system, an organic unity in which each has its own place fixed. It is the completed Method of Philosophy" (*EW* 1:44).

"The New Psychology" has often been cited as evidence that Dewey was as strongly attracted to Hall's as to Morris's vision of philosophy in this period.[3] The paper is, however, an unremarkable example of the neo-Hegelian response to empirical psychology, one that might as easily have been written by Morris as by Dewey. Dewey opens by applauding the rise of the 'new psychology,' in particular its use of physiology as a supplement to introspective analysis of consciousness. Then he announces the purpose of his article: the correction of a "very great confusion and error" about the relation of physiological investigation to psychology, the science of human consciousness. The error Dewey had in mind was the belief that "physiological psychology is a science which does, or at least claims to, explain all psychical life by reference to the nature of the nervous system." He replies: "Nothing could be further from the truth. . . . Explanations of psychical events, in order to *explain*, must themselves be psychical and not physiological." As for the nervous system and the facts of its organization, Dewey proclaims that "it has *of itself* no value for psychology" (*EW* 1:52).

3. See Chapter 1, above, for examples.

Having identified and exposed this popular error, Dewey proceeds to introduce the reader to the neo-Hegelian view of the respective claims of philosophy and physical science to conduct and to interpret the results of the investigation of human psychology. In keeping with that view of mind and body, subject and object, as simply 'aspects' that consciousness presents from different points of view, Dewey depicts 'mental' and 'physical' things and events as phenomena of distinctly different perspectives. But since they are ultimately phenomena of different perspectives on one and the same thing, consciousness, the two orders of phenomena may be presumed to run parallel. On this view, psychophysical parallelism, physiological events never directly reveal the nature of mental events. But they may nevertheless function as valuable clues for the study of mental events. Dewey explains: "[If] a certain nervous arrangement can be made out to exist, there is always a strong presumption that there is a psychical process corresponding to it. . . . In this way, by purely physiological discoveries, the mind may be led to suspect the existence of some mental activity hitherto overlooked, and attention directed to its workings" (*EW* 1:55). Dewey was therefore enthusiastic about the prospects of future psychophysiological cooperative research. He was no less enthusiastic about the contribution to be made by the social and historical sciences, such as cultural anthropology, sociology, and ethnology. Following Hegel, Dewey argues that cultural institutions may be viewed as the 'objective' manifestation of consciousness working toward its self-realization. In such institutions, he writes, we have "a record of the development of intelligence [that] can be compared only to the importance of the paleological record to the student of animal and vegetable life" (*EW* 1:57).

Dewey's 'new psychology' is thus clearly not Hall's Darwinian, empirical science of conscious human behavior. It is instead Morris's neo-Hegelian philosophy of mind, in aid of which physiology and empirical social sciences are to work as handmaidens, supplying observations of the physiological parallels to, and objective manifestations of, consciousness for subsequent philosophical study.

Dewey left Johns Hopkins University in 1884, on the surface at least a signatory to the entente cordiale Morris had tried to establish between academic philosophy and physical science. Moreover, he appeared to believe, as Morris did, that mental and moral phenomena were topics for philosophy rather than empirical science to investigate. But already there are hints in his work of a commitment to a more radical, Hegelian stance on the interrelations of philosophy and science than Morris was, at least publicly, willing to advocate. Most important in this respect are Dewey's comments on method, particularly those in "Kant and Philosophical Method."

Consider the characterization of philosophic method he offers: "The criterion of experience is the system of categories in their organic unity in self-consciousness, and the method consists in determining this system and the part each plays in constituting it. *The method takes the totality of experience to pieces, and brings before us its conditions in their entirety.* The relation of its contents, through which alone this content has character and meaning, whereby it becomes an intelligible, connected whole, must be made to appear" (*EW* 1:43; emphasis added). Dewey's characterization of philosophic method in this passage is a restatement of Hegel's conception, according to which "the method is nothing but the structure set forth in its pure essentiality."[4]

Two important features of this conception should be noted. First, the method is defined by the characteristics of its end product as opposed to the intellectual means used to arrive at that product. Second, there is only one method of knowing anything. From a Hegelian standpoint, there is but one truth to be known: the truth of the absolute whole as an organic system. Anything less than the truth of the whole will be but a partial truth and hence not, strictly speaking, true. Since there is ultimately only one truth, and since philosophy is the science by which the one ultimate truth may be known, philosophy possesses the only complete method for grasping truth.

According to the Hegelian view, the physical sciences use essentially the same method as philosophy, but in a flawed and imperfect way. The physical sciences, in Dewey's words, take the totality of experience and 'bring before us its conditions,' that is, they bring to our attention the general conditions or laws exemplified in particular classes of experience. But physical science does so incompletely because of its reliance on purely empirical means of investigation. By these means alone, it can never determine the fundamental conditions or categories of experience in their 'entirety' or 'pure essentiality.' To do this, we must further determine what is implied in there being general conditions or laws of nature and in our ability to grasp them. To make such determinations, we must go beyond the narrow bounds of the special, physical sciences

4. G. W. F. Hegel, "Preface: On Scientific Cognition," in *The Phenomenology of Spirit*, trans. A. V. Miller (Oxford: Oxford University Press, 1977), p. 28. And see, generally, M. J. Inwood, *Hegel* (London: Routledge & Kegan Paul, 1983), esp. chap. 3.

and apply dialectical philosophical reasoning to the first-order determinations the special sciences yield.

Morris's depiction of the physical sciences as handmaidens to philosophy originates in this conception of physical science as a defective, first-order form of philosophy. But Morris had practical and political reasons for refusing to antagonize his scientific colleagues, either at Johns Hopkins or at the University of Michigan, by characterizing them as defective philosophers or their research as incomplete until reworked by more philosophic minds. And he had similar reasons to downplay the difference between his own and his colleagues' notions of scientific method. Morris, following Hegel, preferred the traditional usage of 'science' as a synonym for 'knowledge,' from which it followed that scientific method was a method of knowing and that any scientific method that yielded something less than knowledge (hypotheses, for example) could not be a 'scientific method.' But increasingly in the late nineteenth century, 'science' was becoming synonymous with the specialized tools and techniques of contemporary laboratory experimentation and statistical analysis. Morris disliked the trend away from the traditional use of 'science,' but on the whole he diplomatically assented to calling 'philosophy' what he would have preferred to call 'science' and to calling 'science' what he would have preferred to call 'special science' or perhaps simply 'inductive generalization.'[5]

Dewey, however, refused to follow Morris's lead. Unwilling to permit even the appearance of dualism in his conception of knowledge, Dewey was less amenable to trends in modern terminology. When, for example, in "The New Psychology" he wrote that knowledge of the physiology of the central nervous system was of no value to 'psychology,' what he was calling 'psychology' Morris would have called 'philosophy' of mind. And when three years later Dewey called for the construction of a "truly scientific ethics" that would be able to "justify the living ways of man to man" in his 1887 paper, "Ethics and Physical Science," it was not an empirical or naturalistic ethics he was advocating.[6] In 1886, Dewey turned his impatience with British neo-Hegelianism's conciliatory attitude toward the 'special sciences' into a platform and published it in a periodical where British neo-Hegelians and empiricists alike would be likely to see it: the British philosophical journal *Mind*.

5. As he does, for example, in the 1882 paper discussed in the previous chapter, "Philosophy and Its Specific Problems."
6. John Dewey, "Ethics and Physical Science," *EW* 1:226.

PHILOSOPHY, SCIENCE, AND PSYCHOLOGY

Through his 1886 series in *Mind*, Dewey introduced himself to the trans-
atlantic philosophical community. It was an important event in his career and he did not waste his opportunity to make an impression. In this
two-part series, "The Psychological Standpoint" and "Psychology as
Philosophic Method," Dewey criticized empiricist claims that empiricism could explain mental phenomena, such as knowledge, without resort to metaphysics or speculation and also idealist counterclaims that
the questions empirical science could answer about mental phenomena
are different *in kind* from those philosophic mental science attempts to
answer.[7]

In "The Psychological Standpoint," Dewey argues that British empiricism's characteristic insistence on the possibility and desirability of constructing accounts of mental phenomena on a purely experiential basis
was to be applauded. Unfortunately, none of the theories actually produced by John Locke, Bishop Berkeley, David Hume, or their suc-
cessors, J. S. Mill and Alexander Bain, met this description. Despite his
stated intentions, each had admitted into his account of mind that
"which does not show itself in experience" (*EW* 1:124). In so doing,
Dewey argues, he revealed that his metaphysical assumptions, rather
than his observations, were the true source of the data on which his
generalizations about mental life were based.

The British empiricists' departure from descriptive scientific investigation, or as Dewey calls it, the psychological standpoint, is peculiarly
evident in their explanations of knowledge. Knowledge is purported to
originate in sensation. But the sensations of which our knowledge is
composed, Dewey charges, are unknown and unknowable, hence
purely speculative postulations. They are certainly not the sensations of
which we do have experience, because these are not given in our experience but rather emerge as the result of processes of discrimination,
attention, association, and the like. The sensations of which we are conscious, being products of all these activities, cannot be the simple, original material of experience from which knowledge is constructed. The
empiricist account of knowledge turns out to rest on a speculative, not
an experiential, basis.

The moral Dewey draws from what he sees as British empiricism's

7. See John Dewey, "The Psychological Standpoint," *EW* 1:222–43; and "Psychology as
Philosophic Method," *EW* 1:144–67.

blunders is the danger of departing from the psychological standpoint on mental life. We must resist the temptation to step outside our conscious experience when conducting our investigations into consciousness and its causes. If we do not, he warns, we immediately find ourselves caught in paradoxes and logical circles. For example, he writes: "All that we can know exists for our consciousness; but when we come to account for our consciousness we find that this too is dependent. It is dependent on a nervous organism . . . upon objects which affect this organism. It is dependent upon a whole series of past events formulated by the doctrine of evolution. But this body, these objects, this series of events, they too exist but for our consciousness" (*EW* 1:132). Since appeals to objects or causes 'outside' consciousness invariably turn out to be appeals to some construct of our consciousness, all such appeals trap us in an inescapable circle. "The problem is to reconcile the undoubted relativity of all existence as known to consciousness, and the undoubted dependence of our own consciousness" (*EW* 1:132). Dewey's answer is that we must think the two points 'together.' He suggests: "If this is done, it will be seen that the solution is that the consciousness to which all existence is relative is not our consciousness, and that our consciousness is itself relative to consciousness in general" (*EW* 1:132–33). Or in other words, everything within and without us is conscious experience. This, Dewey insists, explains how we can construct a purely experiential account of knowledge, without denying the relativity of our knowledge to our particular subjective points of view.

In "The Psychological Standpoint," Dewey acknowledged the debt he owed to Green for his criticisms of British empiricism. But in the second of his *Mind* papers, "Psychology as Philosophic Method," Dewey turned his critical guns on Green's school of idealist thought, not excepting Green himself. Instead of arguing for a distinction between empirical science and philosophy and for the necessity of the latter as a complement to the former, Dewey attacks the distinction and the "post-Kantian" British idealists, such as Green and Caird, who approved it. Like their empiricist counterparts, Dewey argued, these neo-Kantians have succumbed to the temptation to find the source or causes of our conscious experience and of our knowledge in something outside that experience—albeit this time in another consciousness, of whose nature we have little or no direct experience.

Dewey illustrates what he calls the 'post-Kantian' (later, 'neo-Fichtean') idealist position with remarks from an article by Caird. Caird distinguished philosophic from empirical sciences of the mind on the grounds that whereas the former deals with "the conditions of the knowable, and hence with self-consciousness or that unity which is implied in all that is and is known," the latter's contribution is limited to furthering our grasp of "how this self-consciousness is realised or developed in man, in whom the consciousness of self grows with the consciousness of a world in time and space, of which he individually is only a part"[8] (*EW* 1:146). To this Dewey replies:

> When psychology is defined as the science of the realization of the universe in and through the individual, all pretense of regarding psychology as merely one of the special sciences, whose subject-matter by necessity is simply some one department of the universe, considered out of relation to the individual, is, of course, abandoned. With this falls, as a matter of course, the supposed two-fold character of man's nature. If the essence of his nature is to be the realization of the universe, there is no aspect in which, *as man*, it appears as a mere object or event in the universe. (*EW* 1:148)

Hence self-consciousness cannot be distinguished from the absolute self-consciousness, Dewey is saying, without abandoning the psychological standpoint. And to abandon the psychological standpoint is again to land oneself in a paradox. If we suppose there is another, different sort of self-consciousness, we must bear in mind that this other, supervenient, absolute consciousness, on which our limited, finite consciousness is supposed to depend, itself exists in and for our consciousness. British neo-Hegelianism has evidently not sufficiently 'thought together' the ideas of inner and outer consciousness. But this is what must be done if the paradox is to be avoided. We must each recognize that our own consciousness is absolute consciousness, that the two are one and the same. Human consciousness, then, is what absolute consciousness is like when it realizes itself from within one particular, finite perspective.

Of course, in advocating the unity of consciousness to neo-Hegelians, Dewey was preaching to the converted. Green himself had earlier acknowledged that the distinction between finite and absolute consciousness should not be treated as itself absolute. When in his *Prolegomena to Ethics* Green wrote that "our consciousness may mean either of two things: either a function of an animal organism, which is being made . . . a vehicle of the eternal consciousness; or that eternal consciousness itself, as making the animal organism its vehicle . . . but retaining its

8. Dewey is quoting Edward Caird's article "Metaphysic," from the *Encyclopedia Britannica*, 9th ed., 16:89.

essential characteristic as independent of time" (72) he anticipated the objection that the distinction makes his conception of consciousness dualistic. Green adds that he is saying not that man has two varieties of consciousness but rather that "the one indivisible reality of our consciousness cannot be comprehended in a single conception" (73). Our limited capacity to grasp the truth forces us to conceive of consciousness both as universal, absolute, and constructive, and as finite, nonabsolute, and merely reproductive (that is, reproducing within its limited point of view the absolute's self-constructed reality).

Dewey argues that despite such disclaimers, Green's conception of consciousness is dualistic. It is a reformulation of the distinction Kant made between the phenomenal appearance of self and its unknowable, noumenal reality. The cause of the dualism in each man's theories, Dewey argues, is the same. Instead of directing their analyses "into the *actual nature* of experience," Kant and Green both made the object of their analyses "the *necessary conditions* of experience," the *logically* necessary conditions (*EW* 1:153). But experience, Dewey argues, is not merely logical, nor is consciousness merely a logical unity. The rich variety of things and relations that make up conscious existence cannot be captured in the thin strands of a purely logical web of relations.

If absolute idealism is to avoid collapsing into transcendentalism, Dewey warns, it must reexamine its fundamental presuppositions. In particular, it must rectify two serious errors: "First, Philosophy can treat of absolute self-consciousness only in so far as it *has become* in a being like man, for otherwise it is not material for philosophy at all; and, secondly, it falls into the error of regarding this realization in man as a time–conditioned product, which it is not. Time is not something outside of the process of conscious experience; it is a form within it, one of the functions by which it organically constitutes its own being" (*EW* 1:160). It is a mistake to imagine that one can study consciousness in isolation from its manifestations, whether it is human consciousness in isolation from its manifestation in a particular individual or the absolute consciousness in isolation from its particular manifestations. Abstract consciousness from what it does, from any content on which it can operate, he argues, and you have nothing at all. So the philosophical project of studying the absolute consciousness itself as distinct from study of its particular manifestations in natural events and human actions is empty.

The notion that such a project could ever be pursued, according to Dewey, arises from commission of the second error: the error of thinking of the absolute as bringing about its realization in time. This error is implicit in the suggestions that the absolute is working toward its realization and that philosophers, by studying the underlying logic of the universe, can in effect study the absolute's working out of its own nature. But these suggestions are inconsistent with the assertion made by the absolute idealists themselves that time is simply one form of organic interrelation holding between the finite constituents of the absolute and so not applicable to the absolute itself. As the absolute does not exist in time, Dewey argues, it should not be described, even metaphorically, as more or less realized in one or another spatiotemporal configuration. It is thoroughly misleading to speak as if natural or human history reveals to us the absolute's progressive self-realization. The absolute is eternally realized. The fact that human beings happen to experience the universe as temporally ordered does not entail the conclusion that the absolute operates in accordance with the order that finite human minds impose upon their experience.

The point Dewey is trying to make is that no one of the categories or relations of human consciousness is more peculiarly 'real' or revealing of the absolute than another. None is, so to speak, metaphysically privileged. Dewey viewed the emphasis placed on logic by British neo-Hegelians as a survival of transcendentalism, inconsistent with Hegelianism rightly understood.[9] If we truly are constituents of a greater consciousness, an organic whole, then whatever is integral to the internal structure of our consciousness is integral to the internal structure of the whole. Thus if temporal relations are essential constituents of our conscious experience, they must be essential constituents of absolute consciousness. Since logical relations exclude the temporal, logic alone cannot be an appropriate vehicle for the pursuit of philosophical inquiries into consciousness. Dewey sums it up: "If the material of philosophy be the absolute self-consciousness, and this absolute self-consciousness *is* the realization and manifestation of itself, and as material for philosophy exists only in so far as it has realized and manifested itself in man's conscious experience, and if psychology be the science of this realization in man, what else can philosophy in its fulness be but psychology?" (*EW* 1:157).

---

9. Whether he thought Hegel has rightly understood Hegelianism in this respect is not entirely clear. Dewey certainly disagreed with the doctrine, sometimes attributed to Hegel, that a philosophy of nature, including the description and prediction of particular events in nature, could be developed directly from Hegelian 'logic.' But Dewey does not make it obvious whether or not he thinks this interpretation of Hegelian logic is consistent with Hegel's own views.

In saying that psychology was 'philosophic method,' Dewey was not saying that philosophers should cease their ordinary activities, epistemological, aesthetic, metaphysical, or moral, and begin at once to do psychology. He meant that they were *already* doing psychology—a sort of metatheoretic psychology. To do it well, whatever the philosophical specialty, philosophers must recognize that the questions they ask are all ultimately questions about constituents of conscious experience. Moreover, if the answers are to be coherent, they must all be integrated with a theory of mind that can encompass all the varieties of interrelations consciousness manifests. For that matter, every researcher is a psychologist and every subject of research—geology, biology, chemistry, astronomy—is a branch of psychology. That is, the categories and fundamental relations that characterize these aspects of our experience, Dewey believed, will turn out to characterize our experience as a whole. By determining what those categories or concepts are, the philosopher creates (or rather reproduces) a framework or 'method' by which the separate contributions of the special sciences may be organized into a coherent whole. Because these categories composing the framework are 'psychological,' psychology is the 'completed method' of philosophy.

By his rejection of any dualism or distinction in absolute idealism's conception of knowledge or of the self, Dewey committed himself to upholding empirical psychology as a legitimate, if inferior, means by which to begin to try to answer *philosophical* questions about knowledge, mind, and the nature of the world. Green or Caird might brush aside the results of empirical psychology as in themselves irrelevant to philosophic inquiries. But henceforth Dewey could not. Insisting that all special sciences be seen as stages along one and the same continuum of knowledge and truth, he had to be able to show that philosophical psychology is related to and develops out of its more primitive, empirical progenitor, if his program for the reconstruction of neo-Hegelianism was to be made convincing. This condition Dewey attempted to meet in his first book, *Psychology*.

DEWEY'S *PSYCHOLOGY*

Given its origins, the 1887 *Psychology* was necessarily a hybrid text, less remarkable for what it contained than for the fact that it existed at all.[10] George Croom Robertson, editor of *Mind*, was struck by Dewey's capac-

10. See John Dewey, *Psychology*, EW 2.

ity to "reconcile an idealism of the thoroughgoing modern type . . . with an adoption of the spirit and aims of the English psychological school from Locke onwards. It has been interesting to hear such ungrudging allowance of philosophical import to the work of the English inquirers from one . . . of a class of thinkers with whom it has been a common fashion to regard it with a certain disdain."[11] In the *Andover Review*, H. A. P. Torrey, Dewey's undergraduate professor of philosophy, saw it as the author's intent "to make his work an introduction to philosophy in general. And we think his conception of the science the true one, notwithstanding the claim of the 'new Psychology,' that is to say, of the physiological aspect of the science, to the whole field. . . . Dr. Dewey gives about as much of his book to that side of the subject as is due to it, or profitable."[12]

The space Dewey gave to the new psychology, if sufficient for Torrey, a Kantian, was, predictably, insufficient from the more empiricist perspectives of Robertson and the book's severest critic, Dewey's former professor, Hall. Robertson complained of the lack of "a clear and distinct view of the relation of nervous to mental process and a summary of the really important and relevant physiological data."[13] Hall went further. He not only found fault with Dewey's grasp of modern psychological investigation ("the book . . . might have been written half a century ago, and have been poorer only by a number of pat physiological illustrations") but attacked Dewey's project of reconciling idealism and physiological psychology as scientifically naive. "That the absolute idealism of Hegel could be so cleverly adapted to be 'read into' such a range of facts . . . is indeed a surprise as great as when geology and zoology are ingeniously subjected to the rubrics of the six days of creation," was Hall's backhanded compliment to his disappointing former student.[14]

On the basis of its reviews, it seemed unlikely that the book would have any sort of success. Yet it did. American departments of philosophy held more Torreys than Halls. For those of an idealist bent, not ready to see psychology emancipated from departments of philosophy but open to new ideas, Dewey's *Psychology* offered an acceptable compromise. In the 1880s and 1890s, *Psychology*'s hybrid character worked to its advantage.

11. George Croom Robertson, "Critical Notice of *Psychology*," *Mind* 12 (1887): 439.
12. H. A. P. Torrey, review of *Psychology*, *Andover Review* 9 (1888): 438.
13. Robertson, "Critical Notice of *Psychology*," p. 442.
14. G. Stanley Hall, "Critical Notice of *Psychology*, by James McCosh, *Introduction to Psychology*, by Borden P. Bowne, and *Psychology*, by John Dewey," *American Journal of Psychology* 1 (1888): 157, 156.

The Hegelianism into which the reader is introduced in *Psychology* is Dewey's reformulated neo-Hegelianism of 1886. Not surprisingly, this new position is only partly worked out and on occasion collapses into just the sort of dualism *Psychology* was a protest against. Dewey opens by defining psychology as "the science of the reproduction of some universal content or existence, whether of knowledge or of action, in the form of individual, unshareable consciousness" (*EW* 2:11). Or to put it another way, psychology is the science of how universal consciousness constructs for itself particular points of view (subjective selves) from which to view its universal self: "The universal element is knowledge, the individual is feeling, while the relation which connects them into one concrete content is will" (*EW* 2:22).

Why a universal consciousness would want or need to construct particular perspectives, or subjective selves, in order to realize itself is not explicitly discussed. An answer is implied, however, in Dewey's Hegelian conception of the construction of meaning. Dewey gives it as a general rule that "every act of mind involves relation; it involves dependence; it involves *mediation*" (*EW* 2:205). If every act of human minds involves mediation by some network of categories and relations, we may presume that every act of absolute consciousness must do so as well. The relations constituting each one of our peculiar individual perspectives on the universe are the 'mediating' devices the absolute mind uses to know itself.

What there is for consciousness to discover from any particular perspective is of course one and the same organic reality, so Dewey concludes that "were individuals *knowing* individuals only, no one would recognize his unique distinctiveness as an individual. All know the same, and hence, merely as knowing are the same" (*EW* 2:23). But consciousness is not only self-knowing; it is purposeful. And its purpose of perfectly perceiving itself is both aided and hindered by each one of the particular perspectives or subjective points of view it must adopt. The relation of purpose to opportunity is the reason why "in any actual case knowledge has some emotional coloring, and hence is conceived as being one's *own* knowledge" (*EW* 2:23), that is, the view from one's own perspective. Feeling arises as consciousness perceives a perspective as involving a mix of benefits and burdens or limitations. The will to self-realization is what holds a given perspective or self together.

Dualism is at least superficially avoided in the account of psychology and its subject with which Dewey begins his discussion. Nothing so far is attributed to the particular individual self that could not also be in some sense an attribute of universal consciousness and vice versa. And if we conceive of the absolute, universal consciousness as consciousness realizing itself as a manifold of particular selves, which stand in temporal relation to one another but as a whole exist outside time—viewing itself through a kaleidoscope of perspectives but having no 'universal' perspective of its own over and above the kaleidoscope—then Dewey's conception of consciousness does indeed avoid dualism. Yet his initial definitions of the three 'aspects' of consciousness make it difficult and ultimately impossible for him to keep his conception of consciousness entirely monistic. In the book's first section, "Knowledge," no serious difficulties arise. But as soon as Dewey begins the second, "Feeling," dualism creeps in.

The reason is not hard to see. Dewey defines 'feeling' as the subjective appreciation of consciousness's subjective situation as helpful or the reverse. Moreover, a subjective situation is ultimately helpful or the reverse as it does or does not contribute to consciousness's perfect self-realization. Of course, no individual's perspective is adequate to consciousness's perfect self-realization. Thus it turns out that every individual's perspective on the world (or self) will be felt to be unsatisfactory. That is, each individual self feels its self to be an imperfect realization of, and thus distinct from, absolute consciousness. This result is surely as deep and as "inwardly lacerating" a divide between universal and individual consciousness as were the "divisions and separations . . . of New England Culture" that Dewey had expected neo-Hegelianism would help him overcome.[15] As Dewey describes it, "the feeling that a universal self is our own true being is necessarily accompanied by the feeling of obligation and responsibility. We feel bound to realize our own [universal] nature because it is *our* nature, and feel responsible for its non-realization" (*Psychology*, EW 2:289–90). Our only recourse is to act in the faith that the deficiencies of our particular contributions are being made up elsewhere. Dewey writes: "Feeling finds its absolutely universal expression in religious emotion, which is the finding or realization of self in a completely realized personality"; that is, "in religious feeing we find our self expressed in God" (*EW* 2:245). Only in this way can our unsatisfactory subjective selves be disregarded as unreal manifestations of our true nature.

The same problem about the means and objective of conscious activity gives rise to dualist treatment of the topic of the third section, "The

15. See "From Absolutism to Experimentalism," *LW* 5:153, quoted in Chapter 1, above.

Will." Here we are told: "The will is always holding itself before itself. The self has always presented to its actual condition the vague ideal of a completely universal self, by which it measures itself and feels its own limitations. The self, in its true nature, is universal and objective. The actual self is largely particular and unrealized. The self always confronts itself, therefore, with the conception of a universal or completed will towards which it must strive" (*EW* 2:358). No matter how the 'actual self' struggles to realize its full potential as a particular finite self, not even its perfect realization as such a self would satisfy the demand of the will for complete universal self-realization. Again, our only comfort is in the essentially religious faith that our particular subjective selves are in a sense unreal. In the words of the text, relief from the endless demands of the will is afforded by the faith that "God, as the perfect Personality or Will, is the only Reality" (*EW* 2:361).

The distinction Dewey makes between individual, finite consciousness and universal, infinite consciousness in his discussions of moral psychology, the basis for his depiction of personal life as the struggle to make the 'actual' finite self the vehicle of the realization of one's 'true' or infinite selfhood, is drawn straight from the self-realization ethics of Green, Caird, and like-minded neo-Hegelians. It is a distinction that an unreconstructed neo-Hegelian such as Green would be entitled to make—but that Dewey was not. Dewey's position on the self in "The Psychological Standpoint" put him at odds with Green's notions of the self and of self-realization. This was because Green's moral agent's summum bonum is to become what Dewey's agent already is: a realized organic whole. The irreconcilable aspects of consciousness that make up the human self in Green's theory of mind reappear as two irreconcilable conscious ends in Green's theory of morals. In his *Prolegomena to Ethics*, for example, Green states the case as follows:

> The reason and will of man have their common ground in that characteristic of being an object to himself which, as we have said, belongs to him in so far as the eternal mind, through the medium of an animal organism and under the limitations arising from the employment of such a medium, reproduces itself in him. It is in virtue of this self-objectifying principle that he is determined, not simply by natural wants according to natural laws. . . . The conditions of the animal soul, 'servile to every skiey influence,' no sooner sated than wanting, are such that the self-determining spirit cannot be conscious of them as conditions to which it is subject—and it is so subject and so conscious of its subjection in the human person—without seeking some satisfaction of

itself, some realization of its capabilities, that shall be independent of those conditions. (182)

The first problem such a moral agent has in deciding how to lead his life is to differentiate between his true and his ephemeral, animal desires, so as to focus his energies on realizing his true nature. Having discovered that his true nature demands the realization of his latent personal capacities, the agent next must discover some means by which to bring this about. Like Bradley before him, Green argues that social life is the medium both of self-discovery and of ultimate self-realization.

In Green's unmodified neo-Hegelianism, however, what an agent's true self is must be understood in two ways. We must recognize that a moral agent has the potential to act both *as the medium* of the absolute self-consciousness and *as the absolute* reproducing itself in that medium. Consequently, self-realization entails two ideals the agent cannot resolve into a single summum bonum. He interacts in society so as to realize his personality as a finite self. But he is also aware of himself as potentially absolute, as having the capacity for absolute realization far exceeding that afforded by membership in a social organization.

Thus the human agent on this account of self-realization is in the unhappy dilemma of having the means of partial personal realization available while at the same time having capacities within him that transcend the boundaries of any possible social station. Green remarks: "Each has primarily to fulfill the duties of his station. . . . No one so confined, it would seem, can exhibit all the Spirit, working through and in him, properly and potentially is. Yet is not such confinement the condition of the only personality we know?" (192). Self-realization is the struggle to overcome this paradox.

The paradox is a direct consequence of the duality in this conception of human self-consciousness. The particular self is held to exist as a sort of cell of an overmind. By communication with the whole and partial reproduction of the whole within the cell-like self, the particular self is aware of the greater, freer life the whole leads. The freer, fuller life of the whole is the cell-self's ideal. Because it shares in the self-consciousness of the whole, the particular self feels it has, in some sense, the capacity to realize its ideal, to become the whole it participates in. Hence its dissatisfaction with its life as a cell and its hopeless struggle to realize itself as the whole of which it is after all only a cell. In a paper of 1892, Dewey would remark: "No thorough-going theory of total depravity ever made righteousness more impossible to the natural man than Green makes it to a human being by the very constitution of his being."[16]

Since Dewey had rejected Green's account of the self as dualistic, together with the hierarchical relation between the self's two aspects, Dewey's moral agents ought not to find themselves in such a paradoxical position. That nevertheless they do in his *Psychology* is an indication of how much more work was needed to develop his protest of 1886 into a coherent position.

Although Dewey was to revise *Psychology*, first in 1889 and again in 1891, he made no significant changes to the passages on moral psychology.[17] The dualism between human and divine consciousness remained. Whether Dewey failed to dissolve the distinction between the two varieties of selfhood because he was unaware of the problem or because he thought it a minor blemish not worth the trouble of removal is not clear. In the end, he judged the problem serious enough to warrant working out in a full-length text, his 1891 *Outlines of a Critical Theory of Ethics*.

By his protest of 1886 against dualism in the mainstream of neo-Hegelianist thought, Dewey deprived himself not only of classic formulations of idealism as a model for his own, but also of classic formulations of self-realization ethics—with one notable exception. Of the ethical treatises published by the more important figures in the movement, only Bradley's *Ethical Studies* came near to meeting Dewey's requirements for a nondualist conception of self-consciousness and its realization.[18] The 'true' self each of Bradley's moral agents seeks to realize is his or her own particular, actual self with all its actual, if latent, capacities and potentialities, not a distinct, divine self mysteriously supervening upon the actual self. Although Bradley, like Green, believed that moral life was inherently paradoxical, his account of the paradox avoids overt dualism. Like Green's agents, Bradley's agents may expect to find the means of self-realization—social life and social stations—inadequate to their ends. But this is because their social stations may prevent their perfecting the nonsocial talents of their actual selves, not because their

16. John Dewey, "Green's Theory of the Moral Motive," *EW* 3:160.

17. For an analysis of the changes he did make, see Andrew J. Reck, "The Influence of William James on John Dewey in Psychology," *Transactions of the Charles S. Peirce Society* 20 (1984): 87–118.

18. Of British neo-Hegelians discussed in Dewey's 1886 paper, "Psychology as Philosophic Method," Bradley is the only one who escapes criticism as 'post-Kantian.' See *EW* 1:166 n.

true selves transcend the particular, finite lives open to them as actual selves. But while Bradley's *Ethical Studies* provided a suitable model for the development of Dewey's own ethics, it also posed a serious challenge.

Dewey had opted for an uncompromising stance on the relation of empirical science and philosophy. As far as he was concerned, philosophy was science. The empirical, special sciences were just a sort of first-order, preliminary form of the scientific investigations philosophy conducts. To make his case convincing, he had been obliged to indicate how, for example, the generalizations of empirical mental science provided the first-order generalizations for subsequent analysis and interpretation by higher-order, philosophic investigation, both in his papers of 1886 and in *Psychology*. To be consistent, he would be obliged to do the same with moral science. He would have to show that generalizations from the empirical study of morals could be developed and ordered by the application of philosophic methods of analysis and classification. But Bradley denied that any science of morals was possible. He insisted that the moral world, with its character-forming societies and virtue-forming stations, was in a state of constant flux. Because the moral world is internally inconsistent, negotiating it is impossible unless moral agents invent coherent ideals of the world on which to act. However functional these ideals may be, Bradley holds, one cannot be said to *know* what is merely ideal. Nor can one create a scientific scheme for the classification of something that is not a coherent system.

It was for this reason that in the conclusion of *Ethical Studies*, Bradley argued that the incoherence and incompleteness of the moral world can be reconciled only by an act of faith that our struggles to cope with a confused and confusing world do not go unrewarded. We must abandon the scientific attitude and its demand for 'justification by sight' for an essentially religious attitude that takes its justification on faith. This outcome was not acceptable to Dewey, however. He was not prepared to cede half of philosophy's traditional territory to departments of theology. Nor would he accept Bradley's pessimistic conclusion about the unknowability of the moral world. In his 1891 *Outlines of a Critical Theory of Ethics*, Dewey made the first of a series of attempts to prove Bradley wrong about the possibility of moral science.

⌐3⌐ *Outlines of a Critical Theory of Ethics*, 1891

Why has modern philosophy contributed so little to bring about an integration between what we know about the world and the intelligent direction of what we do? . . . [T]he cause resides in our unwillingness to surrender two ideas formulated in conditions which both intellectually and practically were very different from those in which we now live. These two ideas, to repeat, are that knowledge is concerned with disclosure of the characteristics of antecedent existences and essences, and that the properties of value found therein provide the authoritative standards for the conduct of life.

The Quest for Certainty

The development of Dewey's early ethical views mirrored the development of his early theory of mind, metaphysics, and philosophy. Before attempting an original interpretation of his topic, Dewey produced a short series of essentially academic exercises. In 1887, in a paper entitled "Ethics and Physical Science," he first tried his hand at a rebuttal of Herbert Spencer's evolutionary ethics, arguing that ethics is an evaluative enterprise and therefore makes assertions that cannot be confirmed, denied, or justified by inductive scientific techniques.[1] In *Psychology* of the same year, Dewey demonstrated his grasp of mainstream Anglo-American idealist ethics of self-realization. Four years later, he began an overhaul of idealist ethics that led eventually to his rejection of absolute idealism. His first book on the subject, the 1891 *Outlines of a Critical Theory of Ethics*, was to self-realization ethics what *Psychology* was to absolute idealist theory of mind. And as was the case with *Psychology*, the text offered Dewey's answers to problems raised in a preceding journal article. On this occasion, the journal was the first volume of the

---

1. See John Dewey, "Ethics and Physical Science," *EW* 1:205–26.

International Journal of Ethics and the article was Dewey's 1891 "Moral Theory and Practice."[2]

Contemporary neo-Hegelian ethics diverged from such rivals as utilitarianism and Kantianism in denying that moral philosophy could provide any practical guidance for solving moral dilemmas. Neo-Hegelians held that moral philosophy, or the science of morals, is a descriptive, analytical enterprise, whose purpose is to justify judgments about what *is* the case with regard to morality. Moral action is about making real what *is not* the case. But what is not the case cannot be an object of knowledge. Thus moral action cannot be reliably guided by moral philosophy.

Moral character, on the other hand, though perpetually 'becoming,' is at least partially realized at any given moment. To the extent it is realized, it can be an object of knowledge. Thus idealists concluded that moral science is necessarily a science of character, its aim being to grasp the fundamental principles and conditions of personal realization. This conception of ethics grew out of the neo-Hegelian's tendency to see logical relations and conditions as providing privileged access to absolute reality, on the ground that these relations were more 'objective' and independent of finite perspectives on the world than any others and so more likely to be applicable to absolute as well as finite human consciousness.

In 1887, Dewey still accepted this view of moral science and its relation to moral practice, despite its incompatibility with his own evolving conception of absolute consciousness. He had come to believe that the subjective relations constitutive of human conscious experience mirror relations in absolute conscious experience and that absolute consciousness is nothing more than the totality of the particular subjective perspectives of which it is composed. Consequently, he held that all the fundamental categories of human experiences, not merely those of reason, are equally revealing of absolute reality. To be consistent, he should also have rejected the view that self-realization is the attempt to realize one's self as the absolute. He should have argued instead that our realization lies in perfecting our own unique subjective construction of the world, that it is through this that we simultaneously realize ourselves both as finite and as absolute consciousness. Further, he should have argued that the sort of rigid distinction he had made between natural science and morals in "Ethics and Physical Science" was insupportable.

2. See John Dewey, "Moral Theory and Practice," *EW* 3:93–109.

Given Dewey's conception of 'science,' the practical art of managing one's life and developing one's character must necessarily be a prescientific stage in moral knowledge—not on a par with, but of the same order as, theoretical moral philosophy. Dewey began to address these inconsistencies in his ethics in "Moral Theory and Practice."

"MORAL THEORY AND PRACTICE"

"Moral Theory and Practice" was ostensibly a response to four essays published in the first issue of the *International Journal of Ethics*, each arguing that scientific reasoning, natural and philosophical, was irrelevant to individual or collective efforts to elevate private and public morality through the then popular medium of ethics societies. Two of the authors, Felix Adler and W. M. Salter, were founders of the Ethical Culture movement; the other two, Bernard Bosanquet and Henry Sidgwick, were philosophers involved with similar societies.[3] Actually, Dewey's targets are two versions of the view "that moral theory is something other than, or something beyond, an analysis of conduct—the idea that it is not simply and wholly 'the theory of practice'" (*EW* 3:94). On the one hand, Dewey argues, moral theory is mistakenly supposed to be the study of the foundations of morals, that is, an analysis of the physical, metaphysical, ontological, logical, or psychological presuppositions implicit in morality. On the other hand, moral theory is equally wrongly supposed to be the moral equivalent of "a nautical almanac, or an ethical prescription or cook-book" (*EW* 3:94), that is, the setting out of rules for the solution of particular problems. Both versions fall short of the mark. The first conception of moral theory is clearly theoretical but not moral, whereas the second is moral but not theoretical. The first sort of theory analyzes everything but morals; the second analyzes nothing at all.

"What then is moral theory?" Dewey asks. "It is all one with moral *insight*, and moral insight is the recognition of the relationships in hand. This is a very tame and prosaic conception. It makes moral insight, and therefore moral theory, consist simply in the every-day workings of the

3. All four papers appeared in the first issue of the *International Journal of Ethics* (1890). See Felix Adler, "The Freedom of Ethical Fellowship," pp. 16–30; Bernard Bosanquet, "The Communication of Moral Ideas as a Function of an Ethical Society," pp. 79–97; William M. Salter, "A Service of Ethics to Philosophy," pp. 114–19; and Henry Sidgwick, "The Morality of Strife," pp. 1–15. Dewey's paper is supposedly a reply to all four of these works, but only the first three are discussed in any detail.

same ordinary intelligence that measures dry-goods, drives nails, sells wheat, and invents the telephone" (*EW* 3:94–95). As Dewey defines it, moral theory is the theoretical investigation of moral life, investigating that life as biology investigates organic life. Moreover, moral theory is not discontinuous with the sort of practical observations and generalizations ordinary people make, any more than biology is discontinuous with the sort of observations and generalizations farmers, fishers, and hunters might make. Yet when it comes to explaining just what it is in moral life that is analogous to the organic life processes studied by biologists, Dewey is coy. Moral theory, he says, "is the analytic perception of the conditions and relations in hand in a given act,—it is the action *in idea*" (*EW* 3:95). What he does not say is to what end he thinks acts are related or what ideals they are conditioned upon. Presumably, the answer in each case would be self-realization. But this was apparently not an issue into which he wished to be drawn.

Instead, Dewey attacks what he takes to be the first and more fundamental misconception of moral theory: the conception of moral theory as a propadeutic to morals. It is only because of the evident shortcomings of the first misconception, he suggests, that the second misconception has made any appeal. To correct the first error and thus remove any motivation for the second, Dewey argues for a reconstruction of the "aborted conception of theory" in which the error originates (*EW* 3:94). But he might equally have called it an aborted conception of practical reason.

'Theory' was traditionally distinguished from 'practice' on the grounds that theoretical activity involves reason, yielding changes in the state of our knowledge, whereas practice can (and often does) rely on intuition and habituation, yielding changes in the state of the world. Consequently, neither activity seemed integral to the other. Appealing to this traditional distinction, one of Dewey's nominal interlocutors, Felix Adler, had asserted that theories of morals were as inessential to moral practice as theories of aeronautics or locomotion were inessential to the practices of plowing and walking. Dewey replies:

> What the well-worn illustrations of walking without knowledge of the theory of locomotion, of reasoning without knowledge of the syllogism, etc., prove is that a man may know some things without knowing others—others which, in ultimate analysis, are related. Where, however, there is anything which deserves the name of conduct, there is an idea, a "theory," at least as large as the action. Because the theory is narrow in scope it is not lacking; and it is

narrow only so far as the corresponding act is abstract and partial. The average man can walk without *much* theory because walking is not an act of *great* content. (*EW* 3:96)

Dewey's point seems to be this. Theoretical inquiry appears inessential to practical affairs only when we take as our paradigm of theoretical inquiry the sciences that we now call sciences of basic research, such as physics, astronomy, pure mathematics, and theoretical chemistry. Although we hope the products of these sciences will benefit other human practices, none is required to be directly beneficial to any particular practice. But there are, in addition to these special sciences, other genuinely 'theoretic' investigations whose relations to practical activities are considerably more direct. Dewey lacked a term for these practical sciences, which I will group under the general rubric of 'materials sciences.' Materials sciences are those 'practical' or 'applied' sciences that investigate the nature of the resources on which various practical human projects depend. Examples include metallurgy, aerodynamics, and human physiology.

If we expand our paradigm of scientific or theoretical inquiry to include materials sciences, then it appears that every goal-directed human activity can be said to have some body of 'theory' lying behind it. The accomplished plowman will have a working knowledge of soil composition, land navigation, draft animals, and so forth. The accomplished chef must have a considerable grasp of the practical chemistry of foodstuffs and the interactions of their constituents with various other materials (e.g., coloring agents). Practitioners of such arts are never wholly innocent of theories about the materials with which they work.

Turning to the relation of moral practice to moral theory, Dewey argues that it is the same as that which holds between the arts of plowing, bridge building, or cooking and their respective materials sciences. The artisan, no less than the philosopher, has a stock of theoretical notions about moral conduct and character upon which his judgments about his own and others' lives are based. Dewey states: "The sole difference between the idea of a child, that he ought to learn the multiplication-table, or be kind to his baby-sister, and the widest moral theory—the one recognized as theory by every one—is simply one of degree of analysis of what practice is, and not a difference of kind. Action to the child is narrow and partial, and his theory is limited" (*EW* 3:97).

After introducing his own view of moral theorizing, Dewey uses it to attack a distinction drawn by another interlocutor, Bernard Bosanquet,

between 'moral ideas' and 'ideas about morals,' similar to Bradley's distinction between the moral facts (moral perceptions) and moral theory
(generalizations from the facts). On the basis of this distinction, Bosanquet had argued that concrete moral dilemmas cannot be solved by appeal to councils of moral theorists, since their 'ideas about morals' are
ideas about the logic of moral concepts, bearing no special relation to
their realization in practice.

But if every agent acts on the basis of some theoretical understanding
of the materials available for the pursuit of his ends, then it ought not to
be the case that a council of moral theorists would be of no use to agents
in moral dilemmas. The council ought to be able to assist agents by
increasing their understanding of the materials—dispositions and actions—of moral practice. Dewey suggests that if such councils are of no
use to those facing moral dilemmas, it is because they misconceive their
roles as theorists:

> What I am getting at, in a word, is that the ordinary idea of moral theory
> shears off the very factors which make it *moral* theory at all and reduces it to
> the plane of physical theory. Physical theory does deal with abstractions, with
> hypothesis. It says, "If this, then that". . . . Now, the pundit who should allow
> his final deliverances [about a specific case] to go out in the form of "If this,
> then that" (except as a way of saying "I do not know enough of this concrete
> case to have any theory about it"), would be denying the sole condition of
> *moral* theory; he would be mutilating the moral fact, the individualized act,
> till it was a mere bundle of abstractions. (*EW* 3:98)

Because sciences of basic research are not conducted with reference to
any particular human practical activity, the products of sciences such as
physics are universal laws concerning the relations of objects and events
in various hypothetical situations ('if this, then that'). Materials sciences, on the other hand, are conducted on the understanding that the
purpose is to facilitate particular practices and that the products of their
research must bear some relation to actual situations arising in those
practices. Moral theory should be conducted on the same understanding. Dewey goes on: "In the last analysis, then, the value of our council
of pundits will depend upon this: not whether theory helps practice, but
whether the council is capable of the kind of theory demanded" (*EW*
3:99). If moral theorists act on the assumption that moral theory is a
science of basic research, then their analyses of moral ideas may be as
empty of practical value as Bosanquet claims. If, however, they were to

conceive of moral theory as a practical science of the resources available for the construction of a morally satisfactory life, then their analyses would be of enormous value.

Moreover, Dewey argues, once we recognize that moral theory is a practical, or materials, science of the human self and its realization, then the supposed distinction between moral rules and scientific laws will fall away. Contrary to common belief, he argues, moral rules do not in fact 'tell us what to do.' Like the conclusions of any materials science, moral rules and principles are simply general statements of the nature of the resources available to us and about their performance when put to various uses. Dewey writes:

> Some . . . entertain the idea that a moral law is a command: that it actually tells us what we should or should not do! The Golden Rule gives me absolutely no knowledge, of itself, of what I should do. . . . About the specific act to be done it tells, I repeat, not a jot. But it is a most marvelous tool of analysis. . . .
>
> What this rule is, that every rule is which has any use at all. This is the grain of truth in Mill's idea of a nautical almanac. The almanac, after all, does not tell the sailor where he is or how to navigate. It is an aid in his analysis of the required conditions of right navigation. (EW 3:100–101)

In rejecting the traditional conception of moral theory as irrelevant to practical action, Dewey warns, we must not go too far in the opposite direction and begin to imagine that moral theory is nothing but practical guidance or instruction. Nor should we defend philosophical moral science from the territorial advance of the natural sciences by arguing that it consists solely in nonscientific prescriptions and evaluations of conduct. Moral principles such as the Golden Rule, Dewey argues, are descriptive, not prescriptive. He writes: "Taken in any full meaning, the law of gravitation indicates an order of physical fact in which matter behaves thus and so; the Golden Rule indicates an order of social fact in which it is true that persons act thus and so, and not simply desirable that they should act thus and so" (EW 3:106). Here Dewey is clearly leaning on the unstated premise that the moral end is personal realization. His claim that there is an order of social fact that the Golden Rule describes makes sense only if we suppose human beings do not always act as 'persons' do.

Dewey's claim that moral principles are not prescriptive has another source. Moral theory, as Dewey understands it, is not a pure theoretical enterprise, as philosophy is. Moral theory does not pursue knowledge for its own sake. Dewey says that "the difference between a practical and a theoretical consciousness is that the former is consciousness of *something to be done*" (*EW* 3:108). A practical science, such as medicine or engineering, presumes its ends are justifiable. It does not concern itself with the question of what the justification might be. It confines itself to determining how those ends may best be pursued. Consequently, no explanation is given why its recommendations should be acted upon. Similarly, Dewey thinks, no reason need be given by moral theorists why their recommendations should be acted upon. Given the object of moral life, moral theorists simply recommend ways that end may best be pursued.

Of course, this way of dealing with the status of moral principles does not tell us why we ought to adopt the particular end that Dewey presumes moral theory promotes. Dewey's handling of the matter might seem disingenuous until we consider how moral theory would fit into his pantheon of knowledge. Because moral theory is concerned with a limited subject matter (action in relation to the end of self-realization), it would be a 'special science.' As such it would be subordinate to the science of sciences, philosophy. Philosophy, using psychological method, provides the justifications for the basic assumptions of each special science, by appeal to the fundamental categories of the universe that its analysis reveals. All the special sciences are equally defective, on this view, precisely because they operate on the basis of assumptions they are not themselves able to prove. Consequently, justification of the ends of moral theory is a problem for pure philosophy rather than for moral theory. For this reason, Dewey could feel entitled to leave this problem to another day. It is a problem for a higher level of inquiry than that on which Bosanquet's council of moral theorists would be operating when making recommendations regarding specific moral dilemmas.

MORAL JUDGMENT AND IDEALIST LOGICAL THEORY

In "Moral Theory and Practice," one of the reforms for which Dewey called was reconstruction of the theory of moral judgment. Idealist philosophers' efforts to defend philosophy's claim to the realm of values had resulted in a partition of intellectual territory. Idealists argued that morality involves the realization of the self as an absolute self, and since the absolute is not empirically observable, morality is not a subject for empirical investigation. Further, they argued, moral judgments differ in kind from the judgments about events in the natural world, so that the latter are not necessarily relevant to the former. This had been Bradley's position in *Ethical Studies*, as well as the position of most of the papers to which Dewey responded in "Moral Theory and Practice." As was the case in 1886, he objects that the partition is inconsistent with the best tenets of Hegelianism—specifically, the best tenets of neo-Hegelian logical theory. Ironically, Dewey's protest of contemporary idealist treatments of moral reasoning and judgment drew upon the work of the very contemporaries he was attacking, most evidently in the case of F. H. Bradley's *Principles of Logic*, a text Dewey used in his own logic classes at the University of Michigan.[4]

According to idealist logic, the basic unit of meaning is not the word but the proposition. Propositions, however, do not spring from our minds like Athena from the forehead of Zeus. Each is the conclusion of a process of judgment. Therefore, the basic unit of thought, as opposed to meaning, is judgment. Judgment is a tripartite process, including analysis, inference, and predication. First, some portion of an agent's experience is isolated for investigation (analyzed). Next, the agent performs 'ideal experiments' (inferences) upon the isolated fragment of experience. The agent experimentally projects upon it various possible predicates ('blue,' 'winged,' 'heavier than that') in order to discover which predicate(s) fit(s) the isolated element onto which each is projected. The ideal predicate(s) that fit(s) best will then be adopted (predicated or asserted) as the correct characterization of the real.

Working from this conception of judgment, Bradley arrived at three further conclusions: (i) all judgments are logically general, (ii) all judgments are general hypotheses, and (iii) the subject of which all judgments predicate qualities or properties is reality as a whole.

All judgments are general, because the ideas of which judgments are composed are themselves general. Thus they are incapable of referring uniquely to any particular thing. The idea of blueness, for example, may be a particular thing occurring at a particular moment, but it cannot uniquely refer to any one individual thing. The idea of blue refers to a general class of qualities. Consequently, all judgments, being composed

4. F. H. Bradley, *Principles of Logic*, 1st ed. (London: Kegan Paul, Trench, 1883). See, e.g., John Dewey, "Philosophy at the University of Michigan" (1890), a report on course offerings, written for the *Monist* (*EW* 3:90–92). Dewey also used a text by Bernard Bosanquet, *Logic, or the Morphology of Knowledge*, 2 vols. (Oxford: Clarendon Press, [1888] 1911), which espoused a logic and epistemology very similar to Bradley's. Where disagreements arose between Bradley and Bosanquet, Dewey seems to have sided with Bradley (see, e.g., note 5, below).

of general ideas, are necessarily about general classes of things and not about individual bits of reality.

Judgments are hypothetical because any particular entity that we may try to qualify by means of judgment is itself merely a hypothetical entity. What we are given in our immediate experience of the world, idealists agreed, was certainly not a set of discrete objects standing in discrete relations but rather an unindividuated whole of raw feeling. It is the nature of the human mind to analyze what is given in immediate experience, to break it into particulars standing in particular relations. But we cannot know whether the products of our analyses of immediate experience correspond to real objects in real relations. To know this, we would have to be able to step outside our own experience, to compare our analyses with reality itself. Since this is impossible, we cannot know if what we take to be particular objects really are what we suppose them to be. Hence every judgment we make, every judgment that treats a bit of experience as a genuinely discrete, particular bit of reality, is merely hypothetical. Its truth is conditional upon the truth of our hypothesis that the products of our analyses of experience correspond to real particular components of reality.[5]

In which case, Bradley reasoned, all judgments are really general hypotheses about reality as a whole. The propositions in which we express the conclusions of our judgments, such as 'this dog is heavy,' should be viewed as incomplete expressions of the judgment actually made. A fuller rendering would be, 'reality is such that this is a dog and it is heavy,' or 'if reality is what we take it to be, this dog is heavy.' So, for example, Bradley argued that what we ordinarily call 'assertions' should be interpreted as complex predicates asserted as true of an unstated subject: reality as a whole. We do not bother to mention the true subject of our judgments, he thought, because the subject is invariably the same. Only the predicates we assert as true of reality vary from case to case, so only these require overt expression.

As a result, idealists such as Bradley and Dewey arrived at a double-barreled conception of the truth of our propositions about the world. Strictly speaking, to be (absolutely) true, the content of a judgment must

5. One might go another step and argue that since we cannot know the relation of our ideas to reality, we might as well view our judgments as categorical assertions of fictions or of our ideas about how the world ought to be. For an example of an alternative along these lines, see Bosanquet's *Logic*. Dewey appears to have stopped short of this further inference, holding with Bradley that all judgments are hypotheses.

correspond to reality.[6] This, however, we are never in a position to check. All we can be sure of is that some of our judgments 'work' or 'fit' our experience but others do not. Since the truth of our judgments is undeterminable, our judgments can at most be said to be warranted by how well they perform for us. This outcome has led some commentators to argue that idealists such as Bradley, or Dewey in the early 1890s, should be viewed as protopragmatists.[7] The superficial similarity of Dewey's idealist and later pragmatic theories of the 'fixation' of our beliefs (in C. S. Peirce's terms) by their serviceability has considerably complicated the problem of determining when exactly Dewey abandoned idealist logical theory for a pragmatic epistemology. It is important to bear in mind, however, that in 1891 he had not come round to Peirce's view of truth as that to which all men are fated to agree. In this period, truth, to Dewey, meant correspondence to absolute reality, however unverifiable that correspondence might be.

The fine points of idealist logical theory need not detain us, but two implications of this way of thinking about judgment should be noted. First, every proposition is the result of a *process* of judgment. Second, no proposition merely reports the 'facts.' Or in other words, every proposition about the world is 'theory-laden.' There is no such thing as an 'observation statement' pure and simple. Whenever we try to characterize what is given in our immediate experience, we necessarily first analyze or break up the unindividuated experiential whole into discrete 'objects.' What we observe when we do so is always partially a product of our expectations. If we live in a culture that looks for demonic activity in the world, for example, we are likely to observe a demonic activity in

6. Bradley is not usually classified as a 'correspondence theorist' for the excellent reason that in the second edition of his *Principles of Logic* (1922) and other later works, he specifically repudiated this doctrine. But in the first edition of *Principles of Logic*, the edition available to Dewey in 1891, Bradley describes truth as 'correspondence' to reality. For recent commentaries on Bradley's conceptions of truth, see Anthony Manser, *Bradley's Logic* (Totowa, N.J.: Barnes & Noble, 1983); Stewart Candlish, "The Truth about F. H. Bradley," *Mind* 98 (1989): 331–48; James Allard, "Bradley's Principle of Sufficient Reason," in *The Philosophy of F. H. Bradley*, ed. Anthony Manser and Guy Stock (Oxford: Clarendon Press, 1984), pp. 173–89.

7. The locus classicus for this view of Bradley's idealism appears to be F. C. S. Schiller, "The New Developments of Mr. Bradley's Philosophy," *Mind* 24 (1915): 345–66. An influential commentary on Bradley's protopragmatism that links the development of his philosophy with Dewey's is "F. H. Bradley and the Working-out of Absolute Idealism," chap. 8 of J. H. Randall, Jr., *Philosophy after Darwin: Chapters for the Career of Philosophy, Volume 3, and Other Essays* (New York: Columbia University Press, 1977).

our animals, relatives, or crops. If we live in a culture that does not look for such things, what we will observe in similar circumstances will be very different. In no case are our observations untainted by our theories of what the real is like.

Within any theoretical framework, there is always a class of statements that play the role of observation statements, statements arrived at by following what are, for that framework, the primitive, unquestionable rules of analytical procedure, the products of which all accept as unarguably real. These, Dewey and Bradley agree, are our 'judgments of perception,' those judgments that report without further analysis just what any observers operating in a given theoretical framework would observe in a given case; for example, 'this is a tree' or 'that dog has spots.' Scientific judgments, by contrast, involve more specialized analytical procedures, meant to uncover the hidden structure of ordinary perceptual objects, often by reference to a set of theoretical objects (e.g., electrons, genes, forces) that are not themselves perceived. Scientific judgments treat judgments of perception as if they were pure observations reporting the facts of a given case. Nevertheless, the 'facts' are what they are by convention. And conventional rules of analysis are themselves determined by our theories.

Bradley wrote his *Ethical Studies* about a decade before his *Principles of Logic*, but it was in the light of the later text that Dewey would have read the earlier work. And in this light, Bradley's claims in *Ethical Studies* about the nature of moral judgments and their relation to nonmoral practical judgments and to theoretical judgments are insupportable.

First, there can be no basis for Bradley's claim in *Ethical Studies* that there is a difference *in kind* between judgments of perception (such as moral practical judgments) and theoretical judgments. Theories and theoretical judgments must be revised to fit the facts, as Bradley so often insisted. But since facts are determined in part by theories, facts are revised and revisable with revisions in our theories. Since this was held to be true of judgment generally by Bradley, Bosanquet, and Dewey in the 1890s, Dewey had solid idealist grounds for rejecting any distinction between moral practical judgments (moral observations) and theoretical judgments about morals.

And he had grounds for questioning the strong distinction Bradley had made between moral practical judgments and nonmoral practical judgments. Because, on this theory, all judgment is to be interpreted as an activity, we must think of judgment as a goal-directed practice. The goal all specific acts of judgment seek in common is the construction, so to speak, of maps of reality by which we can direct our efforts toward our public and private ends. Consequently the suggestion that there is a type of judgment that is not practical must be rejected. It simply cannot be correct to say that moral judgments differ in structure or kind from nonmoral practical judgments. Moral practical judgments, if they are judgments at all, must have the same structure as their nonmoral counterparts. All are instruments for the achievement of human ends. In rejecting the claim that the plain man's moral judgments differ from the theorist's judgments about morals, and in rejecting the claim that moral judgments differ in kind from nonmoral theoretical judgments, Dewey was simply applying to morality the principles he had drawn from contemporary idealist logic.

MORAL THEORY AND PRACTICE IN DEWEY'S *OUTLINES*

In 1891, Dewey's dispute with Bradley turned primarily on epistemological issues, in particular the interpretation of moral judgments. On most other fundamental moral issues, Dewey followed Bradley closely. Like Bradley, Dewey believed that (1) the object of life and action is self-realization, (2) one can realize one's self as a person only by participation in a social group, and (3) self-realization ethics can and should be defended on the basis of appeals to experience rather than metaphysical reasoning. Dewey's *Outlines* could almost be read as a corrected, revised edition of Bradley's *Ethical Studies* for the American undergraduate student of ethics.[8]

On Dewey's reading of idealist logical theory, there was no bar in principle to treating the practice of self-realization 'scientifically,' that is, as a 'materials science' of self-realization. Still, there remained serious obstacles to be overcome if the idea of making ethics scientific was not to seem naive. In particular, there were the two practical obstacles Bradley had emphasized: (1) the moral world, in contrast to the purely physical world, is in an unfinished state and contains internal inconsistencies making complete and consistent description of its structure a practical impossibility, and (2) there are nonsocial forms of personal realization that cannot be realized except at the expense of the duties of one's stations. Inconsistencies in the moral world and between the means and end of self-realization as we experience them necessarily entail the generation of contradictory conclusions about what our roles

8. See John Dewey, *Outlines of a Critical Theory of Ethics*, EW 3:237–388.

and duties to ourselves and others really are. Thus, Bradley argued, we are regularly obliged to choose between conflicting generalizations that are equally valid on the evidence available. Choosing to accept either one or the other is arbitrary, rationally speaking, and nothing more than the expression of faith in the view adopted. If, for example, an agent chooses to realize some nonsocial personal capacity at the apparent expense of his social duties, Bradley believed, the agent's sole justification is his faith in an underlying identity of his own and others' good. So Bradley concluded that neither private nor public decisions about self-realization can be assisted by scientific methods of inquiry or justification.

If the *Outlines* is any guide, Dewey was not deeply impressed by the first of these practical obstacles. His treatment of the problem is brief to the point of brusqueness. As in "Moral Theory and Practice," he simply asserts that a misconception of scientific or theoretical understanding is involved. Because he agreed that social arrangements evolve over time, Dewey accepted Bradley's conclusion that the social institutions existing at any one time can seem and even genuinely be mutually inconsistent. But social institutions, as Dewey saw them, are only expressions of our judgments about how self-realization is to be achieved. Inconsistencies in these institutions will mirror the inconsistencies in our theories about the best means of arranging for our realization. But he did not consider that the existence of inconsistencies in our theories about the moral world indicated fundamental inconsistencies in the moral world. Nor did he agree that, because choices between conflicting conclusions about the world may be undetermined by the facts, all such choices are, strictly speaking, rationally arbitrary acts of faith. As Dewey rightly points out, if this line of argument were accepted, we would have to say that the physical world was likewise fundamentally inconsistent. As Dewey notes, "all science rests upon the conviction of a thorough-going and permanent unity of the world of objects known—a unity which is sometimes termed the 'uniformity of nature' or the 'reign of law'; without this conviction that objects are not mere isolated and transitory appearances, but are connected together in a system by laws or relations, science would be an impossibility" (*EW* 3:323).

All the special sciences are founded upon such 'acts of faith,' themselves not scientifically justifiable. A special science of ethics must likewise make

> an assumption analogous in kind to that which intellectual experience makes for the world of knowledge. And just as it is not the affair of science, as such,

or even of logic (the theory of science) to justify this presupposition of science, or to do more than show its presence in intellectual experience, so it is not the business of conduct, or even of ethics (the theory of conduct) to justify what [is to be termed] the "ethical postulate." In each case the further inquiry belongs to metaphysics. (*EW* 3:323)

To postulate the existence of an order in the moral world is not to make a leap of faith at odds with scientific inquiry. It is the first step to putting our inquiries on a scientific basis.

Thus Dewey claims the right to assert as a fundamental postulate of the moral world, what Bradley was willing to offer only as an article of faith, that "IN THE REALIZATION OF INDIVIDUALITY THERE IS FOUND ALSO THE NEEDED REALIZATION OF SOME COMMUNITY OF PERSONS OF WHICH THE INDIVIDUAL IS A MEMBER; AND, CONVERSELY, THE AGENT WHO DULY SATISFIES THE COMMUNITY IN WHICH HE SHARES, BY THAT SAME CONDUCT SATISFIES HIMSELF" (*EW* 3:323; capitalization in original). Although it is true that presupposing an underlying order in the world, moral or physical, is a necessary condition of inductive methods of the special sciences, Dewey's postulate is not such a presupposition. It is one thing to postulate that there is order, say, in the movements of astronomical bodies and quite another thing to postulate that their movements are ordered by mutual gravitational attraction. Similarly, it is one thing to say that there must be an order in moral life and quite another to say that it takes the form of a reciprocal identity between private and group self-realization. Dewey's suggestion that his 'ethical postulate' is merely a necessary assumption of scientific inquiry into conduct, analogous to the assumption of uniformity in nature, is incorrect. The postulate is more nearly analogous to Newton's law of gravity or the first law of thermodynamics, neither of which is a fundamental postulate but rather a 'secondary' or 'intermediate' principle standing between the fundamental principle of uniformity in nature and statements about particular objects and events. Had Dewey nothing further to say in support of his postulate, his position would be wholly indefensible.

In fact, Dewey arrived at this not-so-fundamental principle after a lengthy analysis of self-realization meant to show that the facts of personal and social life afford grounds for concluding that the means and end of self-realization are incompatible neither in principle nor in normal practice. That Bradley's second obstacle could be overcome, that personal and public self-realization could be shown to be reciprocal, was to Dewey a foregone conclusion. To deny it would be counterintuitive. If we take the position that to be a person just is to be the holder of a complex of social stations, then a 'personal capacity' or 'personal excellence' that is not a condition or component of a social station(s) seems impossible. So if on Bradley's definitions of 'person,' 'self,' and 'self-realization' there can be 'personal' capacities that are essentially nonsocial, so much the worse for Bradley's definitions. Dewey takes the position that intellectual, cultural, and artistic interests "*are themselves* social, when considered in the completeness of their relations" (*EW* 3:315); each is a species of realization of intelligence, which is both essential to realization of personality (so its realization is a justifiable social function in itself) and an essential ingredient of every social station. But to point out that a claim seems counterintuitive is not to prove it wrong. To back up his intuitions, Dewey had to reconstruct idealist accounts of the nature of personality and the conditions of its realization so as to remove any hint of discrepancy between them.

Dewey's reexamination of personal realization begins with his analysis of the nature of human desire and its ideal. Not surprisingly, he finds that the true object of desire was simpler and more readily realizable than Bradley supposed. Bradley had argued that since our capacity to give particular form to the enduring human ideal was not limited by either logical consistency or practical possibilities of its realization, it cannot itself be conceived as limited. Thus he came to the conclusion that the fundamental ideal is to be an infinite whole or to *be* free of external determination. Dewey also holds that the essential object of desire has an 'infinite' character. But he asserts that the ideal we desire is to *act* freely, to be free of external obstacles to one's activity.

When we analyze human desire, Dewey says, we find three elements: states of feeling, an act of will, and some external object. Like Bradley, Dewey thought it evident that the external objects toward which desires tend are never desired for their own sakes but only as means for the production of internal modifications in one's self. So it would seem that the true 'object' or ideal of desire must be the modification of either one's feelings or one's will. Utilitarians had opted for the first alternative, Kantians for the second. But to conclude that these are the only alternatives, Dewey argues, would be incorrect.

In the course of his critical commentary on hedonistic utilitarianism, Dewey holds that hedonism commits a fatal error in its analysis of the relation of external objects to the production of states of feeling. To say simply that the true end of desire is production of favored states of feeling, and that objects are pursued merely for their ability to stimulate the desired feelings, raises more questions than it answers. It is a commonplace that objects that give rise to pleasure in an individual on one occasion fail to do so on others to all intents and purposes identical to the first. How is the irregularity in the causal operations of external stimuli of pleasure to be explained?

Clearly, hedonists misunderstand what the relation between pleasure and external objects really is. Dewey attributes "the error of the hedonistic psychology" to their "omitting one's consciousness of an *object* which satisfies" (*EW* 3:253). Objects are not simply valued as means to pleasure. Instead, pleasure is a by-product of obtaining the objects for which we have an appreciative desire. What then do we want external objects for? For what we can do with them, Dewey answers. We want external objects for the sake of satisfactory activity. For example, when I say to myself, 'I want that dress,' it is true that I expect to get pleasure from obtaining that dress. But 'dress' in this instance does not stand simply and directly for the physical dress I propose to buy. 'That dress' operates as a symbol of all the activities I will be able to perform once the object is at my command. It is from those activities, rather than from the dress itself, that I expect to get pleasure. Dewey concludes that the "real object of desire is activity itself" (*EW* 3:254)—unobstructed, free, self-absorbing activity.

Appetites and impulses impel all living creatures into activity. Self-conscious creatures, however, know that they act and know that their capacities are realized through their activities. It is through the relations of objects to their ends that self-conscious creatures are able to define the manifold forms their activity might take. Moreover, it is through analysis of objects and their nature that self-conscious creatures are able to discover new ways objects might be used, new varieties of action not hitherto experienced. Take, for example, the definition of hunger:

> To be conscious of an impulse for food means to give up the unreasoned and momentary seizing of it; to consider the relation of things to this want, what will satisfy it best, most easily, etc. The *object* of desire is not something outside the action; it is an element in the enlarged action. And as we become more and more conscious of the impulse for food, we analyze our action into more and more "objects" of desire, but these objects never become anything apart from the action itself. They are simply its analyzed and defined content. Man wants activity still, but he knows better what activity means and includes.
>
> Thus, when we learn what the activity means, it changes its character. To the animal the activity wanted is simply that of eating the food, of realizing the momentary impulse. To man the activity becomes enlarged to include the satisfaction of a whole life. (*EW* 3:255)

Unfortunately, Kantianism is equally guilty of supposing that the external objects toward which desires tend are desired only as instruments for the production of pleasure. But Kantianism does at least correct hedonism's neglect of the role of our wills in desire. At any given time, an agent is subject to a manifold of impulses and appetites that might be channeled into a variety of mutually conflicting lines of action. And one cannot assume that one course of action will always stand out as certainly best, thus determining the agent to pursue that and only that course of action. Usually, a number of comparably fulfilling courses of action seem open to us. In these situations, we must choose or will which of these possible objects we shall desire and pursue and which we shall not.

When, by an act of will, we focus our efforts upon some one possible course of action, Dewey thought, we effectually *identify* ourselves with the modified self that will be the outcome of our choice. We will to be that self, rather than any one of the other selves we might become. Clearly, such choices can be rational or irrational. For one who numbers rationality among her capacities, satisfaction can be found only in realizing her capacity to will her self-realization in accordance with reason. Not to do so would be an act of self-mutilation, to cut one's self off from those activities that are peculiarly human for the sake of those that any animal may enjoy. It is thus to Kant's credit that he showed "the necessity of putting in abeyance the immediate satisfaction of each desire as it happens to arise, and of subordinating it to some law not to be found in the particular desire. He showed that not the particular desire, but only the desire as controlled by the idea of law could be the motive of moral action" (*EW* 3:300).

Dewey then sums up his analysis of desire and its ideal as follows. The ideal of all our particular desires

> is for an entire and continuous activity, and its satisfaction requires that [each particular desire] be fitted into this entire and continuous activity; that it be made conformable to the conditions which will bring the whole man into action. It is this fitting-in which is the law of the desire—the "universal" controlling its particular nature. . . . The problem then is to find that special form of character, of self, which includes and transforms all special desires. This form of character is at once the Good and the Law of man. (*EW* 3:300–301)

Dewey's answer is that such a form of character or personality can be constructed only through collective social action. To become such a self, a person, is to become a member of a group, participating in the group's common project via the filling of socially determined stations within the whole.

But self-realization does not begin and end with the performance of the duties of one's station. Social stations are rarely tailored to individual tastes and needs. As a rule, they are designed as loosely as possible to accommodate the widest possible range of potential performers. Although this is beneficial overall, it might seem a handicap to particular individuals in ill-fitting stations. Some of their capacities may be stifled, some weaknesses reinforced. So it would appear that in most cases, individuals' personal realizations can come only at the expense of attention to the duties of their stations.

But this unhappy conclusion, Dewey thinks, follows only if our analysis of what it is to be or be realized as a person is prematurely cut off. Precisely because social stations are so loosely defined, they can be adapted to each individual's needs and interests. No two people ever can or ever do really fulfill the duties of their stations in the same ways others do. Their capacities are unique to themselves, and they stand in unique relations to the social and physical world. They have simply to bring their own unique capacities to bear on their stations to tailor them to the needs of their own personal realizations.

To be a person then is not only to perform the roles society assigns. That constitutes at most a sort of minimum condition of personhood. To be a person is to make that unique adaptation of a station to one's capacities and to the resources and obstacles the social and physical environment furnishes. It is to find or construct an individualized social station that no other individual possesses. The ideal of desire is to realize not simply personhood but individual personhood, to be *an* individual person. Or in Dewey's words, it is the "realization by a person and as a person of individuality," individuality being defined as "the performance by a person of his specific function, this function consisting in activity which realizes wants and powers with reference to their peculiar surroundings" (*EW* 3:304).

Communities of persons do in a sense share an ideal of personal life, as Bradley had suggested. But for Dewey, this does not entail the conclusion that what the members of communities do is to try to construct and realize a greater self of which each individual is literally an organ. Given his view of the metaphysics of consciousness in this period, Dewey could not have thought this outcome possible in any case. The ideal shared is that a maximum of satisfactory self-conscious activity shall be enjoyed by each individual member—to which end it enjoins the performance of those interactive functions that are essential if persons are to live in close proximity. It is only through proximity, through interaction with others, that each is able to discover and develop one's own individual personal identity.

Although the end each seeks to realize, an individual life of satisfactory self-conscious activity, is unique to himself or herself, the achievement by any one person of his or her end is dependent upon the achievement by other community members of their ends. One cannot learn how to be a satisfied person or learn how to be a person at all except through the example of and interaction with other beings who are already persons. And in achieving a satisfactory personal life for one's self, one is bringing about the conditions necessary for one's fellows to do the same.

Dewey's 'ethical postulate,' the postulate that there is a reciprocal relation between the realization of each individual's interests and the realization of the interests of all, is an induction from the 'facts' of the nature of our desire and the conditions of its achievement. Since it is our own individual realizations that we seek, we must each create for ourselves our own peculiar 'niches' in the social and physical world. In doing so, we must take care how our niches interact with others'. They should not take forms that destabilize the environment that supports us. The relations of persons to persons, as Dewey conceives them, are like the relations that hold between members of a ecosystem. In an ecosystem, no act is without some effect upon the whole. Nor is the failure of any one individual or species to 'realize' its desires for food, shelter, reproduction without effect on the whole. The failure of an organism to adapt itself to the carrying capacity of its surrounding environment may destroy not only itself but the other species dependent upon it. In ecosystems composed of unselfconscious creatures, such disasters do occur, because the members are unable to recognize when their pursuits are destabilizing. Persons, however, have the capacity to understand the interrelation of their good with the goods of others. Thus the rational moral agent will construct his or her own niche in the world with an eye upon the effects upon the whole, recognizing that its preservation and his or her own are inextricably entwined. Individual and communal self-realization are thus mutually interdependent.

With that, Dewey completes his case for rejecting the second of Bradley's two objections to the possibility of rendering the moral world a fit subject for scientific inquiry. On Dewey's definitions of desire, its ideal, and the conditions of its realization, there is no incompatibility between the realization of one's self as an individual and as a member of a social group. Society is a sort of self-generating ecosystem of a multitude of individual yet interdependent niches. Granted, the activities that constitute one individual's niche may be very like those of another. Nevertheless, those activities are never identical, nor do they ever draw on exactly the same capacities of the two individuals in exactly the same ways. Hence my niche, or my individuality, is a unique achievement and makes a unique contribution to the social whole. But although I and my niche are unique, they are not nonsocial. In cultivating my personal capacities for satisfactory activity, even if these are for activities such as aesthetic enjoyment or the acquisition of knowledge, which outwardly benefit no one but myself, I necessarily act for the public or social good. In realizing my own individuality, I contribute to the realization of all my fellows.

If there are no fundamental incoherences in moral life, Dewey reasoned, then there is no bar to the construction of a materials science of moral life, that is, a genuinely scientific ethical theory that could be used to tell us how or by what means we can achieve our special ends with the special materials available. The creation of our individual niches, and the relations of each to the whole, must obey universal principles similar to those observed by other special sciences. Certain sorts of capacities can make use of certain materials and not others. Certain sorts of social arrangements permit of certain niches and not others, and so forth. Scientific inquiry, far from being irrelevant to the promotion of the project of morality, our respective self-realizations, is an indispensable tool of that project's success.

CRITICAL OBJECTIONS TO THE *OUTLINES*

In reply to an appreciative note from William James, Dewey wrote: "The book has received a little of what is called 'favorable comment' as well as more or less of the reverse, but so far as reported you are the first man to see the point,—and that I suppose is the dearest thing to a writer. The present perceptual structure is so great, and such a weighty thing, both in theory and in practice, that I don't anticipate any success for the book, but when one man like yourself expresses what you wrote me, the book has already succeeded."[9] From the philosophical community it was more rather than less of the reverse that Dewey received. Of the seven reviews of the *Outlines* published in English-language periodi-

9. Dewey to William James, May 10, 1891. See Ralph Barton Perry, *The Thought and Character of William James*, vol. 2 (Boston: Little, Brown, 1936), p. 517.

cals, five were highly critical.[10] It must have been a serious disappointment to Dewey that one of his severest critics was a fellow idealist, Josiah Royce, who dismissed Dewey's resolutions of the problems of ethical
theory as the result of his youthful, "untroubled optimism . . . in the
presence of all the harder problems of ethics." Royce commented further that "the deeper problems of ethics, the antinomies of self and task,
of inner and outer, of ideal and fact . . . our author, after all, rather too
gayly ignores."[11] Since it was from idealists such as Royce that Dewey
was most likely to receive support and encouragement, the fact that the
one man who saw the point was a critic of idealism did not bode well.
Few empiricists could be expected to be as broad-minded as James was
toward a neo-Hegelian ethics.

   Dewey's efforts to reconstruct idealist ethics of self-realization had
backfired. His revisions to idealist conceptions of self, the self's ideal,
and the self's realization entailed conclusions so far out of line with
ordinary moral conceptions that not even idealists could readily accept
them. Most objectionable to the reviewers were the conclusions entailed
by Dewey's account of moral good and evil. Royce asked, if morality
were as Dewey depicted, "where would be the true problem of evil?"[12]
Royce's question was echoed in a letter to Dewey from Thomas Davidson, the reviewer for *Philosophical Review*, in which Davidson asked if
Dewey had not created an ethics without evil.[13] The questions are illu-
minating, for their answers reveal the considerable distance Dewey's
revisions had departed from the mainstream of idealist ethical thought.

   According to the ethical theories of Bradley and Green, both the ideal
of desire and its pursuit are social. The ideal is constructed and defined
by a group, and the pursuit of the ideal is a group project. The ideal is
the standard against which the contributions of the group's members
are evaluated. The fundamental principle of this sort of consequential-
ism might be summed up as 'act so as to maximize the realization of
personality in yourself and others.' The obligation to accept and to respect the principle is assumed by all those who voluntarily participate in

---

10. The book received eight reviews altogether, three of which were unsigned: Thomas
Davidson, *Philosophical Review* 1 (1892): 95–99; James Hervy Hyslop, *Andover Review* 16
(1891): 95, and *Educational Review* 2 (1891): 297–98; G. Rodier, *Revue Philosophique* 33
(1892): 97; Josiah Royce, *International Journal of Ethics* 1 (1891): 503–5; *Mind* 16 (1891):
424; *Monist* 1 (1891): 600–601; and *New Englander and Yale Review* 55 (1891): 275.
   11. Royce, review of *Outlines*, p. 505.
   12. Ibid.
   13. See Dewey's reply, Dewey to Davidson, March 14, 1891, Thomas A. Davidson
Papers, Sterling Library, Yale University, discussed in Coughlan, *Young John Dewey*, p. 84.

the group's life as the price of membership. What in particular one is obligated to do depends upon both the opportunities an agent has to realize personality and the constraints imposed by the social roles he undertakes. The morally good man recognizes and respects the duties membership entails. The morally bad man is the free rider or social saboteur who either enjoys the privileges of membership without contributing his due or who actively interferes with the members of the group and their pursuit of the common project.

Dewey meant his theory to incorporate a substantially similar account of the nature and origin of an individual's moral obligations. But he failed to note that it was not the fact that personality is a social construct that alone gave rise to moral obligation in Green's or Bradley's ethics. Obligation arose instead from voluntary assumption of membership in a group. In Dewey's ethics there is no group practice to which individuals can commit themselves in this way. Dewey's moral agents seek the realization of their own 'individuality.' But 'individuality' is an essentially private attribute. Moreover, a principle urging the maximization of individuality in oneself and others would be empty. One's adaptation to circumstance is either unique or it is not. And as defined by Dewey, everyone's adaptation is necessarily unique. So realization of individuality cannot be the goal of a social practice.

Dewey presumably accepted this result because it seemed to translate the neo-Hegelian concept of society as an organism into the metaphysically neutral terms of biological science. Describing the ideal of self-realization as an organic adaptation of capacities to an environment had the scientific ring Dewey was aiming to give his theory as a whole. But he seems not to have seen that on this description the origin and justification of moral obligations is incomprehensible. One does not become a member of an environment or take on responsibilities to an environment, even if that environment happens to contain sentient beings like oneself. It was for this reason that Royce and Davidson concluded that Dewey's ethics had no room for ordinary notions of moral obligation or of moral evil. If no individual has or can have obligations to his environment, no agent can be, or be judged, morally at fault.

A brief examination of what Dewey called 'moral badness' in *Outlines* confirms the concerns of his critics. Dewey writes: "Badness originates in the contrast which thus comes about between *having* the repetition of former action, and *doing*, pressing forward to the new right action. Goodness is the choice of doing; the refusal to be content with past good as exhausting the entire content of goodness" (*EW* 3:374). Lacking any other basis for evaluating action, Dewey resorts to what can only be called self-interest. A good self acts rationally to ensure future satisfaction in a changeable, sometimes dangerous, environment. A bad self irrationally ignores the fact that environmental conditions and personal capacity vary over time and so are unlikely to yield in future the same satisfactions yielded in the past. Such a self becomes 'demoralized,' that is, passive and unresponsive to changing reality. Demoralization unchecked ultimately results in 'disintegration,' the inability to maintain one's niche in the world. It would seem then that 'evil' action is self-destructive or imprudent action and that the ultimate human evil is suicide.

Two reviewers took the criticism of Dewey's account of evil a step further, asking whether Dewey was not bound to consider evil (irrationality) essential to, hence good for, the health of individuals and social groups. Davidson noted in his review that it is through failed actions that Dewey's agents learn the necessity of critical self-examination and prudent deliberation about actions. So it seemed to Davidson that moral badness is integral to the progressive development of Dewey's agents' individuality. The *Monist* reviewer took up the question in relation to social groups. He asked Dewey whether socially disruptive (imprudent) actions were not integral to the health of social groups. He wrote:

> Progress is itself the ideal, since "permanence of *specific* ideals means moral death." But this progress must originate with the individual, who by the formation of the new ideal ceases to be in perfect accord with the community, and will continue to be in disaccord with it until the community has accepted his ideal. A perfect realisation of individuality in the community would be the "fixed millennium" which the author properly objects to, and to escape which it is necessary, that the equilibrium towards which the individual, as well as the social, organism is ever tending shall never be actually attached.[14]

The *Monist* reviewer's point is that rational or 'good' choices of action are paradoxically self-defeating and so evil. Since rational choices can be made only on the basis of an individual self's or society's past experience and past satisfactions, rationality will tend to work to conserve a self or society in one form and promote only those satisfactions already judged good. But conservation of the self or society in a given state and resistance to risk taking for the sake of novel satisfactions is evil, according to Dewey. Consequently, the social group must encourage imprudent, ir-

14. *Monist* 1 (1891): 601.

rational actions by at least some of its members so as to ensure change and variation in its internal organization and idealizations. So it turns out to be in one's own and society's self-interest to ignore or suppress rational consideration of one's own or society's self-interest. In which case, not even self-interest supplies Dewey a coherent basis for the evaluation of actions.

But this complaint is not as serious as it looks. First, it could be in one's self-interest to limit actions to pursuit of guaranteed satisfactions only if one were also guaranteed that one's capacities and environment would not alter in future. No human agent is in possession of such a guarantee. So no rational human agent would limit her pursuit of satisfactions to the repetition of past satisfying actions. Second, even if one's environment and/or capacities were to remain constant, it would still not be rational simply to repeat past lines of action. It could be rational to do so only if one were in possession of a guarantee that no better or other satisfactions were attainable. Again, no rational agent is in possession of such a guarantee. Consequently, it can be both rational and in one's self-interest to experiment with novel actions and forms of satisfactions.

There is, however, a deeper paradox in Dewey's ethics not specifically mentioned in the reviews. If the aim of a Deweyan agent is to realize individuality, then the goal has been achieved at the outset. Any further efforts after self-realization are pointless, and Dewey's ethics devolves into a variety of hedonism. This paradoxical result Dewey would have had to admit because it follows from the theory of the self he had developed in his previous publications. In his metaphysics, consciousness is absolute, but absolute consciousness, he insisted, is simply the concrete universal made up of all the finite worlds of experience that compose it. Since all finite consciousnesses are already fully real components of the system to which they contribute, finite selves cannot become more 'real' over time. There is no room for 'realization' in Dewey's self-realization ethics.

Forced by critical reviews to rethink his position, Dewey came to see that his self-realization ethics of individuality had no coherent account of moral evil, of a group project of self-realization that explained the origin of moral obligation, or even of self-realization as the ideal of desire and action. But instead of trying to remove these flaws and secure his theory, Dewey accepted the flaws as facts about morality and rewrote his theory accordingly. Since self-realization was a paradoxical ideal, he decided it had to be jettisoned and with it all the associated concepts of moral good and evil, obligation, and progress hitherto formulated by idealist moral philosophers. If it was on the basis of a shared ideal of self-realization that idealist ethics evaluated conduct as good or bad, then idealist ethics had no justifiable basis for making those evaluations. If obligation arose from voluntary assumption of a role in a group project, then idealist ethics could not coherently speak of moral obligation.

Dewey decided his revisions of idealist ethics had not gone deep enough. A more thoroughgoing analysis and reconstruction of its fundamental tenets was necessary if idealist ethics was to be put on a firm, scientifically respectable footing. Between 1891 and 1894, Dewey systematically reviewed and attacked what he had thus come to see as the central problems of idealist theories of the self. He forcefully reiterated his earlier criticisms of Green's conception of the relation of particular selves to absolute self-consciousness[15] and then attacked the conceptions of progress with which idealism worked,[16] the notion of volitional determination involved in the notion of progress,[17] and the notion of self-realization itself.[18] In 1894, he published the results of his critique in a new textbook: *The Study of Ethics: A Syllabus.*

15. See John Dewey, "Green's Theory of the Moral Motive" (1892), *EW* 3:155–73.
16. See John Dewey, "The Superstition of Necessity" (1893), *EW* 4:19–36.
17. See John Dewey, "The Ego as Cause" (1894), *EW* 4:91–95.
18. See John Dewey, "Self-realization as the Moral Ideal" (1893), *EW* 4:42–53.

⊰4⊱ Dewey's Reexamination of Self-realization Ethics, 1891–1894

Philosophy in maintaining its claim to be a superior form of knowledge was compelled to take an invidious and so to say malicious attitude towards the conclusions of natural science.

The Quest for Certainty

T*he Study of Ethics: A Syllabus* is probably the most poorly written book Dewey ever published.[1] Readers, then and now, have been reluctant to give this extremely difficult work close critical attention. It received only two reviews in English-language periodicals following publication of the first edition[2] and has been given little critical attention since. Some of the book's unpopularity can be safely attributed to what Royce called the "rough-hewn and fragmentary" nature of what were evidently lecture notes hastily compiled for publication without much attention to style, clarity, or at times even grammar.[3] The quality of the prose was not the only feature to hinder the book's success. Although published as an introductory textbook, the *Study of Ethics* is neither a survey nor an outline of ethical philosophies. It is a study of what Dewey had come to see as the central problems of his own ethical theorizing. As Royce remarked in his review, the book "supplements and extends the *Outlines*" rather than replaces it.[4] Consequently, the text would have been useful only to those instructors who happened to

1. See John Dewey, *The Study of Ethics: A Syllabus* (1894), EW 4:221–362.
2. Reviews appeared by Josiah Royce, *International Journal of Ethics* 6 (1895):110–32, and Roger B. Johnson, *Psychological Review* 2 (1895): 2. Descriptive notices appeared in two French periodicals: *Revue de Metaphysique et de Morale* 3 (March 1895, Supp.): 5, and François Pilon, *Revue Philosophique* 43 (1897):328–32.
3. Royce, review of *Study of Ethics*, p. 113.
4. Ibid., p. 110.

share Dewey's peculiar concerns. Even then, were they unacquainted with the earlier text revised by the *Study of Ethics*, the main points of the latter would have seemed as fragmentary and obscure as Dewey's prose. For all its vices, and they are legion, the *Study of Ethics* is worth reading as a partial statement of a highly original reworking of idealist conceptions of personality and self-realization. Dewey called his revised idealism "experimental idealism."[5] Royce, disapprovingly, called it "ethical realism." Despite his misgivings about Dewey's new idealism, it was for its originality that Royce was willing to recommend the text to his reader. "As a sketch of such a theory," he wrote, "the present volume, despite its hasty form, seems worthy of this somewhat extended notice."[6]

CRITIQUE OF SELF-REALIZATION

Having been accused by the then preeminent American idealist, Josiah Royce, of gaily ignoring the antinomies of self and task, ideal and fact, Dewey set out to prove that such antinomies ought to be ignored. From 1891 to 1894, he devoted his publications in moral philosophy to showing his idealist critics how the antinomies could be dissolved. Beginning with the antinomy of 'self' and its 'task' of self-realization, Dewey launched an outright attack on the conception of self-realization.

In the 1892 paper "Green's Theory of the Moral Motive," he draws upon the epistemology developed by Bosanquet and Bradley in their respective logical works.[7] Dewey argues that the function of judgment and idealization is the construction of adequate representations of our experience. The mark of a successful representation is its agreement with reality as we experience it: its ability to organize our experience into coherent systems of objects and relations. A mark of the failure of a representative conception or judgment is its disagreement with our experience: its inability to work in application to our experience. Green's conception of self-realization, Dewey holds, is a clear example of an unacceptable representational conception. It does not organize our moral experience but instead renders it irremediably incoherent.

Such an argument would naturally be of most interest to idealist philosophers who shared these epistemological conceptions. Dewey leaves no room for doubt in the paper that his fellow absolute idealists are his intended audience. In the course of his criticism of Green's work, Dewey

5. *Study of Ethics*, *EW* 4:264.
6. Royce, review of *Study of Ethics*, p. 113.
7. See "Green's Theory of the Moral Motive," *EW* 3:155–73.

pauses to remark: "I may have appeared to some to have dealt with it rather harshly, though not, I hope, unjustly. But aside from the fact that the truest reverence we can render any of the heroes of thought is to use his thinking to forward our own struggle for truth, philosophy seems, at present, to be suffering from a refusal to subject certain ideas to unswerving analysis because of sympathy with the moral atmosphere which bathes those ideas" (*EW* 3:170). The target here, in other words, is not Green himself but those idealists who refuse to approach Green's work in the same critical spirit they would assume toward any nonidealist moral philosophy.

Whether Dewey included himself among the idealists chastised is unclear. Probably he should have done. In his earlier publications, Dewey had uncritically adopted the prevailing conception of self-realization despite the fact that it was inconsistent with his own stated views on the nature of consciousness. In his papers of 1886, he had argued that time was a mere appearance of the absolute. If so and if, as Dewey believed, whatever is true of the absolute (the concrete universal) must be true of its instantiations (individual selves), then time should also be a mere appearance of individual selves. So in the *Outlines*, Dewey should not have defined the goal of moral agency as 'self-realization.'

The metaphysical views Dewey held were heterodox, and wisely he does not appeal to them in his attack on self-realization. Instead, he simply tries to bring his readers to feel the failure of Green's conception of self-realization to fit or agree with our experience. Again and again, Dewey argues that the conception if applied to experience renders that experience incoherent. At the level of personal experience, for example, he urges:

> Instead of being a tool which can be brought into fruitful relations to special circumstances so as to help determine what should be done, it remains the bare thought of an ideal of perfection, having nothing in common with the special set of conditions or with the special desire of the moment. Indeed, instead of helping determine the right, the satisfactory, it stands off one side and says, "No matter what you do, you will be dissatisfied. I am complete; you are partial. . . . you are a fragment, and a fragment of such a kind that no amount of you and such as you can ever afford satisfaction." (*EW* 3:163)

At the level of the social or historical experience of humankind, the conception of self-realization advanced by Green is equally useless. According to Green, the history of our social development gives evidence of a progressive advance toward absolute self-realization. Dewey responds by asking "whether the thought of an advance *towards* the goal had any meaning, and whether we have any criterion at all by which to place ourselves; to tell where we are in the movement, and whither we are going—backward or forward" (*EW* 3:166). Since each and every social institution that has been or could be constructed fails to realize us absolutely, how can reference to an ideal of perfection afford grounds for choosing one failure over another? The upshot of all this is as follows. In no conceivable concrete situation can Green's conception of self-realization afford any instruction, insight, or aid to intellectual organization of one's experience, nor can it act as a standard by which possible courses of action could be graded. Since it is incapable of guiding action, Dewey insists that Green's conception of self-realization is a demonstrably false representation of the object of moral agency.

A year later, Dewey began to mount a case for a new conception of the object of life and action, one consistent with his own conception of the nature of absolute and human consciousness, in particular his belief that selfhood is not 'realized' over time: 'self-expression.' To make his peculiar conception plausible, Dewey had to give some explanation of why the error of supposing time transforms human beings comes about. This he began to do in an article of 1893, "The Superstition of Necessity."[8]

In this paper, Dewey argues that the error originates in the confusion of the contents of our *judgments* with the contents of our *experience*. The confusion is generated by our failure to recognize that the contents of judgments (and so of our knowledge) are only representations of what is given in immediate experience. What is given is an undifferentiated whole of immediate feeling. Attention and interest pull apart the whole, becoming absorbed in certain elements, leaving the rest a blurred, buzzing, disordered confusion at the periphery of consciousness. The fragments that interests select are used to compose an experiential foreground, the 'landscape' of ordinary perception. Our judgments are about the relations of this constructed landscape with its components to the given from which it was derived. Though all judgments make reference to reality, the given, it is important to recall that they are never about reality *as* it is given.

Interests drive the construction of the landscapes we compose for ourselves. These interests can and do generate inconsistencies in those land-

---

8. See "The Superstition of Necessity," *EW* 4:19–36.

scapes. According to Dewey, we ignore the contradictions that typically arise in their composition so long as they do not hinder our current activities. He writes:

> [The] confused and hypothetical character of our first objects does not force itself upon us when we are still engaged in constructing them. On the contrary, it is only when the original subject-matter has been overloaded with various and opposing predicates that we think of doubting the correctness of our first judgments, of putting our first objects under suspicion. At the start, these objects assert themselves as the baldest and solidest of hard facts. . . . The objects which are the content of these judgments thus come to be identified with reality *par excellence*; they are *facts*, however doubtful everything else. (*EW* 4:23)

Succeeding interests reveal the inadequacies of our first representative schemes of the given. Elements of practical concern to our new interests are discovered to be missing from the conceptual landscape. The mind's first reaction to such discoveries, according to Dewey, is invariably conservative. Rather than solve the problem by reconstructing the whole original representative scheme from the ground up, we first try a less radical course. We retain the original landscape and simply add on the hitherto neglected experiential phenomena. If we have mistakenly identified the original landscape with reality, we explain the addition of new elements to ourselves as product of some transformative process occurring within reality itself. And so the 'myth' of necessitation arises. The landscape is supposed to contain unrealized powers to produce novel effects. Dewey states:

> As time goes on, the series of independent and isolated objects passes through a gradual change. Just as the recognition of incompatible qualities has led to setting up of separate things, so the growing recognition of similar qualities in these disparate objects begins to pull them together again. Some relation between the two objects is perceived; it is seen that neither object is just what it is in its isolation, but owes some of its meaning to the other objects. While in reality (as I hope later to point out), this "relationship" and mutual dependence means membership in a common whole . . . a midway stage intervenes before this one fact . . . comes to consciousness. . . . This passage-way from isolation to unity, denying the former but not admitting the latter, is necessity or determinism. (*EW* 4:25)

Consider, for example, a child whose first interest in mapping her experience results in the construction of a representational landscape, complete with the trees, grass, houses, sky, sun, clouds, as in her earliest paintings and sketches. Later, rain, not built into the original representative scheme as a normal feature, becomes an object of the child's interest. This object is then inserted into the original landscape, its presence accounted for as an effect of one of the original constituents: the clouds. Should the child take further interest in meteorology, she would eventually perform a thoroughgoing reconstruction of her conceptual landscape, doing away with the connective device of 'determination' with which she joined the original object 'cloud' with the subsidiary object 'rain.' She would then see both objects as parts of the definition of one whole fact, 'weather systems.' She would no longer superstitiously think of clouds as *causing* rain.

A few months after the appearance of "The Superstition of Necessity," Dewey repeated his attempt to dissolve our belief that there is, in reality, growth and transformation, but in this case he focused on the belief that there is growth and transformation in ourselves. In the 1893 paper "Self-realization as the Moral Ideal," Green is again the foil.[9] Dewey takes the position that self-realization ethical theories typically commit the error of confusing the contents of judgments with the contents of given experience, citing his earlier discussion of the same error in "The Superstition of Necessity." He writes:

> This division of the self into two separate selves (one the realized self, the other the ideal self), is again the fallacy of hypostatizing into separate entities what in reality are simply two stages of insight upon our own part. This "realized" self is no reality by itself; it is simply our partial conception of the self erected into an entity. Recognizing its incomplete character, we bring in what we have left out and call it the "ideal" self. . . . [and] we insert the idea of one of these selves realizing the other. (*EW* 4:52)

Dewey remarks that "as a *practical* fact we do, at a given time, have unrealized powers, or capacities" (*EW* 4:44) and that 'realization' of these capacities is the end of moral action. But the unrealized capacities or powers are not, he argues, as yet unreal capacities. They are capacities we have not yet come to *recognize* as real.

Just as the self constructs a landscape of 'objects' of interest from the given, so also it constructs a representational image of itself as an actor

9. See "Self-realization as the Moral Ideal," *EW* 4:42–53.

in its landscape. The process by which these representations are constructed is in each case subject to the same flaws. Our first attempts to give representational expression to 'ourselves' as distinct from the landscapes in which we act are incomplete and often inconsistent. The pressure of neglected interests periodically forces us to revise our conceptions of ourselves.[10] Again, Dewey says, our first response to such pressure is conservative. We try to resolve detected problems in our representations by simply tacking on hitherto neglected items of our experience. If we have mistaken our concept of ourselves for the reality of ourselves, we will naturally imagine that the transformation has been effected by some hitherto latent causal power within us, falling prey yet again to the myth of necessitation.

Green's conception of 'capacity' and of the realization of capacity is a manifestation of this error. For example, if we were to describe a child as having artistic capacity on Green's theory, Dewey suggests, what we must mean is that in this partially realized person there are ideal, as yet unreal, powers of action that when realized will transform the child into an artist. Dewey's reply is to demand to know how the child's artistic potential is detectable if it is an ideal, merely latent capacity. If it is detectable, as Dewey sees it, then that artistic potential is neither latent nor ideal but already manifest in the child's behavior. It is an unrealized potential only if by 'unrealized' we mean uncomprehended *by the child.* Parents, educators, or philosophical observers do realize the child's capacity, which is just to say that they better understand the meaning of the child's activity than the child. Dewey says, "It is not a case of contrast between an actuality which is definite, and a presupposed but unknown capacity, but between *a smaller and a larger view* of the actuality" (*EW* 4:45).

Clearly, if 'self-expression' is to be the ideal of a reconstructed self-realization ethics, the concepts of 'self,' 'realization,' and the moral ideal will have to be reinterpreted. 'Realization,' Dewey says, will mean

to act concretely, not abstractly; it is primarily a direction to us with reference to knowledge, not with reference to performance. It means: do not act until you have seen the relations, the content, of your act. It means: let there be for you all the meaning in the act that there could be for any intelligence which

10. By 'neglected,' he presumably means 'not given conscious attention.' The neglected interests would have been operating before they came to be specifically noted. Interests to which we are not attending, then, come to be noted whenever we inadvertently thwart their expression.

saw it in its reality and not abstractly. The whole point is expressed when we say that no possible future activities or conditions have anything to do with the present action except as they enable us to take deeper account of the present activity . . . to see it in its totality. Indeed . . . I think it could be shown that these future acts and conditions *are* simply the present act in its mediated content. (*EW* 4:49)

What Dewey is saying is that reality is given but *meaning* is not. The activity peculiar to self-consciousness (as opposed to mere consciousness) is realization of meaning, that is, a system of ideal relations by which the self organizes its world of experience. A change in the meanings (or representations) we assign to the given does not entail a change in the content of the given; it merely involves a change in our notions of what the given is like. But although meaning is not given or innate, in Dewey's view, the activity of realizing meaning is both. Realization of meaning is an essential activity of the self, not a contingent activity occurring only when certain preconditions happen to be in place. Hence Dewey's assertion that realization has more to do with our knowledge than our performance. That we shall realize meaning is not a matter of choice or dependent on acts of will. But how we shall realize meaning, whether consistently, inconsistently, in piecemeal fashion, or according to a general plan, is a matter we can control. For Dewey, morality and moral realization consist in regulation of the realization of meaning.

Throughout "Self-realization as the Moral Ideal," Dewey uses the term 'self-realization' to cover both the activity of and the object of realization of meaning. But clearly, he does not suppose that just any meaningful interpretation of experience is the moral goal. On the contrary, Dewey holds that some interpretations are better than others. In the absence of any explicit characterization of the goal of realization, the term 'authenticity' suggests itself. Or in case that particular term is too laden with existentialist associations, one might substitute 'soundness' or 'truthfulness.' Dewey stresses that it is the *truest* interpretation of experience that is our goal, the system of meanings that most nearly corresponds to the organic unity of the given itself. His characterization of the difference between selfish and unselfish men illustrates his position. Dewey claims that it is a difference of interpretation, specifically of interpretation of the moral imperative "fiat justitia, ruat coelum." An unselfish man, according to Dewey, takes it as enjoining him to "let the needed thing be done though the heavens of my past, or fixed, or presupposed self fall"; the selfish man, by contrast, takes the same imperative as enjoining him to "let me keep my precious self moral, though the heavens of public action fall" (*EW* 4:51). The selfish man, Dewey says, is bad and selfish because "he has identified himself with his past notions of himself, and, refusing to allow the fructifying pollen of experience to touch them, refusing to revise his conception of himself . . . begins to disintegrate and becomes a standing menace to his community or group" (*EW* 4:51). The selfish man, it appears, is the man who maintains an inauthentic conception of himself (or his world of experience) in the face of obvious disparities between the real and the ideal. The meanings he had assigned his experience are either incomplete or incoherent, distorting or neglecting much that is real though deliberately disregarded in his activities. Presumably, his fault does not lie in his failure to have constructed a truer representation of himself or his activities in the first place. His fault lies instead in his failure to accept the corrections that subsequent experience provides.

Thus far, we have overlooked the fact that latent causal forces are not the only mythic entities to which change and transformation in the self are superstitiously attributed. Idealists and intuitionists (together with some hedonists) also believe in the existence of a nonphysical latent force or capacity that human agents gradually realize over time, the capacity of free volition or free will. By means of this capacity, we are supposed to be able to effect essential changes in our own characters and activities. It should be noted that this view is not advanced or endorsed in "Self-realization as the Moral Ideal."

In this paper, the will is not an essential factor in self-realization. Realization is described as an autonomous process that proceeds without self-conscious initiation or effort. Realization of meaning can and should be directed, according to Dewey. But the regulation is attributed to interest rather than to volition. In the case of the bad or selfish man, it is to be noted that Dewey does not attribute badness to a failure of will. Nor does he urge the bad man to reform his will. Instead, he insists that realization can be regulated only by the knowledge of what our interests really are. He writes: "To find the self in the highest and fullest activity possible at the time, and to perform the act in the consciousness of its complete identification with self (which means, I take it, with complete interest) is morality, and is realization" (*EW* 4:51). The bad man is bad because he fails to understand and act on his true interests. His improvement depends not on the reformation of his will but on the education of his understanding.

In a paper of the following year (1894), "The Ego as Cause," a short discussion of libertarianism, Dewey attacks the traditional attribution of agency to the will as yet another instance of the superstition of necessitation.[11] In brief, he argues that accounts of human agency based upon the premise that human beings have a faculty or power of volition fail so dismally to explain human behavior as to render the premise incredible. Theories defining the will as an efficient cause of action, Dewey calls 'libertarian' to distinguish them from both determinism and indeterminism. Determinism (either as Dewey defines it in "The Superstition of Necessity" or as it is more commonly defined) neither requires nor supports the supposition that the will exists or plays a role in conduct. Indeterminism, defined as the 'liberty of indifference,' likewise neither requires nor supports the supposition that the will plays a role in determining conduct. Libertarianism alone makes this supposition. Nevertheless, Dewey continues, no libertarian has succeeded in explaining how it is that a single 'cause,' in the absence of contributing external forces, can at any one time be the source of alternate incompatible effects. Consequently, libertarianism, when pressed, has invariably devolved into some variety either of determinism or of indeterminism. And so, Dewey concludes, no justification has ever successfully been given to support the supposition that the will exists or plays a role in conduct. Continued assertion of the existence of the will is thus insupportable.

Now this was not the position Dewey held in 1891. In *Outlines*, following Green and Bradley, he had held that the activity of will was what distinguished voluntary from involuntary conduct. Moral agents, persons, were distinguished from nonmoral agents, animals, on the grounds that the latter lacked will—the capacity voluntarily to endorse ideal courses of action. And the will played a role in the *Outlines'* analysis of desire. Will was the element that distinguished human desire from animal passion and impulse. Animal action, it was suggested, was merely reaction to the stimuli of impulse. Moral or voluntary conduct, by contrast, was the manifestation of an agent's willing the realization of consciously endorsed impulses. Development of a theory of conduct in which the will played no role was thus a novelty both for Dewey and for idealist ethics,[12] one that undoubtedly merited Royce's 'somewhat extended notice' in 1895.

11. See John Dewey, "The Ego as Cause," *EW* 4:91–105.
12. Though it was not, of course, such a novelty for ethical philosophy generally, as Royce noted in his review; see Royce, review of *Study of Ethics*, p. 111.

THE END OF MORALITY IN THE *STUDY OF ETHICS*

Dewey's critique of idealist conceptions of the self altered his view of the facts of moral life and, consequently, of moral science. In 1891, moral science was a material science of self-realization. The moral scientist was (1) to describe and explain just what ideal personal capacities had historically been realized by human agents and (2) to suggest ways ideal personal capacities (and so persons themselves) could be more freely and fully realized. By 1894, Dewey's conception of moral science had changed.

First, moral science need not now concern itself with the historical realization of ideal capacities, since Dewey had rejected the existence of ideal capacities whose progressive realization could be the goal of social and personal life. He now held that the only capacities a self may have are the capacities it already has as a self-conscious being. Since the self's capacities are given, all that waits to be 'realized' is their meaning. In effect, Dewey had reversed the relation between the real and the ideal. Instead of trying to grasp how human agents have realized ideals, the moral scientist has now to grasp how agents *idealize* the real.

This further relieves the moral scientist of trying to understand and to explain how persons have come to be what they are. Realization of ideal capacities was a historically determined process. What could be realized by a particular agent was determined at least in part by the historical development of his society or group. This was the case because the social roles or niches available to be realized by any agent are always peculiar to a society's stage of historical development. Dewey's rejection of time as a condition of the self's reality ruled out this sort of historical determination. In the *Study of Ethics*, it is what persons understand themselves to be, rather than what they actually are, that is context-dependent. It is ways of expressing ourselves that we learn from others rather than ways of being.

And so in the *Study of Ethics*, the moral scientist is also relieved of the task of making practical suggestions for the literal improvement of persons. Idealization of the real, not realization of the ideal, is the object of his studies. Any practical suggestions will have to do with the quality of contemporary idealizations. In other words, his practical suggestions will be aimed at reforming his fellows' understanding of their own nature, not at reforming his fellows. The moral scientist has turned out to be a sort of moral psychologist, one who undertakes "a thorough psy-

chological examination of the process of active experience" to improve
our understanding of what "the free and normal living of life as it is"
actually involves.[13] His job is to describe how the expression of impulse
occurs, what constitutes an obstacle to expression, and how these obstacles may be overcome. In one respect, however, the moral scientist's
task is unchanged. It remains practical. For on this account of morals,
the distinction between truth and goodness is wholly collapsed. Since
knowing and expressing the self is our true end, then obviously any
science that increases our understanding of ourselves is inherently
'practical.'

The *Study of Ethics* is divided into two parts of unequal length. Part I is
a brief overview of the main points in Dewey's theory of ethics. Part II,
the bulk of the text, demonstrates and defends Dewey's conception of
ethical theory as a branch of psychology. Central to the project of Part II
is elimination from moral science of those survivals of 'faculty' psychology lingering in common-sense moral views. Dewey had, of course, already attacked the faculty of will in articles preceding the appearance of
the *Study of Ethics*. But his critique had been metaphysical and epistemological, unsupported by a strictly 'psychological' examination of
human thought and action. This deficiency was remedied in the *Study of
Ethics*. Dewey's psychological analysis begins in Part I and continues in
Part II, accompanied by a related analysis of the phenomena of moral
judgment and the 'faculty' of conscience.

Customary analyses of moral conduct, Dewey argues, agree in differ-
entiating moral from nonmoral action on the ground that the former is
voluntary and the latter not. Conduct is voluntary and so of moral significance whenever the agent is self-conscious, well informed regarding
and interested in a given act, whose projected consequences coincide
with the agent's preferences and/or long-term projects. This partial analysis of moral or voluntary conduct Dewey fills out as follows.

All conduct, voluntary and nonvoluntary, originates in conscious impulses—the spontaneous autonomous activity that is the essence of any
conscious entity. To this collection of impulses, self-consciousness con-
tributes another: the impulse to idealize experience that Dewey vari-
ously calls "idealization," "mediation of experience," and "definition."[14]
For example, oysters and infants are similar in that each lives in a world

13. Preface to *Study of Ethics*, EW 4:221.
14. Dewey is also loose in his characterizations of the functions of the self, sometimes
distinguishing them as consciousness and self-consciousness, sometimes as consciousness
and unconsciousness. The first usage seems more precise and is followed in this chapter.

of immediate experience, organized by the percipient's impulsive activity. Neither creature experiences the world as meaningful. The similarity is of course superficial, because the infant has, in addition to the impulses shared with the oyster, the impulse to idealize or define experience. In the child's self-consciousness, impulse and its experiential import will merge, so that the original impulse and its effects on the self-aware agent form one concept. Take, for instance, a child's first experience of a lump of sugar. The results of acting on an impulse to put a white cube in its mouth becomes for the child the meaning of the impulse. The impulse is 'idealized,' or defined, in terms of its experiential concomitants. Dewey writes: "It is not simply that these results *do* follow, but that the child becomes *conscious* that they follow; that is, the results are referred back to the original impulse and enter into its structure in consciousness. It is evident that these mediations, or conscious back references, constitute the *meaning* of the impulse—they are its *significance*, its *import*. The impulse is *idealized*." (*EW* 4:237). Henceforth, the child will see lumps of sugar as meaningful, their meaning being the satisfying experiences they represent.

Dewey warns us not to confuse the self-conscious process of idealization with the merely conscious process of association. Animals can be habituated to associate the impulses with their results and to behave accordingly. But the impulse and result, Dewey theorizes, remain separate events in the animal's consciousness. For the child, associated events merge into one conceptual construction. And this construction replaces the two original experiences in the child's mind. In place of the separate experiences of a white lump and the sweetness experienced from it, the child now operates with a single representative idea, a 'sweet-white-lump.' Dewey goes on to say that "*the expression of every impulse stimulates experiences and these react into the original impulse and modify it. This reaction of the induced experience into the inducing impulse is the psychological basis of moral conduct*" (*EW* 4:236–37).

The child has the capacity to be a moral agent because he has the capacity to know what he is about. This same capacity is the ground from which spring the other two essential characteristics of voluntary activity: interest and the coordination of plans of action. As the child or moral agent idealizes his impulses, defining them in terms of their experiential import for his self, the agent at the same time constructs a representation of himself as possessor of these idealized impulses. The mature moral agent understands that these idealized impulses, which Dewey calls 'interests,' are not necessarily transient but can become long-term commitments. His particular acts, his instantiations of meaning, come to be recognized as concrete expressions of his general lines of interest. So Dewey argues that voluntary activity is essentially creation and expression of meaning. Consistent with this view, he for the most part drops the term 'self-realization' in speaking of conduct and its peculiar function for the self, in favor of 'self-expression.'

Dewey tries to support this account, in part, with an explanation of why voluntary action was erroneously supposed to be the product of a faculty of 'will.' Impulses or interests, he explains, do not operate singly. The organization of experience in terms of any one interest or set of interests invariably has implications for the expression of others. The various interests of the self compete in and for its attention and for space in the self's construction of a world of meaning. The competition of interests regularly requires the agent to revise his representations, to adjust and readjust the terms in which he expresses his impulses in coordinated projects. The feeling of inner turmoil accompanying the thwarting of interests provided the stimulus for postulation of the faculty of will.

Dewey argues that it is "not difficult to detect the source of the error. We necessarily tend, during the struggle, to identify ourselves especially with that phase of the process which is prominent in consciousness, and to regard the other phase (although equally an expression of ourselves) as indifferent or even as hostile to ourselves" (EW 4:254). Different sets of competing interests suggest alternative possible representations of the self and its world. The set suggesting a self-image most attractive to an agent's dominant interests tends to be identified as the 'true' representation. The opposing interests and the self-image they generate are then rejected by the agent as alien, products of external force working against his 'true' self. If the 'true' interests suppress the opposing interests, then the agent rationalizes the outcome as a victory of his true self over alien impulses. If the opposing interests suppress the 'true' interests, then the agent interprets the outcome as the subjugation of his true self by hostile, alien influences. But in fact, Dewey argues, there are no external forces to be feared or opposed. There are only the agent's own real interests collectively driving his activity. The real outcome is establishment of an equilibrium among the agent's interests—the balance that seems best to express all the competing interests demanding recognition.

Having advanced and to some extent defended his account of voluntary activity, Dewey proceeds along established idealist lines to attack the ethical theories of rival philosophies on psychological grounds. The new wrinkle to this old strategy is that in the *Study of Ethics*, self-realization ethics is one of the rival theories attacked. Where Dewey had previously criticized hedonism and Kantianism, he here targets 'empirical idealism' (hedonism) and 'abstract idealism.' This division of rivals to his own theory, called 'experimental idealism,' was not a happy one, fully justifying Royce's complaint of inattention to important details in some of Dewey's discussions. The category of 'abstract idealism' includes Kantianism, intuitionisms loosely derived from Kant (e.g., James Martineau's), and the self-realization ethics of Green, Caird, Royce, MacKenzie, and, to some extent, Bradley. The disparity of the doctrines represented by the term 'abstract idealism' defy reduction to a common set of doctrines. The variety of characterizations Dewey resorted to in his attempt to make the reduction testifies to the difficulty of the task ('abstract idealism,' 'perfectionism,' 'rationalism,' 'ethical rationalism').[15]

So disparate were the views of the philosophers Dewey grouped under the rubric of 'abstract idealism' that he wisely made no serious attempt to refute their 'shared' view. After a few pot shots delivered at random, he argues as follows. Abstract idealists all subscribe to the existence of the will. Hedonistic or 'empirical' idealists do so likewise. In effect, both agree that violating the principle of Occam's razor by postulating the existence of will is necessary to explain human conduct. Dewey then proceeds to attack the hedonistic idealist's doctrine of the will and, by analogy, to undermine abstract idealism at the same time. Neither camp is said to have been able to grasp that impulse and interest are self-originating and thus do not need the assistance of another force to generate (and explain) human conduct. Instead, we are asked to believe that feeling (empirical idealism) or reason (abstract idealism) present the will with potential stimuli of action. A given thing or event becomes an active stimulus only if it is endorsed by the will. 'Desire' names this relation of the will to the thing it endorses. The processes of feeling and reason, though they can provide objects for desire, do not of themselves give rise to action.

Hedonism holds that our infantile reflexive behavior suggested to our infant minds that pleasurable states of feeling result from particular sorts of action, after which they became objects of interest to our developing wills. Henceforth we desired or disliked things or events as means or obstacles to the promotion of pleasant states of feeling. Our reflexive behavior was thus replaced by voluntary acts performed as means to this

15. See, e.g., *Study of Ethics*, EW 4:256, 263, 264, 270.

object. Subsequent efforts to promote (or avoid) pleasure (or pain) provided further insights into the relation of feelings and actions. Experience of new states of feeling suggested new stimuli to the will. But all our voluntary as opposed to nonvoluntary action, whether it proceeds on crudely formed or more sophisticated ideals, originates in the will's endorsement of ideal states of feeling.

Dewey rejects the account as palpably false. He argues: "This theory presupposes that the mind is, like Micawber, passively waiting for experiences to 'turn up'. . . . As a matter of fact, even a child is actually engaged from the outset and all the time in activity. He has his own impulses, or lines of discharge. . . . The child's immaturity chiefly consists not in the fact that it is passively dependent upon external excitations, but in the lack of continuity in the activities set up by the organs themselves." (*EW* 4:267). If the account were correct, it would follow that an infant, like the proverbial ass, set between two equivalent stimuli to reflexive action could not respond to either. Were it true, both children and asses would be a great deal less trouble than we know them to be. The child (and the ass) will move, no matter how we balance the environmental stimuli, because impulses do not require external stimuli to generate action. Impulses are simply spontaneous urges to act. Hence we do not need to postulate a faculty of volition in order to explain how and why agents are moved to act.

Dewey then proposes an alternate account of desire. The relation of desire and the feeling of volitional effort in our experience suggest that they are analogous phenomena of the competition or clash of impulses and interests. The experience of volition, as Dewey has explained, is a symptom of the competition of interests for control of an agent's activity. Desire can be given a similar explanation. In certain situations an impulse may arise that we cannot readily interpret or readily harmonize with the interests and impulses driving our activities. 'Desire' stands for the feeling of frustration that arises whenever an impulse cannot find an outlet for its own expression. Desire, like volition, is to be interpreted as a product of the interactions of impulses in certain configurations.

Dewey raises further objections against hedonistic psychologies, but the analysis of desire completes his main argument against rival theories of voluntary action. And by implication, since the alternatives to 'experimental idealism' have been shown to operate on false theories of voluntary action, Dewey's 'experimental idealism' is left as the only game in town.

Having removed the encumbrance of 'will' from the ground to be covered, Dewey proceeds to show how the phenomena of moral experience, volition, desire, pleasure, pain can be accounted for purely in terms of interactions of impulses or their idealized representatives, interests. But before he could proceed to do the same for the phenomenon of obligation, yet another encumbrance had to be removed: belief in the existence of the faculty of 'conscience.'

MORAL JUDGMENT IN THE *STUDY OF ETHICS*

Dewey's second main line of argument, the attack on the faculty of conscience, also begins in Part I and continues in Part II. Dewey opens this line of argument by pointing out that judgment, moral and nonmoral, is a species of action or conduct. Likewise, voluntary conduct invariably involves judgment. He remarks: "Every act (consciously performed) is a judgment of value: the act done is done because it is thought to be *worth while* or valuable. Thus a man's real . . . theory of conduct can be told only from his acts. Conversely, every judgment about conduct is itself an act" (*EW* 4:224). Or in other words, 'judgment' and 'conduct' are virtually convertible terms. What we call 'judgment' is, of course, a stage within the process of conduct, a stage in which the agent, though active, has not succeeded in determining how some impulse or interest is to be expressed. Common sense, in effect, distinguishes judgment from conduct by spatiotemporal 'location.' Judgment is treated as an 'inner' activity that precedes or follows 'outer' conduct. Dewey does not forbid such distinctions in the *Study of Ethics*, provided the distinction is recognized as one made between elements of a single process. That is, the distinction is permitted as long as the two stages of the expression of impulse are not hypostatized into separate events or things.

Depending on whether we choose to concentrate on the inner or outer elements of the process of the concrete expression of the self, Dewey says, we may define conduct either as *"co-ordinating or bringing to a unity of aim and interest, the different elements of a complex situation,"* or as *"co-ordinating, in an organized way, the concrete powers, the impulses and habits, of an individual agent"* (*EW* 4:232). The first definition characterizes conduct in terms of the relatively internal activity of proposal and selection of possible lines of concrete expression of interests demanding expression ('judgment'). The second characterizes conduct as the expression of interest in accordance with some plan ('action'). Either the internal or the external elements of self-conscious conduct may thus be made the focus of special attention and analysis. But neither occurs or ultimately can be accounted for except in relation to the other.

Judgment, Dewey holds, is itself an expression of impulse: the im-

pulse to idealize our experience. Spontaneous idealization, typical of
small children, automatically refers back to an impulse the consequences of its expression. Judgment is the self-conscious counterpart of
this spontaneous activity. Undirected by self-consciousness, the impulse
to idealize may make incoherent assignments of meaning to experience.
When the incoherence becomes dysfunctional in some striking way, our
attention becomes focused on the idealization process. Our attempts
self-consciously to bring the process to a functional conclusion constitute 'deliberation' and 'judgment'—'deliberation' being that stage in the
process of judging previously referred to as 'inference' or 'ideal experimentation.'[16] It is thus a consequence of Dewey's view of judgment that
every self-conscious act, since it is or expresses a judgment, necessarily
involves deliberation.

This conclusion may seem obviously untrue. Dewey admits that it
would be false if it entailed the further conclusion that every act must be
the outcome of an immediately preceding process of deliberation. He
argues, however, that it entails only the conclusion that every act is
ultimately traceable to *some* prior instance of deliberation. And this is
not obviously false. Mental acts, like their bodily counterparts, can become habitual. Translation of a foreign language, for example, is an
activity that initially involves deliberation but later becomes habitual.
When it does, we no longer need to deliberate about the meaning of
words or sentences in that language. Assignment of meanings to impulses proceeds along the same lines. When an impulse is first felt, deliberation is entered into and an assignment of meaning (judgment)
consciously made. If the process is frequently repeated and no anoma-
lies arise requiring new deliberation, henceforth the impulse will be immediately recognized as having the meaning it was previously assigned.
No deliberation will then take place. Nevertheless, the immediate recognition of the impulse is ultimately due to some one or more acts of
explicit deliberation.

Some but not all of our actions are routine applications of previously
adopted meaning assignments. Hence some but not all of our conduct is
habitual. Some attempts to assign meanings to certain complex acts are
never so complete or detailed as to obviate any need for further reflection. These meaning assignments are the general 'ideals' (or 'life plans')
upon which our lives are centered. Included in this category are actions
taken in the furtherance of complex plans whose general lines need not

16. See above, Chapter 3.

be reconsidered from moment to moment. The complex notions we each have of our careers and the duties they involve are, Dewey says, instances of such meaning assignments that "without being fixed habits, yet form the limits within which one's other acts fall" (*EW* 4:241).

Whenever action is neither habitual nor guided by previous delibera- tions, we are conscious of choices to be made among the alternatives open to us. Deliberation is the process by which we compare and assess those alternatives. The alternatives are alternate ways the agent's repre- sentation of himself or his world may be reconstructed. Since delibera- tion focuses on alternate ways or acts by which reconstruction may take place, Dewey says that when we are deliberating, "only an act (and a conscious act) has moral significance" (*EW* 4:240). In this respect, delib- eration and judgment part company. For judgment, the act is morally significant only as an expression of the agent's character.

But although it is only with the value of acts that deliberation is con- cerned, this should not be interpreted as meaning that our judgments and deliberation are just about the properties of acts. Voluntary actions, Dewey reminds us, are always an expression of the self. (Character, in turn, is a way of acting, the way an agent typically expresses himself.) So when we judge projected options, we judge them not in themselves but *as* expressions of the self. The real if unstated subject of our judg- ments of acts is the relation the act bears to our self-expression.

Dewey describes deliberation as the process of ideal experimentation in which we seek to discover which of the alternatives available to us best fits or represents us as a whole or on the whole. He writes:

> It is a process of tentative action; we "try on" one or another of the ends, imagining ourselves actually doing them, going, indeed, in this make-believe action just as far as we can without actually doing them. In fact, we often find ourselves carried over the line here; the hold which a given impulse gets upon us while we are "trying it on" passes into overt act without our having con- sciously intended it. Particularly is this the case so far as our character is immature. . . . Decision, *resolution*, the definitely formed plan, is the proper outcome of consideration.[17] (*EW* 4:251)

Deliberation investigates the fit between ideal alternatives and the real- ity of our situations insofar as we can represent it. Judgment asserts that

17. Note the close resemblance to Bradley's formulation; cf. Bradley, *Principles*, bk. 1, chap. 2, secs. 46–48, and especially his description of 'ideal experimentation' in *Principles*, bk. 1, chap. 2, sec. 48, pp. 85–86.

the alternative act that performed best in the process of ideal experimentation is the best representation of the self. Hence the subject of judgment is not the act chosen but the self.

As we discussed above, the verbal expressions we give of our judgments are misleading in Dewey's estimation, because they fail to make explicit what is always the case, that the subject is reality and that they predicate our representations of our experience as true to this reality. For Dewey, the subject of every moral judgment is likewise reality, the reality of self in distinction from its world of experience. Taking as his example the purported judgment, 'this act is right,' he offers the following analysis: "The subject, 'this act,' in the judgment 'this act is right,' is an act mediated by reference to the other experiences it occasions—its effect upon the self. The predicate 'is right' simply traces out such effects more completely, taking into account, so far as possible, the reaction into the future character of the self, and in virtue of this reaction, judging the act" (*EW* 4:244). What is offered as a judgment, that is, 'this act is right,' is only the predicate of the judgment actually made: that is, 'I am the sort of person to be truly expressed in this action' or 'I am such that this act rightly represents me.'

Deliberation and judgment in ordinary moral contexts can, Dewey thinks, be explained without reference to nonnatural entities or peculiar psychological 'faculties.' It seems almost as if he means them to be explained without reference to 'reason.' In a way, this is the case. As Dewey conceives of deliberation, what determines the outcome as right is not that it is supported by explicit discursive reasoning (although this could be involved). What makes it right is the outcome's being *felt* to agree with reality—that conflicting impulses be felt to be harmonized in the plan of action arrived at. What makes an act right is its correspondence with reality. But correspondence is not to be deduced from some set of theoretical principles of reality. Theoretical principles are after all just another sort of representation of reality. The best and most ultimate test we are able to apply to any representation is the test of its coherence with our nonrepresentational, raw experience. For this, logical reasoning is not necessarily required. Nor need we suppose that what makes an act true is the endorsement of some special faculty of rationality. Dewey appears to believe that the practical necessity of getting as many of our representations as true as possible is entirely sufficient to account both for how deliberation results in right conclusions and for why we care so much that it should. Logic is a useful tool for reflective deliberation, but we can probably account for its existence without appeal to special mental faculties.

One might object, however, that although ordinary deliberation can proceed along the lines Dewey suggests, the reflective deliberation that issues in remorse, regret, and the effort to reform one's self cannot. An act that is 'right' because it is true to myself may still be wrong because the sort of self I am is a wrong or bad self. The more truly I express this self, the more badly and wrongly I act. Thus it seems impossible that a self who deliberated along the lines Dewey gives us could ever recognize its need to reform or, having done so, feel remorse for its past failings.

Dewey's answer would be that we need not suppose that all deliberation about an act ceases with the judgment that the action is right. Implementation of selected courses of action produces consequences, and these consequences are naturally reflected back into the impulses from which they sprang, modifying their meaning to some (possibly negligible) degree. Dewey remarks:

> The identity of agent and act has been our guiding principle. . . . But so far we have overtly considered this identity only on the side of the passing forth of the agent into act, showing that the act is the conclusion of the process of estimating value entered upon whenever any impulse is referred to its probable consequences. This also means . . . that the act in manifesting character reveals it—makes *it* a subject of judgment. This reaction of a deed back into the estimation of character, the reflective weighing of character and motive in the light of the acts which express it, constitutes conscience. We measure the act by our controlling standard—*direct* approbation; we must equally measure our standard by the act as seen in its expression—*reflective* approbation and reprobation. (*EW* 4:292)

Where we do not act purely from habit, acts are selected as authentic expressions of particular interests (idealized impulses). Because the act was felt to afford 'true' expression of those recognized interests, the act was 'directly approved' and so selected. But every act has unanticipated consequences. These consequences, if significant, may cause us to rejudge the original situation, considering both the expressive value the ideal seemed to have and the actual experienced value on implementation.

If the further import of an act includes unanticipated benefits, the original judgments and ideals are reflectively approved. The experience of reflective approval is, Dewey says, signaled by satisfaction and feelings of pleasure, for there is no conflict between the agent's new and former self-expressive representations. The agent's original pleasure in having resolved his interests into an act is simply increased with the realization of how much more than expected the original act has achieved. In retrospect, says Dewey, the agent sees that "his intent lines up, focuses the demands of life. In doing the deed, then, the universe of Reality moves through him as its conscious organ. . . . Hence the joy, the feeling of full life, and the peace, the feeling of harmonized force, which accompany the good act." (*EW* 4:293).

If the further import of an act is conflict and disharmony in the agent's self-expression, this will be signaled by dissatisfaction and pain. Reflecting back the unanticipated results of an earlier judgment, the agent becomes aware of a tension between the values of the act as predicted and as experienced. The discrepancy indicates a flaw of some kind in the agent's reasoning, possibly his representation of himself and his impulses. What he took to be an interest of a certain sort may turn out to have arisen from quite a different sort of impulse. Or what was taken to be a peripheral interest of no importance may turn out to have been central to the agent's satisfaction. His earlier valuative judgment would be seen on reflection to have operated on a false standard, that is, a false conception of what his impulses and interests really are. So Dewey argues: "The moral condemnation, in other words, is directed essentially at the ideal and standard of the act. Not because the agent consciously aimed at evil does he have the guilty conscience, but because the good (ideal) aimed at was of such a kind as to show a character which takes for good that which in light of enlarged character is seen as evil" (*EW* 4:296).

If the error is detected, Dewey argues, it is sufficient in itself to give rise to reflective deliberation. If the agent appreciates the consequences of his antecedent judgment as dissatisfying, then he is able to imagine outcomes that would have been better and regret his choice. These ideas point the way to reform of one's self-representation. What is needed is a reform of the self adequate to guarantee that in similar circumstances one will not err in the same way again. That entails reconsideration and reform of those ideals of what one really is and wants and needs that were the source of the error. Dewey remarks: "If the agent is still on the same level as that in which he performed the act, no compunctions arise. The act is still good to him, and he is still good as exhibited in that act. Only because the bad act brings to light a new good is its own badness manifested. . . . Only because to some extent the self is moving more organically does it realize the disorganic character of its past efforts" (*EW* 4:297).

Thus the phenomena of regret, remorse, and the desire to reform can be explained without appeal to a faculty of conscience or practical reason. Of course, if we do, we cannot claim infallibility or a priori certainty for our moral judgments. But since humanity's moral judgments were not, in his opinion, marked by either infallibility or a priori certainty, Dewey did not see this as a problem for his theory.[18]

Dewey, as we have seen, was opposed to any sort of faculty psychology in 1894. Thus he was no more inclined to suppose that a faculty of pure practical reason gave rise to remorse and reprobation of the self than he was to suppose conscience did. Dewey thought that even reasoning could be accounted for in terms of the self's expressive impulses. The practical necessity of discovering reasonably adequate ideals of one's self and one's world was sufficient in his view to account for our concern to get our ideals right and for our development of tools, such as 'discursive' deliberation, to facilitate the process. Dewey's discussion of Kant's theory of pure practical reason was constructed to bring the reader to a similar view.

Kant argued against the possibility that obligation could be a product of our impulses and passions. Obligation involves resistance to passions and impulses. Thus there must be in the self some source of directives to action other than impulse and having some higher (if not more powerful) claim to our attention than our passions do. This source of higher authority is the faculty of pure practical reason. Dewey responds that Kant's account begs an important question. How does reason assert its claim over impulses and how is this claim to be distinguished from the claims of our impulses? He writes:

If there is no *intrinsic* connection between desire and reason, how can the former, even when checked and held in by reason, give rise to the feeling of moral humiliation? This presupposes some moral capacity already *in* the desires: something capable of recognizing the authority and value of law— which is not only the thing to be explained, but also impossible if desire had

---

18. Believing the case against the existence of conscience or moral intuition already solid, Dewey was fairly dismissive. He remarks: "The development of historical and comparative science and of the doctrine of evolution have dealt the theory hard blows. The former has revealed the great variety of ideas conscientiously maintained upon matters of right and wrong in different ages and in different peoples, and also largely accounted for this variety of ideas by showing their relativity to types of social life. The latter theory, as it gains in acceptance, leaves no room for belief in any faculty of moral knowledge separate from the whole process of experience, and cuts the ground out from under any store of information given directly and immediately. The modern standpoint and method in psychology also make it almost impossible to attach any intelligent meaning to the thought of a special faculty of knowledge" (*EW* 4:307).

the purely low and selfish character Kant attributes to it. At most, the desire
would simply feel restraint, coercion, and would be . . . desirous of breaking
away—the reverse of humility. . . .

Moreover the whole question is begged from the start. It is only in so far as
the reason is already itself impulsive or moving that it can check and restrain
the sense-nature and thus occasion humility. To hold that "whatever dimin-
ishes the obstacles to an activity, furthers this activity itself" . . . is to admit
that reason already possesses an active, self-realizing power, *i.e.*, is impulsive.[19] (*EW* 4:327)

Dewey argues that insofar as any claim seems truly to express something we believe essential to ourselves, it is an object of reverent attention. That is, its expression is and is felt as deeply important to us. And
anything that takes the form of a demand for expression is an impulse.
Thus if practical reason behaves as Kant supposes it does, then practical
reason must be an impulse. And since Kant thinks the claims of impulse
are all of the same order, practical reason's claims cannot be of a different or higher order than the claims of other impulses. So even if it existed, a faculty of pure practical reason would make no difference to our
moral experience.

Dewey's alternative is an explanation of obligation purely in terms of
the conflict of impulse and interest. Not infrequently, we fail to anticipate or to appreciate fully the undesirable consequences of the actions
we choose, even consequences so bad that we later wonder how the act
could ever have appealed to us in the first place. After the fact, disas-
trous acts force us to ask ourselves such questions: How could I have
wanted such an action? And why did I not recognize the true tendency
of my interests and desires? Probably more of our actions ought to
give rise to these questions than actually do so. But although there are
always discrepancies between expectations and actual experience, the
mind is conservative, overlooking small discrepancies where it can.
Only when the gap between reality and our expectations has become
too wide to overlook do we make the effort to reconstruct our (ideals of)
our characters so as to bring them into better alignment with our experience.

When we have been forced to reflectively reformulate our conceptions of ourselves, we endorse the newly reformed conception as a truer

19. Dewey's reference is to *Kant's Critique of Practical Reason and Other Works on the
Theory of Ethics*, 3d ed., trans. Thomas Kingsmill Abbot (London: Longmans, Green, &
Dyer, 1883).

representation than the old. But we are unaccustomed to interpreting our impulses and actions in terms of this new model. The habit of using the old self-image is hard to break, and the newer self-image, by contrast, seems irksome and difficult to implement. We use it because we feel we must, and we use it despite the existence of an easier, less irksome alternative. Dewey's suggestion is that the experience of 'obligation' is accounted for by the peculiar relation in which we stand to such novel ideals. Because they are truer and better, we prefer them. But because we are not habituated to them, we find them tedious to employ. We act on them neither joyously nor miserably, but 'dutifully,' that is, against our inclinations to ease and comfort.

Because there are two self-images competing for our attention, one on the basis of habit, the other on the basis of instrumental superiority, we can readily understand why the phenomena of volition and obligation so typically occur together and how mistakes are made about their relation. The agent feels drawn to two self-images in different ways. Until the novel self-image becomes familiar, the agent may feel as if he is somehow being constrained against inclination to acknowledge the truer self-image by a force other than inclination. But in fact it is simply *another* inclination constraining the first. The agent's discomfort is a result of an interplay of conflicting inclinations. When eventually the habit of thinking of himself as he was used to doing is broken, the agent will find the conflict and with it the feeling of constraint are ended. He will see that "in spite of all the apparent opposition and resistance between the agent and ideal, the consciousness of duty carries with it the sense of a fundamental underlying identity. The sense of obligation is not the sense of a stronger alien force bearing down; it is rather the sense that the obligatory act is somehow more truly and definitely one's self than the present self upon which the obligation is imposed" (*EW* 4:311–12).

From this point, Dewey returns to the question of the nature of moral science. As we have seen, he believed that moral science is systematic, critical judgment of our ordinary judgments of the value of ideals of self-representation. Its task is to understand how far these judgments succeed in facilitating self-expression and to determine where they manifestly go awry. Dewey no longer supposed, as in his *Outlines*, that moral science had the further task of correcting our ideals as well as our reasoning about them. He here states that although every person estimates ideals in terms of the same standard (completeness and consistency of self-expression), what each has to express is unique. So any one ideal will have a different value to different individuals, or to the same individual at different times. Likewise, one ideal will be obligatory for one agent but not for another, and not for the same agent at a later time. An act that is good in terms of one agent's experience may be wrong and false in terms of another's. So it is not and cannot be up to moral science to say what is good for persons generally or what persons ought to do and be. Dewey states:

> Let theorists deal with the facts as they may, the fact remains that no two persons have or can have the same duties. It is only when we are dealing with abstractions that they appear the same. Truth-telling is a duty for all, but it is not the duty of all to tell the same truth, because they have not the same truth to tell. . . . The great underlying contradiction, the lie, in modern moral methods, is the assertion of individuality in name, and the denial of it in fact. Duty always expresses a relation between the impulses and habits, the existing structures of a concrete agent, and the ideal, intention, purpose which demands a new service of that structure. By the necessities of the case, it is only the general form of duty, the relationship of habit and demand which is alike in different individuals, or in the same individual at different times. (*EW* 4:317–18)

There is a good deal more to the *Study of Ethics* than the arguments I have discussed. I have, for example, ignored most of Dewey's criticisms of Kantianism and hedonism together with his account of the virtues. His treatment of these topics, though not wholly without interest, is neither as original nor as expressive of the developments in his thinking as are the topics on which I have focused. In any case, Dewey's interest in them was clearly subsidiary to his main concern. So hurried are the discussions of these topics that one gets the feeling they have been tacked on solely in order to give the *Study of Ethics* the appearance of a textbook. Dewey's concern throughout was to advance the program of reform for absolute idealism that he had first announced in 1886.

The *Study of Ethics* was Dewey's last and arguably most systematic attempt to demonstrate both that philosophy was a kind of psychology and that philosophy would benefit from the adoption of 'psychological methods.'[20] In this and the papers that preceded it, Dewey articulated a

20. Priority would go to Dewey's earlier book, *Psychology*, but the reforms of absolute idealism suggested in that text are by no means as far reaching as those proposed in the *Study of Ethics*.

radically revised sort of absolute idealism, free of the more peculiar features to which some of its many critics had objected. His was an idealism that was not committed to the existence of an overmind imposing itself on human selves or to a teleological theory of the development of the universe, which idealism's contemporary philosophical audience might reject.[21] Yet he had not abandoned the conceptions central to absolute idealism. He maintained the absolute nature of consciousness, the dependence of relations on the activity of mind, identity in difference, the existence of concrete universals, and the denial of the real existence of temporal succession. Thus Dewey's reexamination of self-realization between 1892 and 1894 was a noteworthy contribution to contemporary idealist thought.

As a contribution to idealist ethics it was equally original. First, by interpreting voluntary activity as self-expression, Dewey eliminated any real distinction between moral and nonmoral conduct. Any and all conduct is after all expressive of the self. Consequently, any and all conduct comes under the purview of ethical theory. Second, by collapsing the distinction between goodness and truth, Dewey offered a definitive answer to Bradley's assertion that idealist ethical theory could not be a practical science. Since good self-expression is just truthful self-expression, any theory that improves our understanding of ourselves is ipso facto practical. Third, Dewey eliminated any and all nonnatural entities from morals. Only impulses, habits, and interests remain. One can readily understand why Royce called Dewey's 'experimental idealism' an ethical realism and why he was reluctant to embrace it.

Nevertheless, the *Study of Ethics* shows no signs of movement toward pragmatism. In 1894, Dewey seems still to have been committed to the idea that a true belief is a belief that corresponds to reality, even though agreement with experience, the only real test of beliefs we have, does not guarantee that our beliefs are true. Although he frequently makes analogies between consciousness and its 'environment,' its experiential world, he had not yet come to think of consciousness as constituted by nature, as simply another natural process. Finally, he was still working with a conception of science and its 'method,' psychology, that is inconsistent with his later pragmatic views. For Dewey in 1894, science is the

---

21. It must be noted, however, that this was something of a mixed blessing. By his ejection of teleology from his absolute idealism, Dewey might gain the sympathy of that part of his audience which viewed teleological explanations as no more than ill-disguised Christian apologetics, but on the other hand, he forfeited the sympathy of absolute idealism's traditional audience, which looked to philosophy to support natural theology.

construction of classificatory schemes elucidating the underlying structure of human experience, with each classificatory scheme of each special science ultimately being subsumed under the psychological categories that constitute philosophy's 'method.' It is still the product rather than the tools or techniques that distinguishes science from other forms of investigation. Thus Dewey's moral science is scientific just because the end product is an interpretation of human conduct in terms of its underlying (psychological) categories and relations. His *Study of Ethics* testifies to a considerable dissatisfaction with contemporary absolute idealism, but it does not testify to a conversion to pragmatism.

True to the logic of his own arguments, Dewey was to merge his research in ethics and psychology in the final years of the nineteenth century. To be more precise, he merged it with theoretical and child psychology upon his appointment in 1894 to the joint chairmanship of the Departments of Psychology and Pedagogy at the University of Chicago.

Part II   Pragmatism: 1894–1908

⊰5⊱ Years of Transition, 1894–1903

Neither the scientific nor the philosophical change came at once, even after experimental inquiry was initiated. In fact, as we shall see later, philosophy proceeded conservatively by compromise and accommodation, and was read into the new science, so that not till our own generation did science free itself from the basic factors of the older conception of nature.

The Quest for Certainty

In 1894, Dewey accepted the chairmanship of the Departments of Philosophy and Pedagogy at the University of Chicago. In accordance with tradition, the Department of Philosophy included both the mental and the moral sciences: psychology and philosophy. But at Chicago, the psychology faculty was made up of men well grounded in the new experimental techniques, who worked cooperatively with members of the university's life sciences departments. Although Dewey did not himself take active part in the experiments conducted by the psychology professors and students, he was, for the first time in his professional career, in close daily contact with colleagues actively engaged in scientific psychological research. Through the graduate students in psychology, Dewey had direct contact with members of the life sciences departments, in particular with neurologist H. H. Donaldson and physiologist J. Loeb, both of whom assisted in the direction of psychology students' dissertation research.

Dewey's influence on his colleagues in psychology is well documented.[1] Histories of American psychology cite Dewey as one of the founders of the school of Functionalist Psychology, for which the University of Chicago became known.[2] The influence was not one-sided.

1. See, e.g., Darnell Rucker, *The Chicago Pragmatists* (Minneapolis: University of Minnesota Press, 1969).
2. See, e.g., John M. O'Donnell, *The Origins of Behaviorism: American Psychology, 1870–1920* (New York: New York University Press, 1985), and Ross Stagner, *A History of Psychological Theories* (New York: Macmillan, 1988).

During Dewey's time in Chicago, his own views were influenced in ways that had a lasting impact on his philosophy of mind, knowledge, and morals.

Throughout his early career, Dewey had been deeply impressed by the advances of modern experimental sciences and their technological and industrial applications. If to some of his contemporaries modern science seemed to make philosophy an outmoded, redundant discipline, to Dewey the achievements of experimental science only proved that eighteenth-century philosophies of empiricism and transcendentalism were outmoded and redundant. The explanation and justification of the success of modern science demanded a new and better philosophical foundation: absolute idealism.

Dewey continued to espouse idealist logical theory, despite his substantial revisions of the metaphysics on which it was based, because he thought idealism alone had the material for a comprehensive explanation of the processes by which inquiry (discovery) is practiced and its results justified. To his way of thinking, classical logic picks up where inquiry leaves off. How inquiry is initiated and by what rational processes it is directed are questions classical logic neither asks nor answers. Dewey looked to idealist logicians to provide an integrated account of thought that would illuminate and relate both varieties of mental processes.

In his enthusiasm for the 'new' idealist logic, Dewey argued that scientists would themselves benefit from acquaintance with absolute idealist philosophy. Scientists believed they were better off without the aid of philosophical theories of justification because the only theories they had come up against were 'redecked scholasticisms.' Rightly regarding classical theories of reasoning as irrelevant to their own practices and problems, scientists had often turned against philosophical interpretations of knowledge altogether. Unfortunately, in doing so, Dewey believed, they had missed recent advances in philosophical logic that ought to be of interest to them. Could scientists be induced to consider the newer idealist logic, he predicted, they would see that

> the speculative critical logic worked out in the development of Kantian ideas, and the positive, specific work of the scientific spirit will be at one. It will be seen that [idealist] logic is no revised, redecked scholasticism, but a complete abandonment of scholasticism; that it deals simply with the inner anatomy of the realm of scientific reality, and has simply endeavored . . . to dissect and lay

bare, at large and in general, the features of the subject-matter with which the positive sciences have been occupying themselves in particular and in detail.[3]

The naiveté of Dewey's prediction points up an important point about his understanding of science in the early 1890s. Despite his enthusiasm for modern science and its potential in this period, Dewey seems to have had little or no idea how scientists actually worked or what they took the nature of experimentation, observation, explanation, and justification to be. By his own confession, Dewey's grasp of the fundamentals of physical science in this period was rather limited.[4] His grasp of recent developments in the organic sciences was scarcely less so. He was aware of evolutionary theories of the development of biological organisms and as early as 1891 had incorporated a notion of 'adaptation' into his ethical theory. This notion bore little resemblance to Darwin's, however. As Dewey described an agent's adaptation to his environment in 1891, adaptation was the intentional acquisition of interests, activities, and capacities. In 1894, he distinguished the activity of persons and animals purely on the presence or absence of self-consciousness, suggesting that he was continuing to think of adaptation as a intentional act rather than as the effect of the natural selection of fortuitous variations in inherited characteristics. His rather free use of this and other terms drawn from evolutionary biology does not argue a close acquaintance with, let alone comprehension of, either Darwinian theory or subsequent developments in the life sciences.

Dewey had become acquainted with experimental psychology under G. Stanley Hall and had followed developments in the field after leaving Johns Hopkins University for the University of Michigan. But even in this area, his appreciation of experimental science is suspect. Psychology, as Dewey knew it, had barely begun to establish itself as an experimental science—or even as an independent discipline. In the 1880s and 1890s, psychologists in American and British universities were philosophers whose training and interests were primarily philosophical. In Germany, home of physiological psychology, experimental psychology had

3. John Dewey, "The Present Position of Logical Theory" (1891), *EW* 3:141.
4. In a letter to Arthur Bentley, Dewey said: "Years ago I had a copy of Maxwell's little book [*Matter and Motion*]—I think when I was at Ann Arbor. I remember thinking it was the only thing on physical science principles I could understand." See *John Dewey and Arthur F. Bentley: A Philosophical Correspondence, 1932–1951*, ed. Sidney Ratner and Jules Altman (New Brunswick: Rutgers University Press, 1964), p. 523.

begun as a subdivision of comparative anatomy. As it became recognized as a branch of mental science, German psychologists were often incorporated into departments of philosophy. The reigning schools of psychological thought of the day agreed in treating consciousness and its operations as the proper subject matter of psychology and in viewing introspection as their primary mode of observation. When in 1887 Dewey argued that introspection ought to be supplemented by observation of the subjects' behavior, his stand might fairly be called progressive. But he made no original contributions to the field, nor did he take active part, before 1896, in the debates among psychologists about how psychology could be elevated to the status of a positive science. Years later, Dewey admitted he had had no real interest in such issues. His main interest throughout had been in the ways that the science of psychology could be made to serve the science of philosophy.[5]

Dewey's treatment of the topic of experimentation in his writings on psychology and elsewhere, from 1884 to 1894, further reveal his cursory acquaintance with modern scientific practice and its problems. When, for example, Dewey advocated use of experiments in psychology, he nowhere provided a detailed description of what such experiments would be, how they should be designed, or how their results ought to be interpreted. The recent and important innovation of statistical analysis is rarely mentioned, even though it ought to apply to our own ideal experiments (judgments) as well as to scientific experiments. Like Bradley before him, Dewey believed that ordinary ideal experiments are confirmed or disconfirmed by the correspondence of their results to reality. And like Bradley, Dewey was unable to explain how that correspondence could be detected or assessed. Apparently, he did not see this as an important or interesting problem. In contrast to Bradley, who did discuss contemporary theories of induction in his *Principles*, Dewey ignored the manifold problems of scientific reasoning. From this relatively dogmatic slumber, he was roused by his involvement in debates about scientific method conducted by the Chicago psychologists and their opponents.

The leading figure among the psychologists at Chicago was J. R. Angell, a former student whom Dewey appointed to the post of professor of

5. Dewey's *Psychology* was after all a textbook written as an introduction to philosophy. Many years later, Dewey remarked in his correspondence with Arthur Bentley, "I do not pretend to be a psychologist anyway, and what I've written on that subject has been mostly for the sake of clearing up my own mind about something in either ethics or logic"; see Ratner and Altman, *Dewey and Bentley*, p. 53.

experimental psychology. The group also included A. W. Moore, first a graduate student of Angell's and later a faculty member, and their graduate students and assistants.[6] One may also number among the functionalists G. H. Mead and J. H. Tufts, who worked with Angell and Dewey in developing applications of functionalism to be tested in the laboratory school Dewey directed.[7] Dewey's work reinforced the group's distrust of associational and faculty psychology, as well as its preference for viewing consciousness as organic and its activities as analogous to the unconscious functions by which lower organisms maintain their existence in a changing environment. The group largely ignored Dewey's idealist metaphysics, in favor of more realist interpretations of consciousness and its functions. Rather than looking to idealism for the inner anatomy of the science of psychology, it looked to biological theories of the structures and functions of living organisms. According to Angell's recollections, the problems the Chicago psychologists sought to solve were these: construction of a theory of mind on analogy to biological theories of the evolution and nature of organisms, development of a program of experimentation suitable to the investigation of mental processes so conceived, and explanation and justification of that program against criticisms that a scientific theory of mental processes must necessarily be reductionist in some sense. In Angell's words:

> For myself, to analyze and describe correctly the major aspects of mental experience and to try to bring it into context with the physical organism, to do this in the general atmosphere of recognition of the necessity for adaptive behavior, and to seek at each point to discern what peculiar service conscious processes render in these adaptive acts, both social and physical—that is the essence of what I understood by functionalism and as such set over against a psychological atomism, or a rigid structuralism.[8]

6. These included M. C. Ashley, K. Gordon, W. C. Gore, S. F. McLennan, A. K. Rogers, A. Tanner, H. B. Thompson, and H. W. Stuart, some of whom contributed to the *Studies in Logical Theory* of 1903. E. B. Watson, developer of classical behaviorism, was also a student of and briefly an assistant to J. R. Angell.

7. By all accounts Mead had the most significant and enduring influence on Dewey of all his Chicago colleagues. The paucity of Mead's publications, however, makes it impossible to separate his influence from that of the others, which would in any case have been mutually reinforcing. For a helpful account of Mead's own philosophical development, see Gary A. Cook, *George Herbert Mead: The Making of a Social Pragmatist* (Urbana: University of Illinois Press, 1993).

8. J. R. Angell, "James Rowland Angell," in *A History of Psychology in Autobiography*, vol. 3, ed. Carl Murchison (Worcester, Mass.: Clark University Press, 1930), p. 27.

Solutions to the first two problems were mutually dependent. A theory of mind on analogy to evolutionary biology's conception of organisms would be of merely academic interest, unless the analogy could also be shown to generate hypotheses and predictions that could be experimentally tested. The latter was perhaps the more difficult task. Biologists were not in agreement as to how theories of organic functions and adaptive mechanisms were to be experimentally confirmed and so could not provide functionalist psychology with a model. On the other hand, physiological psychologists had amassed an impressive quantity of observations of conscious operations from which they had generated lawlike generalizations. Their apparent success in developing laws of conscious operations seemed to support their theories that conscious phenomena were reducible to interactions of psychic 'atoms' consistent with the mechanical interactions of physical atoms and macroscopic objects.

A chief objective of the early research of Angell, Moore, and their students was to provide counterexamples to their opponents' assumptions, in particular the assumption that mental operations are mechanical (i.e., in that antecedent conditions fully determine consequent mental events). One of the hypotheses they first sought to undermine in this way was the 'reflex arc': the interpretation of conscious reflex actions as mechanically induced reactions to particular external stimuli. Dewey took no active part in these efforts, but he was sympathetic to his colleagues' aims. In 1896, he offered philosophical support by attacking the mechanistic interpretation of reflex action in "The Reflex Arc Concept in Psychology."[9] This paper eventually came to be viewed as the first plank in the functionalists' platform. But aside from its interest for students of the history of psychology, the work is important because in it Dewey first made original use of a concept derived from William James's *Principles of Psychology*, James's "psychologist's fallacy."[10] Adoption of this Jamesian concept, together with adoption of the functionalists' goals for psychology, as we shall see, gradually transformed Dewey's theory of mind to such an extent that it was no longer compatible with idealism.

DEWEY ON THE REFLEX ARC

The target of attack in "The Reflex Arc Concept in Psychology" was the theory of mental operations then known as 'psychophysical parallel-

9. See John Dewey, "The Reflex Arc Concept in Psychology," *EW* 5:96–109.
10. See William James, *Principles of Psychology*, pp. 96, 195–96.

ism,' advocated, among others, by American followers of German psychologist Wilhelm Wundt.[11] In contrast to Dewey's earlier idealist version of psychophysical parallelism, according to which mental and physical processes were each simply 'aspects' of a single underlying reality, empiricist psychophysical parallelism treated mental and physical processes as separate, independent entities. Its aim, unlike Dewey's, was to liberate psychology from metaphysics rather than redeem metaphysic's scientific status. This liberation was to be achieved by the adoption of the empirical methods of natural scientists. Scientific psychology would henceforth seek to uncover mechanical principles of the interaction of mental objects, on the model of Newtonian mechanics. In the case of reflex action, this meant analyzing reflex acts into a series of mechanical interactions between the subject and the surrounding environment.

On this view, reflex action is not one but two types of mechanical operation, running along parallel lines. Take, for example, an infant's 'reflex' act of reaching toward a bright light. Where earlier empiricists had argued that there is here only one causal process going on (an external stimulus, light, inducing a bodily response, reaching), parallelists argued that there are two: one inner, one outer. The external light source stimulates the infant in two respects: it stimulates the infant's mind, catching its attention and causing it to focus on the stimulus, and at the same time, it stimulates the infant's body to shift toward the source of the external stimulation. The child's mind 'reacts' to the stimulus by forming some conscious attitude toward the stimulus, such as fear, desire, or amusement. Simultaneously, the infant reacts physically to the stimulus according to the pattern of its psychological response; he recoils, reaches, chuckles, and so forth.

Dewey, as we know, had no love for the British empiricists' theories of mind. And he had little more for this latest attempt at a mechanistic interpretation of conscious operations. In "The Reflex Arc Concept in Psychology," he attacks psychophysical parallelism as grounded in scientifically insupportable metaphysical assumptions that ultimately distort the nature of consciousness. Specifically, he charges that psychophysical parallelism is just another species of mind-body dualism, a metaphysical theory of mind and body. He writes:

> We ought to be able to see that the ordinary conception of the reflex arc theory, instead of being a case of plain science, is a survival of the metaphysi-

11. Dewey does not actually use the term in this paper but leaves no doubt which contemporary psychological doctrine is being attacked.

cal dualism, first formulated by Plato, according to which the sensation is an
ambiguous dweller on the border land of soul and body, the idea (or central
process) is purely psychical, and the act (or movement) purely physical. Thus
the reflex arc formulation is neither physical (or physiological) nor psychological; it is a mixed materialist-spiritualistic assumption. (*EW* 5:104)

Dewey argues that there is no scientific support for the thesis that
mind and body operate on parallel lines, rather than as an integrated
organic unity. Moreover, the thesis has no explanatory value. It assumes
rather than proves that these two materially different entities exist and
act in tandem and thus only succeeds in perpetuating the insolvable
problem of mind-body dualism.

The claim that observation supports the hypothesis that conscious reflex action operates on analogy to mechanical interactions in nature is
simply false. Parallelists have misinterpreted their observations, through
commission of a form of James's psychologist's fallacy. This is the fallacy
of confusing the psychologist's point of view on his subject's experience
with that of the subject, so that the psychologist treats his subject's reports of his experience as confused or awkward reports of what (the
psychologist supposes) the subject *must* have experienced. Dewey
claims that parallelists fall into a species of this intellectual trap, which
he calls the 'historical fallacy.'

The points of view they confuse are those we have on our experience
before and after it takes place. What in hindsight the psychologist believes to have been the stimulus of a subject's action, the psychologist
presumes to have been perceived as such by the subject. Yet in the first
instance, it is usually only after his 'response' that the subject becomes
aware of its stimulus. Of course, when subjects are put repeatedly
through the same experimental situation, they can eventually learn to
experience events in the order in which the psychologist presumes them
to have been experienced. But if we accept this as evidence that in the
first instance the subject really acted in response to a perceived stimulus,
we would be wrong. We would be ignoring the fact that human subjects
can learn to respond automatically to what they have been taught to
perceive as signals to act—that they can, in other words, develop habitual responses. And we would be confusing a habit, a learned response,
with a genuine case of reflex action.

Imagine, for example, that a test subject is to be exposed to a sudden
loud noise. Can we predict how the subject will 'respond' to this 'stimulus'? Can we even predict that it will act as a 'stimulus' in this case?

Certainly not, Dewey replies: "If one is reading a book, if one is hunting, if one is watching in a dark place on a lonely night, if one is performing a chemical experiment, in each case, the noise has a very different psychical value; it is a different experience. In any case, what precedes the 'stimulus' is a whole act, a sensori-motor co-ordination. What is more to the point, the 'stimulus' emerges out of this co-ordination; it is born from it as its matrix" (*EW* 5:100). Whether the sudden noise will have any effect upon our test subject—let alone the effect of inducing a response—depends on what the subject is doing at the time and what her expectations for the immediate future happen to be. If, for example, she expects her experiment to produce explosive chemical interactions at any moment, then a sudden loud noise may induce no response, although the same loud noise on another occasion, perhaps a lonely night, would yield a dramatic response.

Suppose now the sudden loud noise is unexpected: what is its effect? Does the effect take the form of a re-*action* by the agent? Does she do something in response? Or is it not more usually the case that the effect is in fact a *cessation* of action? The subject momentarily ceases all activity.

The subject at length responds, but not to the noise. The response is to the disruption of activity. The subject searches for the locus of the disruption in order that it may be dealt with and the original activity reinstated. Whatever responsive act succeeds in achieving that reinstatement 'defines' the locus of the disruption for the agent. If fastening a loose shutter, stumbling over a dog, or looking at one's television set, for example, resolves the situation for the subject, then she defines the disruption of her activity (the 'stimulus') as the flapping of a shutter, the abrupt arrival of her dog, or a gunfight on the television set. Having located and apprehended the disrupting stimulus, the subject returns to whatever she was doing.

It is only after the subject has found a way of responding to a change in her situation that she is able to perceive its 'stimulus.' When it occurred, the stimulus was not itself perceived as the cause of anything, not even the cause of the disruption to which the subject in fact responds. If this sort of situation regularly recurs, the subject will soon learn to make instantaneous identifications of particular noises as signals requiring response (as we all learn to make instantaneous identifications of a ringing telephone, for example, as a signal to action). Thereafter, she will respond 'mechanically' to the stimulus. But then her response will be a product of habit, not an expression of a native conscious process predating habits.

Dewey concludes that observation of conscious reflex acts does not support the hypothesis that such acts are simple mechanical reactions to external forces. Nor does observation support the supposition of a regular causal connection between any one sort of stimulus and one sort of response. The subject's situation is a factor in determining both what features of the environment are capable of blocking her activities, thus stimulating a search for the source of the blockage, and what form her response will take. As a result, the theory of human reflex action as a series of mechanical 'jerks' is appropriate only to habits that have become virtually automatic so that consciousness plays no active role. A better analogy for conscious reflex action, Dewey suggests, would be a loop or circuit. That is, reflex action should be thought of as a loop by which consciousness reconnects disrupted phases of a short-circuited activity.

It has been claimed more than once, and with some justification, that this paper marks the real end of Dewey's allegiance to idealism. Why this is so may not be readily apparent, because the account of reflex action looks like a simple application, to this type of action, of the theory of the idealization of impulse Dewey advanced in the *Study of Ethics*. As such, this paper would hardly appear to constitute a rebuttal to the metaphysical position Dewey held in 1894. What justifies the claim (at least in part) is his appeal to what he calls the 'historical fallacy.' Its significance in this context makes Dewey's description worth quoting: "A set of considerations which hold good only because of a completed process, is read into the content of the process which conditions this completed result. A state of things characterizing an outcome is regarded as a true description of the events which led up to this outcome; when, as a matter of fact, if this outcome had already been in existence, there would have been no necessity for the process" (*EW* 5:105–6). If in 1896 Dewey thought it fallacious to assume that the results of a conscious process are necessarily 'contained' in its initial phase, that is, that nothing can emerge from a process that was not contained in the materials from which it starts, then he ought to have regarded his 1894 account of personal capacity as fallacious. His 1894 claim that an adult's capacities for action were already present in that adult's babyhood would be an instance of the historical fallacy. Furthermore, he ought to have judged his earlier description of the goal of action, the ideal of learning to express one's true capacities fully, as an inexplicable reduplication of effort. Why should any agent struggle through successive stages of self-knowledge in order to attain true self-expression when, in Dewey's words, 'there would have been no necessity for the process'? The agent was already truly expressed in the activities of his infancy.

So there are grounds for saying that by 1896 Dewey ought to have abandoned his elaborately revised idealist metaphysics of the self. But to go further and say that he actually saw or accepted the implications of the arguments of "The Reflex Arc Concept in Psychology" would probably be a mistake. In the same year, Dewey published a paper on child psychology, "Interest in Relation to Training of the Will," in which the goal of education is presented as the encouragement of a child's self-expression.[12] There is no intimation in this paper that the self to be expressed is in any way altered through or as a result of the educative process. The contemporaneous appearance of these two papers suggests that Dewey did not (at least as yet) see his arguments against psychophysical parallelism as inconsistent with his idealism.

The Chicago psychologists hailed Dewey's paper on the reflex arc as a major contribution to psychology. Although Dewey could not be said to have disproved the theory of the reflex arc (or psychophysical parallelism), he had at least undermined the theory by giving grounds for interpreting it as an artifact of its proponents' presuppositions. Moreover, he presented a functionalist alternative that appeared to be experimentally fruitful. His conception of reflex action as functional and adaptive, rather than mechanical, looked to be testable in laboratory conditions. Generally speaking, experimental observation should be able to confirm or deny that the operative force of a given stimulus is always relative to the situation in which it occurs, that situation being constituted by the agent's interests and capacities. The agent's responses should manifest regular and observable variations with variations in the situation and not merely with variations in the stimuli provided. Further, the assertion that all conscious processes are of the same order, functional for the subject, should also be confirmable by experiment and observation. As the Chicago psychologists interpreted it, Dewey's paper provided theoretical justification for the development of a new and improved form of experimental psychological science, one taking its fundamental presuppositions from biology rather than metaphysics.

PRAGMATIC DEVELOPMENTS IN DEWEY'S THOUGHT

On this conclusion, the consensus did not extend far beyond the precincts of the University of Chicago. Critics argued that functionalism was unscientific in its assumptions. E. B. Titchener, a student of Wundt, argued vehemently that functionalism did not practice proper scientific

12. See John Dewey, "Interest in Relation to Training of the Will," *EW* 5:111–63.

methods. First, he maintained that functionalism did not limit its investigations to the objective phenomena of consciousness, focusing instead on the subjective significance that mental operations and events have for the experiencing subject. Second, he held that functionalism reinstated the metaphysics of the 'final cause' in psychology, thus constituting an intellectual regression, not a scientific advance. Titchener warned:

> There is further, the danger that, if function is studied before structure had been fully elucidated, the student may fall into that acceptance of teleological explanation which is fatal to scientific advance. . . . Psychology might thus put herself for the second time, and no less surely though by different means, under the dominion of philosophy. In a word, the historical conditions of psychology rendered it inevitable that, when the time came for the transformation from philosophy to science, problems should be formulated, explicitly or implicitly, as static rather than dynamic, structural rather than functional.[13]

To emphasize his own view that a science of the mind ought to follow the method of the biologist studying the morphology of organisms, Titchener labeled his approach "structuralism."

The functionalists' response to the challenge posed by Titchener's attacks was to try to amass a body of experimental data sufficient to rebut the charge that functionalism could not produce good scientific results. In these efforts Dewey took no direct part. He acted instead as a partisan for his colleagues, urging philosophers to accept functionalist methodology and replying to criticisms that functionalism's theoretical assumptions were nonscientific. For example, he offers and defends functionalist explanations of conscious operations, including thought, perception, and judgment, in the 1900 article "Some Stages of Logical Thought" (in which thought is described as a doubt-inquiry process) and the 1902 paper "Interpretation of Savage Mind."[14] He defends the scientific respectability of functionalist psychological methods in his 1899 article "Psychology and Philosophic Method," his 1902 papers "The Evolutionary Method as Applied to Morality" (a two-part series), and the 1903 publications "Thought and Its Subjectmatter" (Dewey's contribu-

13. E. B. Titchener, "The Postulates of a Structural Psychology," *Philosophical Review* 7 (1898): 453. See also Titchener's article of the following year, "Structural and Functional Psychology," *Philosophical Review* 8 (1899): 290–99.

14. See John Dewey, "Some Stages of Logical Thought," *MW* 1:151–74; and "Interpretation of Savage Mind," *MW* 2:39–52.

tion to *Studies in Logical Theory*) and "The Logical Conditions of a Scientific Treatment of Morality."[15] In these papers, Dewey argued with increasing force against the conception of science on which Titchener based his criticisms of functionalism. In his efforts to flesh out and defend a conception of science consistent with the functionalist program, he made increasing use of concepts and arguments derived from both Peirce and James.

The functionalist approach to human mental acts and events, as Dewey understood it, was genetic. As we saw, for example, in the case of reflex acts, the stimulus and the response were defined in terms of the process from which each emerges. It was to this that Titchener objected as potentially reintroducing natural teleology into psychology. Titchener's and other similar objections thus presented (at least) two theoretical problems for Dewey, functionalism's party theoretician, to resolve: how to show that a genetic method is not inconsistent with paradigmatic cases of scientific practice, and how to show that a genetic method could be practiced without the importation of unscientific, speculative assumptions about the basic furniture of the world.

Dewey had, in addition, his own theoretical interests, which presented him with a third problem. He wanted to establish ethics as well as psychology as legitimate science. This made his own views vulnerable to a charge that they involved a form of the genetic fallacy—a confusion of questions of origins with questions of justification. In the fall of 1901, he used his course in the history of ethics to develop his ideas about how these difficulties might be handled. By the end of the course, he had worked out answers to functionalism's two problems, first delivered in an address to the University of Chicago's philosophy club, "The Historical Method in Ethics." This work was subsequently expanded and published in 1902 as a two-part article under the title "The Evolutionary Method as Applied to Morality."[16] Dewey's answer to the third problem came shortly after, in the 1903 monograph "The Logical Conditions of a Scientific Treatment of Morality."

In "The Evolutionary Method as Applied to Morality," Dewey argues that the 'historical' or genetic method he proposes as suitable to the

15. See John Dewey, "Psychology and Philosophic Method," *MW* 1:113–30 (where it appears under a later title, "'Consciousness' and Experience"); "The Evolutionary Method as Applied to Morality," *MW* 2:3–19; "Thought and Its Subjectmatter," *MW* 2:293–378; and "The Logical Conditions of a Scientific Treatment of Morality," *MW* 3:3–39.

16. See John Dewey, "The Historical Method in Ethics," *LW* 17:351–60; and "The Evolutionary Method as Applied to Morality," *MW* 2:1–38.

practice of ethical inquiry is not unscientific in its focus on processes or emergence or in its assumptions about their metaphysical status. First, it is not true to say that the properly 'scientific' natural sciences of the inorganic world concern themselves with questions of *what* things are like rather than of *how* things come to be as they are. On the contrary, it is how things come to be, he argues, that defines for science what those things are. He explains:

> The essence of the experimental method I take to be control of the analysis or interpretation of any phenomenon by bringing to light the exact conditions, and the only conditions, which are involved in its coming into being. Suppose the problem to be the nature of water. By "nature" we mean no inner metaphysical essence; its "nature" is found only by experiencing it. By nature, in science, we mean a knowledge for purposes of intellectual and practical control. . . .
>
> What experimentation does is to let us see into water in the process of making. Through generating water we single out the precise and sole conditions which have to be fulfilled that water may present itself as an experienced fact. If this case be typical, then the experimental method is entitled to rank as genetic method; it is concerned with the manner or process by which anything comes into experienced existence. (*MW* 2:4–5)

In other words, the study of dynamic processes by which things come to be what they are is not a special feature of the organic sciences, distinguishing them from the inorganic sciences. Every science using the experimental method, Dewey argues, treats dynamic processes as fundamental and treats objects as reducible to stages of processes. All that differs is the degree of complexity involved.[17] And the organic sciences, he insists, use experimental techniques every bit as much as the inorganic sciences, even such sciences as anthropology, sociology, and human physiology. He concedes that the organic sciences are often unable to confirm their hypotheses by laboratory experimentation. But laboratories are not the only places in which experiments take place. Nature performs experiments regularly. Consequently, human history is a record of human experience of natural and artificial experimentation for those who care to read it.

17. For example, as the processes yielding water are simpler than those yielding, say, budgerigars, the definition of chemical processes that yield water ($H + O_2$) is simpler and more readily reduced to a formula than is (as yet) the definition of the processes that yield budgerigars.

Sciences such as psychology, sociology, ethics, and zoology rely on experiments, Dewey says, but their experiments are primarily historical. He notes: "We cannot take a present case of parental care, or of a child's untruthfulness, and cut it into sections, or tear it into physical pieces, or subject it to chemical analysis. Only through history, through a consideration of how it came to be what it is, can we unravel it and trace the interweaving of its constituent parts. History offers to us the only available substitute for the isolation and for the cumulative recombination of experiment" (*MW* 2:9). In this respect, organic sciences are like geology, astronomy, or cosmology.[18] Practitioners of these inorganic sciences do not rely as heavily on laboratory experiments as physicists or chemists do. Yet no one would deny that geologists or astronomers are scientists practicing scientific method. So the fact that a zoologist or sociologist does not perform experiments in a laboratory does not prove that the zoologist or sociologist is not a scientist practicing scientific, 'experimental' methods of inquiry.

Dewey's response to the second issue Titchener's remarks had raised, the metaphysical assumptions of genetic and experimental science, comes in his reply to the stock argument that any attempt to study ethics experimentally will collapse into some form of materialism. That is, if scientists were to apply the genetic method to ethics, eventually the trail would lead back to some protohuman 'missing link'—with the following result: "If, for example, the earlier stage shows only social instincts on the part of the animal, then, somehow or other, the later manifestations of human conscience are only animal instincts disguised and overlaid. To attribute any additional meaning to them, is an illusion to be banished by a proper scientific view" (*MW* 2:11). In which case, the attempt to 'explain' values scientifically would result in their being explained away and the assertion of some form of materialism.

Dewey argues that his critics confuse materialism with science. Materialism does indeed operate on a 'medieval' ontology, holding that the real qualities of an effect of some process must have been communicated or passed on to the effect by its antecedently real 'causes.' It holds, as Dewey puts it, "the earlier stages, being 'causal,' somehow are an exhaustive and adequate index of reality" (*MW* 2:10). Consequently, materialists infer that the only real qualities of a given effect are those reducible to qualities of the antecedent cause. Any qualities of the effect

18. In "Psychology as Philosophic Method," Dewey explicitly compared psychology to paleontology, which was at that time a subspecies of geology.

not so reducible are rejected as mere appearance. Dewey adds, "It is this supposed reduction of the later into the earlier, that the idealist rightly holds is not to explain but to explain away; not to analyze but to ignore and deny" (*MW* 2:10).

Thus philosophers opposed to materialism, especially idealists, have felt obliged to oppose empirical investigations into the mental and moral sciences. But modern experimental science does not suffer from this confusion. Experimental scientists, Dewey assures us, do not understand a 'cause' to be something distinct from the process by which its 'effect' is produced or the source of the latter's reality. All that they understand by the term 'cause' is a preliminary stage in our experience of a process. Likewise, all that is understood by the term 'effect' is the final stage in our experience of a process. Consequently, scientists committed to belief in the uniformity of nature are not committed to supposing that causes and effects are substantially identical. A scientist is only committed to supposing that processes work uniformly, that is, proceed through the same sequence, from one occasion to the next. And the belief in a uniformity of process neither supports nor requires the additional assumption of a uniformity of the content processed on each occasion.

Returning to the topic of idealism, Dewey argues that idealists have also committed the error of supposing that causal processes are to be interpreted as the communication of real attributes by one object to another. Having rejected the antecedent conditions that are the source and communicators of 'reality,' idealists substitute the final product. Dewey charges:

> Just as the materialist isolates and deifies the earlier term as an exponent of reality, so the idealist deals with the later term. To him it is the reality of which the first form is simply the appearance. He contrasts the various members of the series as possessing different degrees of reality, the more primitive being nearest zero. To him the reality is somehow "latent" or "potential" in the earlier forms, and, gradually working from within, transforms them until it finds for itself a fairly adequate expression. . . . We have here simply a particular case of the general fallacy just discussed—the emphasis of a particular term of the series at the expense of the process operative in reference to all terms. (*MW* 2:14)

Or in the language of Dewey's 1896 discussion of the reflex arc, absolute idealism commits the historical fallacy.

Dewey's attack on absolute idealism is here specifically aimed at the sort of idealism espoused by Green, according to which objects of perception are real to the degree that they reproduce absolute reality. But clearly, it applies as well to Dewey's own revised metaphysics of the self. In 1894, Dewey supposed that the self was a real object and that intellectual grasp of the self was the goal of knowledge, scientifically or otherwise pursued. He interpreted our experience of ourselves as growing, becoming mature, and (presumably) decaying as confused interpretations of what we actually experience, the absolute existence of absolute unchanging capacities. In effect, Dewey had committed what in 1902 he called the error of 'emphasis of a particular term of the series at the expense of the process operative in reference to all terms.' Then he went on fallaciously to infer that the mature capacities of the self are invariably present throughout the series, however those capacities may appear to us to alter.

Jane Dewey's biography of her father describes his break with idealism as complete by 1903.[19] The evidence of "The Evolutionary Method as Applied to Morality," and Dewey's 1901 address on the same themes, indicates that the date could be pushed back a bit further, at least as far as 1901. Whether it could safely be pushed back much before then is doubtful. Before 1901, Dewey had taken positions inconsistent with his earlier idealism (e.g., in "The Reflex Arc Concept in Psychology"). And he had begun to offer functionalist accounts of mind that anticipate his mature instrumentalist views (e.g., "Some Stages of Logical Thought"). But his 1901 address (followed by the expanded version published in 1902) for the first time combines both these features with a direct attack on idealism to which his own idealist metaphysics was clearly vulnerable. For this reason, I argue that we may safely conclude that by 1901 Dewey was no longer an idealist.

DEWEY'S REFORMULATION OF THE RELATION OF NATURAL AND
ETHICAL SCIENCE

"The Evolutionary Method as Applied to Morality," Part I, defends Dewey's and his functionalist colleagues' common conception of scientific method against the sorts of criticisms Titchener had raised. Part II offers an impressionistic sketch of what Dewey imagines a science of ethics will be like. It will not, he suggests, be primarily concerned with

19. See Jane Dewey, "Biography of John Dewey," p. 33.

such questions as, "What is the validity of the moral point of view as such?" Questions of this sort can be left to "logic, to the theory of points of view" (MW 2:21). A scientific ethical theory will instead focus on such questions as, "How is the validity of a given moral point of view or judgment determined?" It is no more the business of ethical science to justify the existence of ethical values than it is the business of the physical sciences to justify the existence of the external world. Given the existence of the external world, physical sciences tell us how to justify particular judgments about what it is like. Similarly, given the existence of the moral point of view, an ethical science will provide us with "ways of passing upon questions of specific validity; ways of determining the respective values of this or that particular judgment"; in other words, "discovering, testing, and elaborating adequate modes of *finding out what is really given*" from the moral point of view (MW 2:21).

Dewey is infuriatingly vague about the specific techniques an ethical science will use to perform its tests and make its discoveries. The vagueness is excusable, however, since the paper purports to show only that such a science is possible, not how it is to be practiced. Less excusable, however, is Dewey's unwillingness to come to grips with the objection that 'normative science' is a contradiction in terms, that knowing the history of a practice tells us nothing about its ethical value.

In his 1901 address, Dewey brushed this issue aside as "more specious than sound," insisting that "there are ought facts just as much as there are is facts,"[20] so that ethical science need not be limited to the description of what is. But as he does not explain what an 'ought fact' might be, this is no answer at all. In the 1902 version, Dewey was just as impatient and just as uninformative. Ethical science must concern itself with fact, he admits, but he insists this does not entail that it will be merely descriptive, complaining that "a continual pigeon-holing of such consideration as mere 'description' becomes irritating when it assumes that the description cannot go beyond the *prima facie* and obvious appearance of the material dealt with" (MW 2:23). But the reader is given no explanation of how the transition from fact to evaluation or to the justification of evaluative judgments is accomplished. Possibly, Dewey did not yet have one. At any rate, in 1903, he finally found the patience to explain precisely why the issue is more specious than sound in "The Logical Conditions of a Scientific Treatment of Morality" (MW 3:3–39).

Published in the same year as the better-known *Studies in Logical Theory*, from which Dewey's break with idealism has traditionally been

20. "Historical Method in Ethics," LW 17:351.

dated, "The Logical Conditions of a Scientific Treatment of Morality" has been sadly neglected, despite indications that Dewey himself considered the text to mark a watershed in his development.[21] In this paper, he laid the groundwork for his eventual reconstruction of self-realization on a pragmatic basis, that is, on the basis of a pragmatic conception of science. In his opening remarks, Dewey considers and explicitly rejects conceptions of science and scientific method that he had formerly espoused. In the past, as we have seen, he had defined science as 'knowing' and scientific method in terms of its product: knowledge of the real. In 1903, Dewey proclaims: "We need to throw the emphasis in using the term 'scientific' first upon methods, and then upon results through reference to methods. As used in this article, 'scientific' means regular methods of controlling the formation of judgments regarding some subject-matter" (MW 3:3). Science, it seems, is no longer a form of knowing the real. It is, as Charles S. Peirce would say, simply a method of 'fixing belief.'

But of course, science is not the only method of fixing belief. Before we can define it, we must isolate the distinguishing characteristics of scientific procedures. These Dewey holds are the requirements that judgments about phenomena (1) follow from an accepted set of descriptions and hypotheses about a given subject matter and (2) be confirmable by empirical test. By the latter, he means that it must be possible to generate, from our hypotheses, predictions about actual events that can be checked against future experience. As it is the recognition and use of these procedural rules for the formation of judgments which essentially distinguish science from other forms of inquiry, Dewey argues, nothing bars the application of science to value. It is not a prerequisite of scientific procedures that the terms in which a given inquiry is conducted be the terms physical scientists happen to use. He writes: "[This] point of view expressly disclaims any effort to reduce the statement of matters of conduct to forms comparable with those of physical science. But it expressly proclaims an identity of logical procedure in the two cases" (MW 3:5). As Dewey now sees it, what is distinctive about science is how it justifies its judgments, not what its judgments are about. So the claim that he wants to make, the claim that ethics can and should be treated scientifically, is not and does not entail a claim that value statements are (or ought to be) reduced to statements about the properties of natural objects.

21. Assuming, of course, that his daughter's biography is a reliable guide on this point. See Jane Dewey, "Biography of John Dewey," p. 33.

Clearly, it does entail the claim that in some sense scientific and ethical reasoning are the same. Dewey's contemporaries might be inclined to reject this claim as absurd for three reasons. First, scientific reasoning generates merely probable conclusions, whereas moral reasoning is supposed to generate absolutely certain conclusions. Second, scientific reasoning aims at stating the relations of classes of things, not unique, unreproducible things or events, whereas moral reasoning aims instead at statements about unique cases of action that never exactly recur. And third, scientific reasoning attempts accurately to describe what is the case, testing its descriptions against our experience, whereas moral reasoning attempts rather accurately to determine what *ought* to be the case, thus requiring a different method of confirmation, since normative conclusions cannot be derived from or confirmed by statements of scientific fact.

Anticipating these objections, Dewey responds as follows. He first says that if we define science in terms of the products identified with it, for example, probabilistically warranted laws covering classes of things or events, then 'scientific' judgments may look very different from moral judgments—so different that we might suppose different methods of reasoning must have been used to produce them. If all scientific judgments were like this, Dewey says, there would be no dispute:

> When, however, it is argued that this direct and obvious concern of science with generic statements exhausts the logical significance of scientific method, certain fundamental presuppositions and certain fundamental bearings are ignored; and the logical question at issue is begged. The real question is not whether science aims at statements which take the form of universals, or formulae of connection of conditions, but *how* it comes to do so, and *what it does with* the universal statements after they have been secured. (*MW* 3:9)

In the premises above, from which the conclusion that scientific and ethical reasoning differ is supposed to follow, 'science' and 'scientific' are used in this sense. But this conception of scientific judgment, Dewey argues, excludes just those features that really are definitive of scientific practice: the practice of inquiry in accordance with general rules that every modern scientist commits himself or herself to follow. To be a scientist, after all, is to agree to abide by the judgment of the consensus about how scientific practice is to be carried out, to treat those judgments about how science is to be conducted as categorical, and to evaluate one's own and others' judgments about particular kinds of phenomena on the basis of those rules alone. Consequently, scientists arrive not only at probable or 'hypothetical' judgments about how the world acts. They also arrive at normative categorical conclusions about what ought to be thought, done, or avoided by themselves and others in a variety of practical situations.

Consider the following example. After being kept awake all night with a sore shoulder, one goes to the doctor for diagnosis and treatment of the problem. If the doctor, a practical scientist, were, as the objections hold, capable only of general, hypothetical, descriptive judgments of fact, then the visit would be pointless. But it is not pointless. The doctor, using hypothetical generalizations as instruments in his inquiry, diagnoses the problem as bursitis and judges that it ought to be treated in such and such a manner. How is the doctor able to make this judgment about an individual case? Where does the 'ought' come from? The answer, according to Dewey, is to be found in a more careful analysis of scientific judgment.

The content of the claims scientists assert often do take the form of general, hypothetical descriptions. But, Dewey points out, even these claims have an implicit normative basis. Or to put it another way, if we were to parse out the process of judgment that actually led to the conclusion that 'x is y,' we would find that its premises were normative as well as descriptive. Let us, for example, parse out the doctor's judgment about the sore shoulder. Now every doctor who knows his or her business is bound, in a sense, to judge that a certain sort of tenderness is a symptom of bursitis and that it can be relieved in a given manner. The patient, on the other hand, is not similarly 'bound' to make the same judgments. The patient is not bound to do so just because the patient is not a doctor and does not presume to judge as a doctor. This points the way to uncovering what the doctor's judgment, 'this pain is a symptom of bursitis,' really involves. The doctor's process of judgment, with its implicit assumptions spelled out, would run roughly thus: 'If one is a doctor, a person with certain intellectual commitments, and is presented with a case of shoulder pain of such and such a description, then one must conclude that the pain is caused by bursitis.' Because the content of the normative premises of every medical doctor's judgments about human physiological processes is the same, the doctor will not (normally) bother to state them outright either to patients or to colleagues. Nevertheless, the doctor's judgments always proceed in part on the basis of normative premises about what is to be believed and what beliefs are to guide his or her professional actions. As Dewey sees it, all scientists' judgments proceed in part on some such, normally unstated, premise or set of premises, although the content of the normative premises will differ somewhat from field to field.

If we compare the process of scientific judgment with that of ordinary practical judgments, including ethical judgments, we will find the same underlying structure in each case. A person who says, 'this act ought not to be done,' whether the act is judged for its instrumental value or value in itself, is reporting not her whole judgment but only its conclusion. She suppresses the rest of her judgment, that is, the premises upon which the conclusion emerged, because she supposes they are understood by her audience. Parsed out, the judgment proper is analogous to the doctor's judgment discussed above. The speaker has judged that 'if one is a person, having certain intellectual commitments, and so forth, then presented with this act of so and so characteristics, one must conclude that this act is wrong.'

If scientific and practical judgments all really have the same underlying form, one might well ask why the fact had not been noted earlier. Dewey replies: "Every sort of judgment has its own end to reach; and the instrumentalities (the categories and methods used) must vary as the end varies. If in general we conceive the logical nature of scientific technique, of formulae, universals, etc., to reside in their adaptation to guaranteeing the act of judging in accomplishing a purpose, we are thereby committed to the further proposition that the logical apparatus needed varies as the ends to be reached are diverse." (*MW* 3:20–21).

This explanation may seem to raise more questions than it answers. Dewey is saying that the reason moral, practical judgment has been thought to differ from scientific judgment is simply that the purposes for which these forms of judgment are instruments are different. Differences in function have been mistaken for differences in the process of judgment itself. And the mistake has been reinforced by the fact that confirmation of judgments functional for purpose X may be different from the confirmation of judgments functional for some purpose Z. Hence the real need of different 'logical' apparatuses of inquiry and justification in different contexts.

Dewey's assertion that the function a judgment serves determines its logical form is not happily expressed. Similar statements in subsequent publications became the target of withering criticism. In an exchange with Dewey roughly a decade later, Ralph Barton Perry objected that such an analysis of judgment would reduce logic to chaos. Every judgment (or proposition) would have to be classified in accordance with the function it serves, case by case, turning logic textbooks into menageries of "verbal judgments, visual judgments, private judgments, public judgments, German judgments, American judgments, German-American judgments" and so forth.[22] And as the functions that determine the forms of these acts of judgments are so varied, one might well ask what justified the logical zookeeper's belief that his captives were actually all members of one species. Like Titchener before him, Perry insisted that functional analysis of judgments would be useless or worse unless preceded by analysis of their structure.

Dewey's insistence on using the term 'logic' in what was rapidly becoming an antiquated sense, including both what we would now call epistemology as well as what we now call logic, seems to be the source of the problem here. Dewey did not really mean, either in 1903 or in the later debate with Perry, that what we or Perry would call the 'logical' structure of assertions actually varies with variations in context. On the contrary, Dewey says that the structure of acts of judgment is the same whether the context is scientific or practical. He meant instead that what counts as *evidence* for an assertion varies with variations in the context of inquiry, which is by no means a bizarre claim. Had he been willing to adopt the recent distinction (still current) between logic and epistemology, he might well have saved himself and his readers considerable trouble. For what Dewey's remarks about the misinterpretation of differences in judgments seem to come down to is a claim that hitherto logic and epistemology have been confused. Differences in the nature of the evidence required to justify moral and scientific judgments have wrongly been taken as evidence that they differ in form. Thus interpreted, Dewey's claim that the function a judgment performs plays a role in determining its justification is not ridiculous. In what follows, I continue to interpret his claims about the logic or logical form of moral and scientific judgments as claims about their respective epistemological warrant.

Any judgment, on this view, rests on implicit assumptions about the person making or accepting the judgment. The function the judgment is used to perform determines, at least in part, what is implicitly assumed. Though some will be the same whatever the judgment, the implicit assumptions may differ considerably in scope and so differ also in the

22. Ralph Barton Perry, "Dewey and Urban on Value Judgments," reprinted in *Dewey and His Critics*, ed. Sidney Morgenbesser (New York: Journal of Philosophy, 1977), p. 598. Although the remark occurs in an attack on W. M. Urban, Perry clearly considers Dewey's position vulnerable to the same charge.

scope of the evidence that will be required to justify them. A geophysical scientist, for example, implicitly assumes that she and any scientist in her field is a rational agent, that they all have a certain character, certain intellectual commitments, and certain interests. But rational agency in itself is not an object of interest to the geophysicist or to her colleagues. To avoid the distraction from her own interests and projects that construction of a theory of rational agency would involve, she and her colleagues construct rules for the pursuit of inquiries in such a way as to be conditional upon the smallest possible set of assumptions about agents who are geophysicists: that whatever their character, personal likes or dislikes, age, sex, and so forth, geophysicists are agents who conform all reasoning about a given matter to agreed rules for the formation and testing of hypotheses.

Rational agency is by this means relegated to the status, as Dewey puts it, of a 'practical condition' of any act of scientific judgment. No particular geophysical scientific judgment requires for its justification evidence about the agents making or accepting a particular judgment beyond evidence that they have conformed to accepted procedures. One of the practical consequences of this is that facts about a given scientist's character are irrelevant to evaluation of any one of her professional scientific judgments. Her judgments are not assumed to be conditional upon her having any particular sort of character, or sex, or age. They are conditional only upon her acceptance of agreed rules for the conduct of inquiries.

By contrast, moral judgments incorporate a much wider and more complex set of assumptions about rational agency, because rational agency is the object of interest in moral reasoning. Moral judgments are judgments about the action-guiding beliefs all rational agents ought to accept as the basis of their reasoning about conduct. Thus moral judgments differ in important ways from scientific judgments, which no one who is not a scientist is considered to be 'bound' to accept or arrive at. Because moral judgments incorporate sweeping assumptions about what rational agency involves, we rightly demand of moral reasoners that they be able to explain and support the theories of agency underlying their particular conclusions. As Dewey remarks:

> Character as a practical condition becomes *logical* when its influence is preferential in effect—when instead of being a uniform and impartial condition of any judgment it is . . . a determinant of *this* content-value of judgment rather than that. Put from the other side, in the "intellectual" judgment, it makes no

difference to character *what* object is judged, so be it the one judged is judged accurately; while in the moral judgment the nub of the matter is the difference which the determination of the content as this or that effects in character as a necessary condition of judging *qua* judging. ("Logical Conditions," *MW* 3:22)

One practical consequence of this is that the character and behavior of moral reasoners are considered relevant to overall assessment of their arguments and conclusions. If a moral reasoner's behavior is manifestly inconsistent with the set of assumptions about rational agency which seems to underlie his particular judgments, we have prima facie grounds for disputing his assertions.

This difference in the scope of the implicit claims about rational agency made in setting up moral and scientific judgments is sufficient, Dewey thinks, to explain the differences in their respective modes of inquiry (and subsequent confusion as to their relation). But it is to be noted that the difference is epistemological, not 'logical,' as the latter term is now used. The structure of inference does not differ in the two cases. It is the scope of the antecedent assumptions and the evidence required to support those claims that differ.

And since inference has the same form or structure in moral and scientific judgments, Dewey concludes there is no reason to suppose that moral inquiries and judgments cannot be made 'scientific.' Every scientist acts in accordance with procedural rules for the performance of his or her inquiries, rules that determine what will count as confirmation, disconfirmation, and so on. One of the most fruitful of these is the rule that inferences about one's subject must be experimentally confirmed. Simply put, no inference is to be considered more than provisionally warranted until it has been shown, directly or indirectly, to entail accurate predictions about human experience. Commitment to such rules, Dewey holds, is the essence of science. It is in this respect that he believes ethical theory ought to become scientific.

Dewey argues that the single greatest obstacle to the advance of ethical theory has been the failure to construct procedures for inquiry analogous to those used in the physical sciences. He writes: "Theorists have been attempting to tell what the ideal of man is, what is *summum bonum*, what is man's duty, what are his responsibilities, to prove that he is possessed or not possessed of freedom, without any regulated way of defining the content of the terms 'ideal,' 'good,' 'duty,' etc." (*MW* 3:26). The efforts of ethical theorists to do without theories of evidence and explanation on a par with those of the physical sciences explain the relative lack of progress ethical theorizing had made over the years. To date, the only check on the nature or content of theories of moral agency has been the strain put on human credulity. Not surprisingly, this method of controlling the process of judgment about moral agency has failed to produce a consensus about either the nature of moral agency or its object. If moralists are to achieve the sort of consensus physical scientists enjoy, similar methods will have to be employed. As a first step, Dewey advocates adoption of the 'scientific' (i.e., pragmatic) method of defining the constituents of the subject of our inquiry for which moral terms are supposed to stand. As Peirce described it, that method is to "consider what effects, that might conceivably have practical [experiential] bearings, we conceive the object of our conception to have. Then our conception of these effects is the whole of our conception of the object."[23] As Dewey rephrases it, we are to recognize:

> Only reference to a situation within which the categories emerge and function can furnish the basis for estimation of their value and import. Otherwise the definition of ultimate ethical terms is left to argumentation based upon opinion, an opinion which snatches at some of the more obvious features of the situation . . . and which, failing to grasp the situation as a whole, fails to grasp the exact significance of its characteristic terms. Discussion, for instance, about what constitutes the ethical standard—whether conduciveness to happiness, or approximation to perfection of being—must be relatively futile, until there is some method of determining by reference to the logical necessity of the case what *anything* must be and mean in order to be a standard at all. (*MW* 3:25)

Because it is the components and capacities of rational agency with which morals are concerned, Dewey suggests that particular effort be directed to formulating and testing pragmatic definitions of character and its components: dispositions, habits, emotions, desires. Analysis of the psychology of persons as we find them is a necessary condition of any adequate theory about the judgments persons have reason to make in virtue of being persons. And since social conditions influence the development of dispositions, desires, and preferences, Dewey argues, a second necessary condition of a theory of rational agency is the posses-

23. C. S. Peirce, "How to Make Our Ideas Clear," reprinted in *Philosophical Writings of Peirce*, ed. Justus Buchler (New York: Dover, 1955), p. 31 (first published in *Popular Science Monthly*, 1878).

sion of operational definitions of those sociological factors that partly determine persons as we find them.

Dewey concludes his monograph by noting that because psychology and sociology merely describe how persons think and act, ethical theorists have frequently concluded that psychology and sociology are largely irrelevant to determining what choices of beliefs and actions persons ought to make. He rejects the conclusion as nonsensical. Before we can determine what choices of belief and action persons ought to arrive at, we must first be able to say what persons are and what their capacities for rational decision are. To suppose that psychological and sociological analysis are irrelevant to ethical inquiry is to Dewey equivalent to supposing that chemistry or physics is irrelevant to medical practice.

Medical doctors, for example, do not treat the discoveries and generalizations of other special sciences as irrelevant to their own just because these may go beyond their own area of expertise. They assume as a fundamental postulate of scientific reasoning that all hypotheses are ultimately about the same thing: human experience. If the generalizations about the chemistry of particular organic molecules are of use in forming hypotheses, predictions, and judgments about pathogenic processes in human bodies, medical doctors will gladly make use of the chemist's discoveries. The attitude of the ethical theorist toward his colleagues in the natural sciences, Dewey argues, should rest on the same fundamental postulate, that is, judgments of the natural sciences are instruments for getting at the nature of one and the same thing: human experience. To Dewey, this just is the reason science is practiced by persons. The scientific professions are a network of related industries for the production of intellectual instruments to facilitate rational choice of beliefs about actions and thereby improve the chances of our obtaining the sorts of experiences we desire to have.

Dewey's rejection of neo-Hegelianism's conceptions of mind, self, knowledge, together with the Hegelian conception of scientific method, evidently did not shake his confidence in the essential unity of philosophy and physical science. On the surface, it might even appear that little has changed. Although Dewey no longer defines science in terms of its product rather than its procedures, he continues to urge philosophers to look to their physicist colleagues as 'handmaidens' or research assistants for the better conduct of their own philosophical inquiries.

But under the surface, a revolution has taken place. Consider, for example, the transformation that has occurred in the role of the 'categories.' In the 1880s, Dewey understood scientific method to be a methodical arrangement of the phenomena of experience in accordance with the fundamental categories of experience. The categories themselves were ultimate and unrevisable, confirming interpretations of experiential phenomena without requiring confirmation by experience in turn. But in 1903, the categories have been transformed into instruments of pragmatic inquiry. The sorts of fundamental definitions, concepts, and relations that constituted the categories of Dewey's idealist period are in 1903 simply the apparatus by which particular scientific hypotheses receive preliminary theoretical warrant. As Dewey reinterprets the categories, they are just those 'antecedent' judgments about the fundamental nature of some phenomena which set the parameters for subsequent inquiry. Only those phenomena that fall within the space defined by the particular categorical definitions and concepts of each special science are for that special science 'real' features of its area of inquiry. As the hypotheses provisionally warranted by each special science's fundamental categorical principles come to be experimentally confirmed, they are presumably added to the stock of fundamental principles, fleshing out the conceptual framework with which subsequent scientists will work.

How these antecedent or categorical principles that provisionally warrant hypotheses are confirmed is not spelled out for us in Dewey's 1903 paper but is easily reconstructed. The test, naturally, will be functional. That is, the categorical principles will be tested and confirmed or disconfirmed by their ability to distinguish between competing hypotheses coherently and reliably. Those principles or sets of principles that reliably pick out coherent sets of experimentally fruitful hypotheses, for example, fulfill the function for which they are required and thus are so far warranted. Those principles or sets of principles that tend to pick out incoherent or unfalsifiable hypotheses do not fulfill their proper function and thus their use is so far unwarranted.

By 1903, Dewey had worked out what the structure of a pragmatic ethical science would be. He had yet to work out what its reformulated categorical or first principles should be, what sorts of hypotheses they should be used to warrant, or how ethical hypotheses were to be experimentally confirmed. In cooperation with J. H. Tufts, Dewey set to work on fleshing out his own conceptual framework for the science of ethics. The result of their joint effort was a textbook—the 1908 Dewey and Tufts *Ethics*.

⟨6⟩ Pragmatic Ethical Science: The 1908 *Ethics*

It is not claimed, therefore, that there is no philosophical problem of the relation of physical science to the things of ordinary experience. It is asserted that the problem in the form in which it has chiefly occupied modern philosophy is an artificial one, due to the continued assumption of premises formed in an earlier period of history and now having no relevancy to the state of physical inquiry. Clearing the ground of this unreal problem, however, only imposes upon philosophy the consideration of a problem which is urgently practical, growing out of the conditions of contemporary life. What revisions and surrenders of current beliefs about authoritative ends and values are demanded by the method and conclusions of natural science?

The Quest for Certainty

The 1908 Dewey and Tufts *Ethics* was remarkable in two respects.[1] First, the text was so popular that it was reprinted at least yearly from 1909 to 1931 (when it was replaced by a revised, second edition). Second, *Ethics* originally appeared as a volume in the Holt Company's American Science Series. And it was the 'scientific' character of the work that most recommended it to some of its early reviewers. G. A. Tawney, writing for the *American Journal of Sociology*, said that "probably no more convincing effort to construct a system of moral philosophy by a strictly scientific method has ever been carried out."[2] Norman Wilde wrote in the *Journal of Philosophy, Psychology, and Scientific Methods* that *Ethics* "marks the end of the abstract, speculative treatises and the beginning of the positive studies of established human values."[3] In the *Psychological Bulletin*, E. B. McGilvary described *Ethics* as "well worthy to take

1. See John Dewey and J. H. Tufts, *Ethics*, 1st ed., *MW* 5.
2. G. A. Tawney, review of *Ethics*, *American Journal of Sociology* 14 (1908–9): 690.
3. Norman Wilde, review of *Ethics*, *Journal of Philosophy, Psychology, and Scientific Methods* 5 (1908): 636.

its place beside James's *Psychology*, Remsen's *Chemistry*, and Chamberlin and Salisbury's *Geology*."[4]

In retrospect, it may be hard to believe that the publishers, the reviewers, or Dewey and Tufts themselves took any of these claims very seriously. On the surface, *Ethics* bears little resemblance to a scientific text. It neither describes ethical experiments performed nor provides directions for sample experiments to be run by students entering the field. Indeed, there is no evidence that Dewey or Tufts ever tested, or intended to test, any one of their hypotheses experimentally. Not surprisingly, the use of the term 'science' by authors and reviewers alike has subsequently come to be read as merely honorific. It might even be argued that sympathetic criticism demands such a reading. Only if we refuse to credit Dewey with claiming his ethics was scientific, the argument would go, can we save his ethics from absurdity.[5] But it is unlikely that Dewey would have welcomed such sympathy. The development of his moral philosophy shows that there was nothing about which he was more serious than a reconciliation of ethics and experimental science.

In any case, more is lost than saved by this sort of sympathetic interpretation—including the key to the structure of the book. Unless *Ethics* is read as an introduction to a unified, scientific inquiry, the organizing thread that binds the three parts into a whole is lost. The damage that results is exemplified by Arnold Isenberg's struggles to explain the relation of Dewey's theoretical Part II to Tufts's historical and social Parts I and III. Isenberg wrote: "Part II *came at the right place* between Parts I and III; but it is in no way *dependent* for the coherence of its argument upon anything that comes before or after. [It] . . . is not 'open-ended' at

4. The texts mentioned were earlier volumes in the same American Science Series. Evander B. McGilvary, review of *Ethics*, *Psychological Bulletin* 6 (1909): 14–22, p. 14.

5. It is difficult to be sure precisely why Dewey's sympathetic critics ignore or pass over his insistence that ethics could and should be rendered 'scientific,' since defenses are rarely offered. Presumably, some believe that an ethics that operates on scientific principles must somehow violate Hume's proviso. Others appear to believe that if ethics can be a science, then, in Richard Bernstein's words, "'value' or 'good' is the name of an empirical property that could be *discovered* by science" (Richard Bernstein, *John Dewey* [Atascadero, Calif.: Ridgeview, 1966], p. 117). Since Dewey is committed to the position that values are constructs, it is thought that for him a science of ethics ought to be a contradiction in terms.

Neither fear is well founded. A scientific ethics, as Dewey conceives of it, does not necessarily commit Hume's fallacy (see Chapter 5, above). Nor does it entail that values are 'discovered.' 'Values' are an ethical science's analogues of the 'facts' of physical sciences. Since, as Dewey sees it, facts are constructs rather than discoveries, values too will be constructs rather than discoveries (see Chapter 7, below).

either end; it would be a disappointment . . . if a good reader should form the opinion that it is."[6]

One can only wonder why Isenberg thought the right place for Dewey's discussion of moral theory was between the two parts written by Tufts, if he saw no important connections between them.

For *Ethics* to make sense as a whole, the book must be read as its authors intended, as an overview of what ethical science is (or should be) like. This brings us to the question of how we can possibly do so. What would justify our treating it as a scientific work despite the notable absence of experimentation and experimental results?

THE FUNCTIONS OF SCIENTIFIC THEORIES

In one respect, *Ethics* is rather like an introductory science text. The possibility of the subject's being treated scientifically is neither raised nor defended explicitly. Like an elementary science book, *Ethics* demonstrates the applicability of scientific method to the subject matter by its use. Only its (presumably) evident serviceability in advancing our understanding of ethics justifies its adoption. For those fortunate enough to have access to Dewey's "The Logical Conditions of a Scientific Treatment of Morality," no explanation would have been needed. But such readers would have been few and far between. To the majority, Dewey's methodology and his reasons for adopting it must have been something of a mystery.[7] Happily, we are better placed.

Putting together what we have learned about science from "The Evolutionary Method as Applied to Morality" and "The Logical Conditions of a Scientific Treatment of Morality," we can construct a general statement of what Dewey believes the method and object of scientific *ethical* inquiry are. We know that scientists define and explain the phenomena of ordinary life in terms of the processes that produce them. Scientists experiment in order to reproduce those processes in laboratories, in order to determine what conditions must be in place if a given phenome-

6. See Arnold Isenberg's foreword to a reprint of *Ethics*, 2d ed., Part II, *Theory of the Moral Life*, ed. Arnold Isenberg (New York: Holt, Rinehart & Winston, 1960), p. v. The structural relations on which Isenberg comments are identical in both editions.

7. In the years following 1908, Dewey made intermittent replies to calls for further explication of his conception of moral and evaluative reasoning, including especially "The Logic of Judgments of Practice" (1915), *MW* 8:14–82; "Valuation and Experimental Knowledge" (1922), *MW* 13:3–28; "The Construction of Good," in *The Quest for Certainty* (1929), *LW* 4:203–28; and *Logic: The Theory of Inquiry* (1938), *LW* 12.

non is to occur. So it would seem that the *object* of any scientific inquiry is to discover and explain the principles of design of natural objects and events with a view to facilitating judgments about their future occurrence. And from the second of these two papers, we know that the method by which scientists construct and confirm their judgments about the principles of design of natural objects and events includes (1) provisional warranting of hypothetical judgments by their coherence with antecedent judgments (i.e., warranting for further investigation) and (2) the warranting proper of a hypothetical judgment by the experimental confirmation of the predictions it yields.

But we also know ethics is a practical science and that its aims differ in some important ways from those of 'basic research' sciences. The objects with which such practical sciences as civil engineering, architecture, and medicine concern themselves are artificial rather than natural, things and events that would not occur at all, in the same way, or as often, were it not for human activity. So we might say that practical sciences concern themselves with discovering and constructing principles of the artificial design of things and events, with a view to facilitating our judgments about their future occurrence. Although the principles of design in these cases are artificial rather than natural, the same general method of testing should be used. We should provisionally warrant hypotheses about future experience by their coherence with our antecedently established judgments, and then check the provisionally warranted hypotheses against our experience in experimental conditions.

Human experience is a natural event. But the construction of a coherent, satisfying life requires artifice. Thus ethical science would be a project of constructing hypothetical judgments about the design of a special class of artificial objects or events—satisfactory life or selfhood—and of confirming these hypotheses (depending upon the type in question) in one of two ways: (1) by their coherence with our antecedently constructed theoretical 'categories' and previously confirmed hypotheses and their coherence with our experience under experimental conditions or (2) by their adequacy to fulfill the function of fundamental principles.

Ethical hypotheses would, of course, be descriptive on this view. But it would not follow from this that ethical science cannot make recommendations about what ought to be believed or done. As Dewey sees it, any special science is capable of justifying some conclusions about what ought to be believed or done. This is because being scientific is something we choose to do. In general, what we choose when we choose to be scientific is to join in a social practice defined by rules of procedure that are categorical for that practice. It is this commitment to a practice of investigation that obliges us to treat certain outcomes of investigation as guiding or compelling belief and action on our parts. Not everyone chooses to be a scientist, natural or ethical. But virtually everyone chooses to be a rational agent, that is, to engage in a practice defined by peculiar rules of procedure, rules included among and underlying the more specialized rules and procedures of the sciences. As a result, everyone who chooses to be a rational agent is (to some extent) obliged to adopt certain attitudes toward the outcomes of properly conducted scientific investigations. By the same token, everyone who chooses to be rational is (to some extent) obliged to adopt certain attitudes toward the outcomes of properly conducted scientific *ethical* investigations.

Read as an introduction to a newly emerging ethical science, the peculiar structure of the 1908 *Ethics* begins to make sense. Tufts's Part I, "The Beginnings and Growth of Morality," reviews the background data available to the ethical scientist of 1908 about how different peoples have organized their lives and characters and then, in an elementary way, tries to single out the processes—social, psychological, environmental—that participate in producing these ways of living and being. Part II, "Theory of the Moral Life," takes the first step toward scientific investigation of the principles of the design of the sort of life persons want to lead by selecting and provisionally warranting a set of fundamental principles, defining the field of inquiry and its constituents. The outcome of Dewey's Part II is a set of theoretical principles by reference to which specific hypotheses about conduct or character may be provisionally warranted. Tufts's Part III, "The World of Action," demonstrates the functional adequacy of Dewey's Part II theory, by showing that it can be used to warrant experimentally fruitful hypotheses about the outcome of designing lives in certain ways (i.e., by instituting certain specific social and political arrangements). As a rule, Tufts's demonstration of the functional adequacy of Dewey's Part II theoretical framework stops short of actually experimentally confirming the hypotheses the theory provisionally warrants. Occasionally, particular social or legislative experiments proposed or under way in 1908 are cited as means of achieving (some) experimental confirmation.

Virtually none of the hypotheses selected by means of Dewey's theory is actually shown to be fully scientifically warranted. Does this constitute a problem for the claim that the authors had constructed a 'scientific theory' of moral life? The answer is no. It is not required of scientific theorists that they should actually experimentally confirm hypotheses provisionally warranted by the fundamental principles they construct, so long as they do not claim that the hypotheses are anything more than provisionally warranted. They are only required to show that the principles they construct can fulfill the function for which they were designed. This is all Dewey and Tufts claim to have done: to have constructed theoretical underpinnings for subsequent experimental confirmation of various hypotheses.

The hypotheses and the predictions they yield must eventually be experimentally tested—a task for which moral philosophers are singularly ill-fitted. But this is less of a problem than it might appear. For reasons discussed below, the hypotheses a pragmatic ethical science will need to confirm are primarily hypotheses about the development, suppression, and expression of settled dispositions to action; the roles of specific dispositions in forming a harmonious, stable, and satisfactory character; and the relations of dispositions to the surrounding environment, social and physical. Such hypotheses should in principle be experimentally confirmable by existing sciences, such as sociology, anthropology, physiology, and psychology. The frequent calls for social scientific investigation into labor conditions, class divisions, family organization, and education issued by Tufts in *Ethics*, Part III, indicate that it was to the existing human and social sciences that Dewey and Tufts looked for confirmation of ethical hypotheses.

So although *Ethics* neither records nor gives directions for the performance of ethical experiments, the reader is not left in the dark about the sorts of experiments to be used. Nor is the reader left wondering about what 'experimental fruitfulness' means for ethical science. An ethical scientist's hypothesis is experimentally fruitful if it suggests or generates predictions that can (in principle) be confirmed by social scientists. Moreover, we can see that although the 'coherence,' as Isenberg put it, of the principles of moral life and conduct Dewey arrives at in Part II may not 'depend' upon what goes before or after, the justification of those principles most certainly does. Internal coherence is not sufficient warrant for the adoption of a given set of principles as the fundamental principles of a science. Nothing but the demonstration of the principles' ability to fulfill the function for which they were designed warrants their adoption—which is why Dewey's Part II had to be followed by Tufts's Part III.

FIRST PRINCIPLES OF MORAL SCIENCE: MORAL AGENCY AND ITS OBJECT

The fundamental principles of any special science will include rules of procedure as well as definitions categorizing the phenomena to be studied. The most basic of the rules of procedure are those common to every science: rules about the selection and warranting of hypotheses. What Dewey has to supply, and justify, over and above these basic procedural rules are definitions categorizing moral phenomena, together with any special rules of procedure unique to ethical inquiry. This is the task of *Ethics*, Part II.

The method of construction he adopts is pragmatic. In formulating definitions, he will not accept as a real constituent of the field of ethics anything that lacks 'practical bearings,' that is, anything whose absence would make no difference to our experience. If, for example, Dewey can leave out the faculty of 'will' without finding a 'remainder' of human experience uncaptured, then he will not hypothesize the existence of such a faculty or seek to define it. On the other hand, if a proposed definition of some class of phenomena seems to leave a remainder unaccounted for, he will question or reject that definition. No definition visibly failing either test is to be accepted, even tentatively, as a building block of his theory.

What then does he need definitions for? Dewey gives several (inconsistent) lists of phenomena.[8] From these lists it appears that a minimally adequate ethical theory must be able to define moral agency, the object of moral agency, the nature of the reasons we have to pursue that object, and what grounds, if any, there are for adjudicating between action-guiding reasons where these appear to conflict.

Opening Part II with a relatively uncontroversial definition of an agent as a self-conscious being whose choice of ends is amenable to rational foresight and deliberation, Dewey then notes that not all agency is considered moral: "As currently conceived, stirring the fire, reading a newspaper, or eating a meal are acts with which morality has no concern"[9] (*MW* 5:190). What distinguishes these acts from acts of moral agency, he suggests, are the "two differing ways in which activity is induced and guided by ideas of valuable results" (*MW* 5:191). The difference lies in the complexity of the deliberations and choices that moral and nonmoral agency involve.

8. See his introduction and Chapters 10, 11, 12 (*Ethics, MW* 5:7–20, 187, 199, 220).

9. Dewey is quoting from Herbert Spencer, *Principles of Ethics*, vol. 1 (New York: D. Appleton, 1892), p. 5.

Nonmoral choices and acts, Dewey argues, are guided by a single type of end or 'value.' When, for example, our deliberations are guided by the single end or value of amusing ourselves, all that has to be decided is which of the acts open to us will be most amusing: reading a newspaper, stirring a fire, or eating a meal. Nonmoral agency is essentially "a technical rather than a moral affair" (*MW* 5:191). Agency becomes moral only when a second and incompatible end or value begins to compete with the first. Then, as Dewey puts it, "there is no longer one end, nor two ends so homogeneous that they may be reconciled by both being used as means to some more general end of undisputed worth. We have alternate ends so heterogeneous that choice has to be made. . . . The problem now becomes what *is* really valuable" (*MW* 5:192).

Because our objectives are incompatible, moral situations raise questions technical situations do not; most significantly, questions about the relation of our ends to our moral characters. Dewey argues, "This is the question finally at stake in any genuinely moral situation: what shall the agent *be*?" (*MW* 5:194). As he sees it; "When ends are genuinely incompatible, no common denominator can be found except by deciding what sort of character is most highly prized and shall be given supremacy" (*MW* 5:195). The ends we reject represent roads not taken, leading to experiences we are not to have. Consequently, the choice between incompatible ends is always potentially a choice between significantly different ways of life. Thus a decision about what course of action is most desirable is at the same time always a decision about what sort of life and character it is most desirable to achieve.

Dewey now has the constituents of a definition of moral agency. Moral agency is activity in a situation where a voluntary choice is made between incompatible, character-determining courses of action by an agent exercising some degree of foresight and deliberation. At the same time, we have a definition of moral agency that is controversial. Although Dewey does not draw attention to the point, his definition of moral agency entails that neither classical hedonism nor Kantianism can be theories of *moral* conduct. For example, classical hedonism holds that all objects of desire are commensurable, since all desires are ultimately for the same end: pleasure or happiness. Consequently, all hedonistic deliberation about action is technical rather than moral. So if we accept Dewey's definition of moral agency, we must conclude that hedonism is a critical theory of nonmoral conduct.

It might appear that Kantianism could claim to be a theory of moral agency, as Dewey defines it, because Kant recognized the existence of two incommensurable ends of choice and action: happiness and good. But in Kant's ethics, the determination of which end is *really* valuable is not open to debate. There is only one correct answer. Good is by definition the one unconditionally valuable end. So it turns out that a Kantian agent's deliberations about how to act are technical rather than moral. The Kantian agent is always on the lookout for the course of action most likely to realize the one certainly good end. Although Dewey's definition of the moral agent is one that Kantians and hedonists could possibly accept, his definition of moral agency is not.

This brings us to the question of the object of moral agency. Agency becomes moral whenever a situation presents us with a choice between incommensurable ends. And the object of this sort of agency, Dewey holds, is to achieve a solution with the best overall implications for the future development of our characters. But how is this determined? What is to be counted as a positive implication for one's character and how can it be reliably detected?

According to Kant, the positive implication we should be concerned for is the reinforcement of our devotion to duty by courses of action that suppress desire. The method by which we detect this is analysis of our intentions. So long as our analysis shows our intention to be of the right sort, we may safely go ahead with the action. By contrast, hedonistic utilitarians have argued that the significant implications of actions are their pleasant and painful consequences alone. Naturally, the methods of detection favored by utilitarians are empirical and probabilistic. Dewey rejects both sorts of suggestions.

As he sees it, the Kantian account of the object of moral agency fails in two respects. It defines the object without reference to 'practical bearings,' and its implications conflict with ordinary or common-sense moral experience. It follows from Kant's moral theory that the consequences of an act are not directly relevant to its moral worth, since it is the intention alone that is the focus of moral consideration. But people do not ordinarily treat the consequences of one another's acts as irrelevant to an agent's moral character (although on occasion bad results will be overlooked if they can be attributable to something other than the agent's intentions). Indeed, if we are not to treat consequences as directly relevant to the worth or essential character of an agent's intentions, by what verifiable means are we to detect or measure intention or character? The answer, of course, is none. Third parties have no access to an agent's intentions. The agent's own access via introspection is private and unconfirmable by any public, scientifically admissible means.

The only public, scientifically admissible means available to determine what a person's intentions, desires, or dispositions to action may be in any given case is observation of the person's acts. And this is true, Dewey holds, not only for others' intentions, desires, and dispositions but for our own as well. Just as we divine another's state of mind as angry, fearful, charitable, or ambitious by attending to the consequences of that person's acts, so we learn to detect anger, fear, charity, or ambition in ourselves by the same means. Because hedonism defines dispositions, desires, and intentions in terms of the consequences of the acts to which they regularly give rise, Dewey credits hedonism with a claim to scientific consideration.

What vitiates hedonism's claim is its conflation of the plurality of desires and dispositions for distinct ends into one desire: the desire to maximize pleasure. Although it is true that the satisfaction of urgent desires or dispositions is typically accompanied by pleasure, Dewey argues, it does not follow that pleasure is the object of our desires and dispositions. For example, a majority in the Electoral College is an indicator of success in a campaign for the presidency of the United States. But it does not follow from this that a presidential candidate's object is a majority in the Electoral College. The candidate's object is to become president. Similarly, Dewey argues, the experience of a preponderance of pleasure over pain is (usually) an indication that one of our active dispositions has successfully achieved its object. It does not mean pleasure was the object of that disposition.

Moreover, since moral agency is agency in a situation presenting incommensurable ends, it cannot be the case that all our dispositions and desires are aimed at the production of pleasure. So although hedonism is correct in emphasizing the importance of consequences for defining and distinguishing intentions, desires, and dispositions, its account of the object of moral agency is fatally flawed. In this respect, Dewey claims, Kant was more nearly on the right track in looking to the internal rather than the external concomitants of action. What we choose in a moral situation has implications for who we will be and how we must see ourselves in the future, because we choose (in effect) the suppression of certain of our dispositions to action for the sake of enhancing the expression of others. So Dewey recommends that we 'synthetically' define the object of moral agency as the construction of a satisfactory *character* overall and our immediate objective in problematic moral situations as the discovery of the option most conducive to our long-term ends.

THE GOOD AND THE RIGHT

The definition of the object of moral agency as the development or construction of a satisfactory character, together with the suggestion that the pleasure we take in our characters is an indicator of moral success, gives *Ethics* a decidedly naturalistic—even utilitarian—ring. Though Dewey certainly meant *Ethics* to offer a naturalistic ethical theory, utilitarianism was not the theory he had in mind. In his discussion of the evaluation of character and character-determining conduct, he sought to distinguish his view of the significance of pleasure for motivating and assessing possible acts from utilitarianism's.

Mature moral agents faced with a problematic situation understand themselves to be faced with mutually exclusive courses of action toward incommensurable ends. Based on past experience, they can predict the likely outcomes of each course of action. And using those predictions, they can discriminate and define the dispositions urging them toward those outcomes. Now classic utilitarianism, Dewey argues, sees the prediction of pleasurableness of options as directly determining the selection of the most pleasant option in more or less complex ways. For example, Jeremy Bentham sees the prediction of pleasure in a given outcome as directly determining the agent to act for that outcome. John Stuart Mill, on the other hand, sees the outcome as being reason-giving rather than directly determining, but holds that only the maximization of pleasure or minimization of its opposite provides adequate reason for action. Of Dewey's replies, the one to Bentham is particularly interesting, as it suggests how Dewey might have responded to the common charge that his ethics is essentially Hobbesian.

As Dewey understood Bentham's position, we are determined by nature to desire the expression of a disposition whenever we foresee that the results of doing so will be pleasurable. It is the pleasure foreseen that makes the expression of the disposition good to an agent. And the greater the pleasure, the greater the value of expressing the responsible disposition. What is good is at the same time right, for there is nothing else about the good foreseen result that can motivate our pursuit of it but that quality that makes it good to us. What the eulogistic terms 'good' and 'right' eulogize is pleasure. Thus 'good' and 'right' must be synonymous terms.

This account Dewey rejects as inconsistent with our experience of how we order our competing dispositions to action. Even were it correct to say that we are causally motivated to act from a disposition by the anticipation of the pleasure it would produce, this motivation is not the only influence on our decision. The presence of another factor is revealed by certain ambiguities Bentham is forced to introduce into his account of moral agency. Bentham claims that it is for pleasure and pain "alone to point out what we ought to do as well as to determine what we shall do"[10] (*MW* 5:241). To this Dewey replies that "if happiness is the *natural* end of all desire and endeavor, it is absurd to say that the same happiness ought to be the end" (*MW* 5:245). To say that we *ought* to base our estimates of possible acts on the likelihood of their producing pleasure or pain implies that (1) it is open to us to reject the pleasant alternative, which further implies that (2) ends other than pleasure or the absence of pain attract our interest. Either then we have ends other than pleasure that give different sorts of reasons or motivations for choice and action (which Bentham denies) or there must be different *kinds* of pleasures, giving different kinds of reasons for action. If so, then 'good' and 'right' would not be synonymous. Acts would be evaluated for their 'goodness' as sources of pleasure without thereby settling the question of the 'rightness' of choosing any particular one.

Is this argument specious? Could Bentham reply that the only real difference between the ends of particular acts is the quantity of pleasure they involve? Anticipations of pleasurable results causally motivate us to perform particular acts with a force proportionate to the quantity of pleasure anticipated. A greater quantity of pleasure provides a stronger, not a more rational, motivation to act from the disposition that would produce it. Dewey does not directly deal with this question, but from what follows in his text, his answer would probably go like this. When two foreseen and incompatible results each promise us pleasure, though in differing degrees, Bentham should say that we *will* pursue the greater. But instead, he tends to say that we *ought* to pursue the greater. What grounds does Bentham have for holding this? Why 'ought' the agent to prefer the greater pleasure? Presumably, Bentham must feel that we desire not only to be pleased but to be rationally pleased.

Dewey sees another ambiguity in Bentham's account of how the process of selection of foreseen pleasures takes place. Or rather, he sees it in the fact that a selection takes place at all. Were we simply causally determined to pursue pleasure foreseen, foreseeing pleasure in the results of acting from a particular disposition would set us moving toward that

10. Dewey quotes from Jeremy Bentham, *An Introduction to the Principles of Morals and Legislation*, rev. ed., vol. 1, chap. 1 (London: W. Pickering, 1823).

pleasure before any other results could be foreseen and compared with the first. No genuine selection or deliberation about alternatives could take place. But Bentham holds that we can foresee and compare several alternative possible pleasures before we act from any one. Dewey continues: "From Bentham's own point of view, there is a difference between the good which *first* presents itself, which *first* stirs desire and solicits to action, and the good which being formed *after and upon the basis of consideration of consequences*, is the *right* good. In calling the latter the *right*, we mean it has supreme authority over the end which first appears. . . . So it is again evident that we are using happiness in two quite different senses" (*MW* 5:245). These ambiguities in Bentham's explanation of the motivation of our choices of actions in moral situations and in his account of the meaning of 'good' and 'right' decide the case against both. What we foresee as the results of acting from a given disposition is action-guiding but not directly determining.

Other hedonistic utilitarians, such as Mill, mindful of these sorts of problems with Bentham's ethics, had also come to the conclusion that anticipations of pleasure or pain do not directly determine us to act in one way rather than another. Moreover, Mill argued that pleasures do differ in kind and thus differ also in the kind of reason they give us for action. Choices between competing courses of pleasant ('good') action will be more or less rational ('right') depending on the kind of pleasure chosen. Mill argued that Bentham's error was his failure to recognize that pleasures differ in quality as well as in quantity. So whenever we are faced with a choice, we have but to consider the relative value of the different kinds of pleasure available to us, to isolate and identify the 'higher' kinds of pleasure, to have adequate reason for making a selection and considering it right. All pleasure is reason-giving, but some pleasures give better reasons than others.

To adopt Mill's interpretation of rational choice of action, we would also have to adopt his hypothesis that pleasures are qualitatively distinct. As Dewey points out, this we have absolutely no reason to do. Thus if there are qualitative differences between the ends that would 'please' competing dispositions to action, Dewey reasons, they must reflect qualitative differences in the dispositions themselves. But surely this is going too far. If we grant that differences in 'pleasures' cannot do the work required in either Mill's or Bentham's theories, and that the differences in the worth of ends depend on differences in our dispositions, does it follow that the differences are qualitative? Why not consider Thomas Hobbes's suggestion that desires and dispositions themselves differ quantitatively, that is, in force or urgency? Hobbes's theory, moreover, does not violate Dewey's first principle of scientific moral theory: his definition of moral agency as involving choice among incompatible or incommensurable ends. Hobbes does not hold that all our desires are for pleasure or that the desires we have for food, shelter, security, power, esteem, and so forth, are commensurable in any single end. Instead, he treats the conflicts of our desires on analogy to conflicts of nonrational forces in nature. The stronger of two mutually interfering forces cancels out the weaker. Similarly, the stronger of two mutually interfering desires cancels out the weaker. Thus selection from among a set of competing dispositions to action can be accounted for without appeal to qualitative differences between dispositions.

It is a pity that Dewey did not consider this possible objection. Had he done so, the popular misconception that his ethics is a species of Hobbesianism might have been avoided. Still, a Deweyan answer can readily be constructed on the model of Dewey's argument against Bentham, discussed above. Given Hobbes's view of how deliberation occurs, Dewey could argue, there can be no meaningful distinction between 'good' and 'right' in respect to possible objects of desire, because what we ordinarily speak of as being a true good or a right good is simply the most compelling good of which we are aware. There would be no sense in speaking of the chosen good as rightly or wrongly chosen. Yet this is precisely how Hobbes does speak of the results of deliberations. In *Leviathan*, he writes:

> In Deliberation, the Appetites, and Aversions are raised by foresight of the good and evill consequences, and sequels of the action whereof we Deliberate; the good or evill effect thereof dependth on the foresight of a long chain of consequences, of which very seldome any man is able to see to the end. But for so farre as a man seeth, if the Good in those consequences, be greater than the Evill, the whole chain is that which Writers call *Apparent*, or *Seeming Good*. . . . so that he who hath by Experience or Reason, the greatest and surest prospect of Consequences, Deliberates best himself; and is able when he will, to give the best counsel unto others.[11]

If selection between goods was achieved through an internecine war of desires, it would make no sense to speak of the result as right or wrong, more or less reasonable. We could, at most, call an individual fortunate or unfortunate in the sorts of desires he has. If, however, the

11. Thomas Hobbes, *Leviathan*, ed. C. B. MacPherson (London: Penguin, 1968), p. 129.

conclusions of deliberations can be called either right or wrong, then the strength of our competing desires and dispositions does not alone determine the outcome of our deliberations.

Like Mill, Dewey holds that the pleasure we feel as we anticipate a certain result does give us reason to call that result 'good' and to prefer it to imaginary plans of action in which we can take no pleasure. But unlike Mill, Dewey holds that the reason given is simply reason to believe that a desire or disposition will be satisfied by that result. As in the *Study of Ethics*, he argues that pleasure is to be viewed as a 'subjective signal' of a relation between a disposition demanding expression for its own sake and the courses of action through which it might be expressed. When in the course of the thought experiments we perform in our search for satisfactory choices of action we hit upon a plan of action that could express an active disposition, our subjective experience of the 'fitness' of the plan to the disposition is a feeling of pleasure. When an imagined plan of action gives us pleasure, we have reason to believe that the plan would satisfactorily express at least one of our dispositions. That is, the imagined plan of action is pleasant because it is the means to a desired end, the expression of a disposition.

In a problematic moral situation, when mutually incompatible and incommensurable dispositions compete, we review the possible solutions open to us, using the 'subjective signal' of pleasure to screen out the acceptable from the unacceptable alternatives. Solutions whose imagined results are unpleasant even to contemplate are solutions that we have no reason to think satisfactory to any one of our active dispositions. Those that are pleasant to imagine are solutions that we have prima facie evidence to believe satisfactory in some respect and so 'good.'

Dewey argues, however, that the pleasure we take in imagining a possible option does not necessarily give us sufficient reason for selecting that option. Since more than one disposition is in play in a moral situation, more than one option will be prima facie good. And an option that is prima facie good when viewed as a means to express one disposition may also be prima facie bad when viewed in terms of another with which it is incompatible. So although pleasure felt at the idea of acting in a certain way gives us reason to call that act 'good' and even to pursue it, pleasure does not give us reason to prefer that action to any alternate goods that may be available to us.

What makes one disposition qualitatively superior to another and thus its satisfactory expression more desirable than another's? According to Dewey, it is the nature of the contribution that the disposition and its expression will make to a satisfactory character overall. So in order to determine which dispositions will make the most valuable sorts of contributions, we must first understand what the necessary conditions of such a life and character may be. These will form the basis of our subsequent evaluations of acts and choices in problematic situations. In keeping with his pragmatic conception of definition, Dewey attempts to define a set of minimum necessary conditions of a satisfactory character in terms of their practical bearings. Whatever these conditions may be, he reasons, they will be manifest in the character and conduct of a truly good man. So we should consider what such a man might be like—a man truly good by nature, who is able to maintain the goodness of his character and conduct over time.

No matter how the naturally good man has come by his natural goodness, we can infer that his character and dispositions must necessarily have the following features. First, his character must be a complex of fairly *coherent* dispositions. Were they not, the frustration ensuing from the good man's effort to act from his incoherent dispositions would have moved him to reflect on and to reform his character. Second, since the good man remains good over time, the coherence of his active dispositions cannot have been achieved by fiat, that is, simple arbitrary closure of the set of dispositions to be acted upon, thereby excluding incompatible alternatives. Over time, our dispositions and capacities to realize them in action change. New capacities are developed, old ones diminish. Thus the good man would eventually have become frustrated and unhappy acting from the same fixed set of dispositions and so would have altered his character and conduct accordingly. His dispositions must form a harmonious system that is flexible or adaptable to changes in the agent's capacities for action.

Third, the realization of the dominant dispositions in the good man's character must be relatively independent of any specific environmental conditions. If, for example, the good man's dominant desires were like the desire to possess rare objets d'art or climb hitherto unscaled mountain peaks, then the naturally good man would be unlikely for the most part to find his conduct satisfactory. In which case, the naturally good man's conduct would not seem good to him, and again we would find him abandoning his naturally good conduct.

The necessary conditions of the naturally good man's being naturally good over time, Dewey argues, may be taken as necessary conditions of a rational choice of prima facie goods by a moral agent who is not naturally good. The good man's character is naturally *harmonious, flexible,* and *stable* in the face of changing environmental circumstance. Those of us who are not so fortunate as to be naturally good should consider whether the alternative prima facie goods we are faced with in moral situations are such as to contribute to a life of harmonious, flexible or adaptive, stable character and conduct. These qualities, Dewey argues, are "the signs of a true or moral satisfaction" (*Ethics, MW* 5:259).

If this is correct, we have material for the construction of minimum conditions for determination of the worth of conflicting prima facie goods, or as Dewey puts it, for constructing a "standard" for the evaluation of competing but incompatible good courses of action. Anticipation of possible future conduct gives prima facie reason for action if the act anticipated is (to some degree) immediately satisfactory or pleasant. The reason is sufficient for action if it also promises to contribute to realization of a harmonious, flexible, and stable, character and conduct. According to Dewey, there is one and only one set of dispositions whose selection is justifiable on his criteria, and this one set that "fulfills these conditions is the social good" (*MW* 5:261). Only social or other-regarding dispositions cooperate to form a character that is harmonious, flexible, and stable in its predominant dispositions.

This last assertion might provoke one or both of the following objections. First, how do we know that social or other-regarding dispositions actually are good to the agents who have them? Even if social dispositions meet all the criteria Dewey proposes, this is beside the point unless agents do in fact find these dispositions pleasant in anticipation and so prima facie good.

Second, if we do suppose that social dispositions are actually good to the agents who have them, surely self-regarding, nonsocial dispositions may be good as well. Is it not possible that an agent could form a stable, harmonious, flexible or adaptive character from predominantly nonsocial dispositions? A life devoted to realizing one's artistic talents could result in a harmonious integration of nonsocial desires for one's own education and training, health, self-discipline, production, and so forth. Such a life might be practiced over the course of a lifetime, adapted and reformed harmoniously as the agent's capacities developed and altered.[12] It could be adapted to a variety of environmental circumstances and so would revolve around relatively stable goods. If so, the sociability

---

12. Consider, for example, Matisse's switch to collages from painting as his eyesight failed, Beethoven's continuing to compose after the loss of his hearing, the ability of some notable pianists to continue playing after the loss of a hand through the commissioning of special works, the fact that some dancers are able to continue in creative dance despite age or injury by switching from performing to choreography, and so forth.

of a given set of dispositions would not seem to give one sufficient reason to prefer it to a set of nonsocial dispositions.

Evidently, Dewey anticipated both sorts of objections. He responds with appeals to experience intended to show that we have every reason to suppose that social dispositions are good to their possessors and that qualitative differences exist between these and other nonsocial dispositions. Replying to the first, he argues that common sense has always treated the possession of social dispositions as good for their possessors. What grounds have we for holding that centuries of human experience is mistaken? Dewey insists the answer is none.

Replying to the second, Dewey argues that the testimony of both common sense and human history is that human beings are inherently social beings, unhappy and frustrated when prevented from participating in social activity. In support of his point, he notes that even utilitarians accept that we are inherently social, and he cites John Stuart Mill: "The social state is at once so natural, so necessary, and so habitual to man, that except in some unusual circumstances or by an effort of voluntary abstraction, *he never conceives himself otherwise than as a member of a body*. . . . Any condition, therefore, which is essential to a state of society becomes more and more an inseparable part of every person's conception of the state of things he is born into and which is the destiny of a human being"[13] (*MW* 5:268). As Dewey interprets him, Mill is saying that "we cannot separate the idea of ourselves and of our own good from our idea of others and of their good" (*MW* 5:268). But what of it? Does it follow from the fact that human beings have tended to think in this way, that they must continue to do so in future? Why may they not distinguish themselves and their own private interests from the community and the community's interests henceforth, if they choose? It appears that Dewey has made the elementary mistake of imagining that he can derive an evaluative conclusion from purely descriptive premises.

Arthur Lovejoy's review of *Ethics* was highly critical of Dewey's failure to make clear his reasons for holding that an individual's happiness is a function of that individual's pursuit of communal happiness. Lovejoy noted:

> The moral criterion at which the author arrives is not—in itself or in its premises—so thoroughly distinct from the "self-realization" standard of Green and his disciples as it seems meant to be. The crucial transition in the argument

13. Dewey is quoting from John Stuart Mill, *Autobiography* (London: Longmans, Green, Reader, & Dyer, 1869), pp. 143–44.

seems to depend upon the observation that the individual's real good or happiness demands social well-being because the self is essentially a social self . . .
—a characteristically abstract, loose, and shifty piece of neo-Hegelian
phraseology that is susceptible of several senses and is, in some of its senses,
decidedly open to question.[14]

Had Dewey left the matter as it stands, he would indeed have been
open to the charge, so often made against naturalistic ethics, of having
fallaciously derived an evaluative conclusion from purely descriptive
premises about human nature and human society. In fact, he does not
leave the matter as it stands. But oddly, the argument that would fill in
the gap appears in one of the two chapters Dewey contributed to Part
III, rather than in Part II, where it belongs. Odder still, nowhere in Part
II is it indicated that a further argument exists or where it can be found.
Why Dewey undercut his own case in this way is something of a mystery.

The argument offered in Part III for the qualitative superiority of our
social dispositions as constituents of a satisfactory life and character is
simply a highly compressed version of the rationale for a functional definition of selfhood we first saw in Bradley's *Ethical Studies*. Dewey argues
that personality or selfhood is not a property of human beings, like their
natural endowments. It is instead a complex set of functions that these
natural endowments may be used to perform. One *becomes* a person as
one learns to perform the functions constitutive of personality, in accordance with the social rules for their performance. Dewey explains "Only
in participating in already fashioned systems of conduct does [a child]
apprehend his own powers, appreciate their worth and realize their possibilities, and achieve for himself a controlled and orderly body of physical and mental habits. He finds the value and the principles of his life,
his satisfaction and his norms of authority, in being a member of associated groups of persons and in playing his part in their maintenance and
expansion" (*MW* 5:386–87).

Social interaction is a necessary condition of moral agency in at least
two important respects. "Apart from the social medium," Dewey says,
"the individual would never 'know himself', he would never become
acquainted with his own needs and capacities" (*MW* 5:388). To 'know'
is to assign meanings in controlled ways to one's experiences. To be able
to assign meanings in controlled ways requires an apparatus, a system of

14. Arthur O. Lovejoy, review of *Ethics*, *American Journal of Theology* 13 (1909): 143.

signification and symbolization together with rules for their application. No such apparatus is part of our natural endowments. Such systems are social institutions. By participating in this sort of social institution, we learn to know ourselves.

Second, Dewey holds, "social conditions not only evoke what is latent, and bring to conscious recognition what is blind, but they select, encourage and confirm certain tendencies at the expense of others. They enable the individual to discriminate the better and the worse among his tendencies and achievements" (*MW* 5:389). Language is a necessary condition of knowing, that is, a system for the symbolization of experience, by which experiences may be conveniently stored (in memory or via writing) or communicated. But another institution is necessary if we are to choose among possible symbolic representations of experience: judgment. Judgment can occur only when there is, in addition to a system of symbolic representation, a system of rules for relating symbolic meanings to one another and to the world. Judgment, he argues, is not a natural endowment; it is a function our natural endowments can be used to perform. Rule-governed functions, like judgment, are the products of social interaction and social construction. No individual can make agreements with himself of the sort indicated by the term 'rule of logic.' Thus participation in social institutions is a necessary condition of one's being a *self-conscious* and a *rational* agent. Because these are necessary conditions of moral agency, participation in social institutions is a necessary condition of one's being a moral agent.

Whatever sort of moral agent one may choose to become, one chooses to be a moral agent, that is, free, self-conscious, and rational. And in choosing to be a moral agent, one must at the same time choose that the social institutions necessary to one's being a moral agent exist to sustain and enrich one's personhood. Now these social institutions cannot and will not exist unless individuals cooperate in their formation and continuation. Thus the exercise of social dispositions is necessary to one's attaining and sustaining personality. Social dispositions turn out to be constitutive of personal flourishing in a peculiarly fundamental way. All one's dispositions and desires go to make up the sort of person one is. But one's social dispositions determine not only what sort of person one is but whether one is (or will be likely to remain) a person at all. And so it seems that common sense is right in supposing other-regarding or social goods as peculiarly right or true goods. Social goods are those that no rational agent could rationally choose permanently to forgo. To neglect the exercise of one's social dispositions, once recognized for what they are, is knowingly to invite or permit the dissolution of the institutions necessary to the maintenance of personal life. Nonsocial goods, however prima facie good they may be to oneself, are never necessary constituents of satisfactory moral agency in the same way. It will always be rationally permissible (in principle) to forgo or ignore a possible nonsocial good. So it turns out that Dewey's claim that social dispositions and their satisfactions are qualitatively superior to their nonsocial counterparts is not after all fallaciously derived from a set of merely factual statements about human sociability.

Why was this argument not included in Part II where it belongs? One can only guess. But Lovejoy's remarks may provide an important clue. Dewey's conception of personality as a social construct and thus of social cooperation as constitutive of personhood is characteristically neo-Hegelian. It was as a neo-Hegelian that Dewey had originally made his philosophical reputation. Throughout his career as a pragmatist, he was to face recurrent skepticism about whether he had really abandoned idealism and its assumptions altogether.[15] In 1908, when he had yet to produce the major works of his pragmatic period, the skepticism must have been rife. In this case, he might have feared that if he were to allow his ethics to be identified as characteristically neo-Hegelian in any one of its components, the whole would be written off as simply one more attempt to update idealist ethics. Could he have been certain that most readers would understand that the 'self-realizing' character of certain prima facie goods only provides grounds for *preferring* those to other sorts of goods, as Lovejoy seems to have done, rather than being the reason that they are good, Dewey might have stated more openly why he thought prima facie goods should be judged on the basis of their likelihood to be harmonious, flexible, stable, and social or self-realizing.

In sum, then, Dewey holds that any disposition or disposition-expressing plan of action whose realization is pleasant is prima facie good for the agent in question. Rational choice among prima facie goods is to be based on other qualities of the goods available and their relation to the agent's other projects. Prima facie goods whose qualities taken together are harmonious, flexible, stable, and social are the goods any rational agent ought to prefer. In a moral situation, these are the sorts of goods the agent would be right to pursue. Dewey states: "For all alike, in short, the chief thing is the discovery and promotion of those activities and

---

15. Consider, for example, the argument over whether or not Dewey's aesthetics is really pragmatic. For a helpful discussion of this debate, see Alexander, *Dewey's Theory of Art, Experience and Nature.*

active relationships in which the capacities of all concerned are effectively evoked, exercised, and put to the test" (*MW* 5:275).

MORAL JUDGMENT

The first six chapters of *Ethics*, Part II, are devoted to analysis, criticism, and construction of theoretical principles and categories with which we may screen and provisionally warrant hypotheses about particular varieties of moral phenomena. In the following four chapters, Dewey turns from the construction of fundamental principles for scientific moral inquiry to their explication and defense. In effect, he 'tests' them against our common-sense notions of what moral life involves, in order to show that his principles and categories can capture or adequately explain such phenomena as conscience, obligation, egoism, altruism, and the virtues. In this section, I discuss only the first, his treatment of the phenomenon of 'conscience,' or moral knowledge. There is probably no aspect of Dewey's pragmatic ethical constructivism that it is more essential to grasp if his position as a whole is to be understood—and no aspect of his position that has been more often or more disastrously misinterpreted.

A modern scientific investigator's facts are not given, they must be discovered or uncovered through observation and experimentation. Moreover, those facts must in principle be verifiable by others—that is, the observations and experimentation cannot be inherently private events. Traditional moral philosophies, however, have not infrequently claimed that moral data are given. Though some theories hold that intuition, a sort of observation, is involved, experimentation is not supposed to be required to uncover 'hidden' moral qualities. Moral data differ from scientific data in their immediate availability to some special faculty: 'conscience,' moral sense, or practical reason.[16]

Consequently, most moral philosophers have held that there are significant disanalogies between moral and physical inquiry. First, discovery plays little or no role in morals, since the data of morals are immediately or directly accessible. Public procedures for experimental confirmation are unnecessary. Second, moral inquiry and deliberation are not primarily inquiry and deliberation about whether given acts, choices, or persons are good or bad, right or wrong. These facts are known, or at least readily knowable. Moral deliberation and inquiry are as a rule deliberation and inquiry about whether to do what one ought

16. Classic utilitarianism is an exception.

to do or whether instead to follow one's nonmoral inclinations and egoistic impulses.

To dissolve the disanalogies, Dewey tries to show that there is no faculty either of moral perception or of a priori moral knowledge that obviates the need for the discovery of moral data. Only if, as he puts it, "the relevant bearings of any act are subtler and larger than those that can be foreseen and than those which will be *unless* special care is taken" (*MW* 5:278) will it be reasonable to claim that 'special care,' in the form of experimental investigation, is required. He begins by attacking the two versions of the traditional claim that moral data are always immediately accessible represented by Kant and by moral sense theories.

If Kant's account of moral deliberation were correct, as Dewey sees it, deliberation about the morality of a maxim would be purely a matter of a priori reasoning. Kant assumes that every agent values rationality and thus cannot rationally approve the satisfaction of desire at the expense of his rationality. To be rational is to be consistent in one's actions and one's selections of ends of action. And so Kant believed a simple a priori test can be applied to any problematic proposal. One has simply to consider whether a proposed act is one the agent could consistently approve if it were acted on universally. If he cannot, performing the act would be irrational and clearly wrong.

Dewey charges that the a priori appearance of Kant's method is misleading. Assume, for example, that I am to consider the coherence of universal theft. I may be able to determine that it would be irrational and wrong of me to commit an act of theft. Yet how do I know that the act I am contemplating is an act of 'theft'? And how have I come to know what 'theft' involves? Clearly, I must have made inductive generalizations from the observations of acts of theft or be relying on the inductions of others. In either case, if those observations are incomplete, poorly formulated, or misinterpreted, I may unknowingly arrive at a wrong conclusion. Thus it is not the case that we can or do rely on a priori reasoning alone in our moral inquiries. Nor is it the case that the state and amount of our empirical data about the objective features of the dispositions and conduct being considered have no effect upon our moral estimations.

Even less credible to Dewey was the hypothesis that humanity possesses a special sense or faculty by which it can invariably gather sufficient data for correct moral judgments of the rightness or goodness of motives and acts. For though it is certainly the case that we sometimes seem immediately to perceive values in given situations and to make immediate estimations of the rightness of competing ends, there is no good reason to resort to the postulation of a faculty of moral perception to explain this. After all, we know from *Ethics*, Part I, that individuals' perceptions of moral qualities and moral principles have varied widely from age to age, culture to culture, and within cultures, even from class to class. This wide variation in people's moral perceptions argues against our being endowed with a faculty of moral perception analogous to our faculties of sense perception.

Moreover, we can readily explain the phenomenon of immediate perception without positing the existence of a special sense or faculty. As a matter of fact, frequent repetition of any activity causes its performance to become habitual, virtually mechanical. Although the original performances of the act required thought and conscious effort, subsequent repetitions may involve little or none. Judgment is itself an act. And very similar judgments may be repeated so frequently in the course of one's life that arriving at a given conclusion eventually becomes a habit. Thereafter, the conclusion immediately comes to mind upon apprehension of the situation that stimulates that particular habit.

Although every problematic situation is potentially a moral situation, presenting a morally significant variety of options, Dewey argues that very few ever become genuine moral situations. Typically, decisions made in past dealings with similar situations are adequate to present needs. One simply scans the current situation one is in for options previously approved. And when discovered, they are immediately recognized as appropriate. This process of recognition is no more mysterious than recognition of any familiar object. Immediate recognition is possible only because of prior investigation and discovery. The frequency of moral 'recognition' relative to the infrequency of any need for deeper investigation of the competing options with which situations present us accounts for the traditional belief that the question of what is good or right is either immediately given or accessible a priori. At the same time, it reveals the inadequacies of the traditional account. A problematic situation resolvable by an immediate recognition of previously selected options is not a genuinely moral situation. It is merely a 'technical' rather than moral affair, to use Dewey's words, where the problem solved is the problem of the best means to a previously determined end, rather than a problem of deciding what one's end is to be.

Moral deliberation, Dewey argues, is never immediate. It begins with an effort to discover what the options of a problematic situation really are or involve so that a rational selection from among them may finally be made. He writes: "Deliberation is a process of active, suppressed, rehearsal; of imaginative dramatic performance of various deeds carrying to their appropriate issues the various tendencies which we feel stirring within us. When we see in imagination this or that change brought about, there is a direct sense of the amount and kind of worth which attaches to it, as real and direct, if not as strong, as if the act were really performed and its consequences really brought home to us" (*MW* 5:292). By means of this process, which Dewey refers to as "dramatic rehearsal," we discover whether and how particular dispositions are expressed in the various courses of action open to us, by imagining ourselves acting out those options. The 'direct sense of worth' we get as a result is a sense of relief or frustration, pleasure or pain. That pleasure or relief is a subjective signal that the course of action anticipated will express some one of our active dispositions. Dewey continues, "When many tendencies are brought into play, there is clearly much greater probability that the capacity of self which is really needed and appropriate will be brought into action, and thus a truly reasonable happiness result" (*MW* 5:293).

Our appreciation of possible lines of conduct is thus genuinely immediate. We feel some immediate satisfaction in the idea of expressing a disposition in a certain way, and this immediate satisfaction stamps that course of action as good. We rehearse another option and feel immediate dissatisfaction at the idea of conduct along that line, and this dissatisfaction stamps the conduct as bad. Of course, the quality of our background information about the physical and social worlds is not without influence on our direct appreciations of goodness. Ignorance or faulty reasoning might prevent us from foreseeing consequences of an act that would, had we foreseen them, have caused us to stamp as prima facie good what we in fact stamp as bad or indifferent. Nevertheless, it is the direct appreciation of an idea or plan of action that gives it its prima facie value.

When at the conclusion of a dramatic rehearsal of the opportunities of action open to us we have perceived which possibilities are good, a decision about what goods to pursue still has to made. This judgment is *not* immediate. Thus 'dramatic rehearsal,' as Dewey describes it, is not a method of making moral judgments. Dramatic rehearsal is a method of *gaining information necessary for moral judgment.* Moral judgment takes place when the incompatible goods giving conflicting reasons for action are evaluated in terms of the principles discussed above.

The distinction to be made between the processes of moral judgment and moral discovery has frequently been overlooked, thanks in part to Dewey himself. Because we normally think of deliberation as involving both the gathering of evidence and the drawing of conclusions, it has been natural to suppose that dramatic rehearsal *is* Dewey's account of both the gathering of moral data and of how we arrive at conclusions from that data. Of the various innovative features of Dewey's theory of moral deliberation, from 1908 onward, the process of discovery is invariably given the greatest emphasis. That this should have been so is not surprising when we consider the weight of philosophical opposition to the idea that anything like empirical discovery plays a role in moral decision making. Unfortunately, in his effort to dispose of one problem, Dewey spawned two more. He fell into the habit of describing the process of moral discovery, "dramatic rehearsal," not merely as part of the process of moral deliberation but *as* moral deliberation, as for example, in the statement that "deliberation is actually an imaginative rehearsal of various courses of conduct" (*MW* 5:293).

Having been educated in the neo-Hegelian tradition, Dewey never conceived of definitions as exclusive. That is, 'definitions' merely direct attention to some distinctive aspect of a given phenomenon, without excluding the possibility that other equally distinctive aspects may exist. So, for example, Dewey could define morality as a matter of conduct at one point, of character at another, and see no contradiction between the two 'definitions.' Similarly, he could define deliberation as dramatic rehearsal, the discovery of prima facie goods in a problematic situation, and subsequently hold that deliberation is the evaluation of discovered goods in accordance with rationally constructed principles of judgment, and yet see no contradiction between his definitions.[17]

Critics, on the other hand, expecting Dewey's definitions actually to exclude properties, processes, or characteristics not mentioned, have understandably been puzzled to know what they are to make of his conception of pragmatic moral deliberation. Perhaps the most common response is to interpret dramatic rehearsal as the whole of Dewey's account of moral deliberation, in which case, of course, the theory collapses into a form of Hobbesianism for which it is then duly criticized.

---

17. In his review of Dewey's 1887 *Psychology* (discussed in Chapter 2, above), G. Stanley Hall complained that "definitions make the fibre of the book, and even the favorite form of sentence. The author is always working from partial to complete definitions or conversely" (Hall, "Critical Notice," p. 156). Definition was still Dewey's favorite form of sentence, probably because it seemed to him such a flexible form.

Charles L. Stevenson's introductory essay to the recent critical edition of the 1908 Dewey and Tufts *Ethics* provides a classic example. As Stevenson describes it, dramatic rehearsal "provided a *method* for reaching evaluative opinions—a method of *reasoning*, since it required an individual to foresee consequences. Dewey was not merely pointing out the possibility of such a method; he was taking it to exemplify the only sort of reasoning that had a place in ethics" (*MW* 5:xiii). It is by this method, Stevenson continues, that Deweyan moral agents will determine both which possible acts have consequences they desire and which one of those acts they would be right to pursue. For Deweyan agents, then, to say 'act X is good' is to say that desire for the consequences of X has been discovered through a dramatic rehearsal. To say 'act X is right,' Stevenson goes on, is to say that "a dramatic rehearsal based on scientifically true propositions, if the speaker were to carry it out completely, would lead [the speaker] to have a predominating favor of X" (*MW* 5:xx). If Stevenson were correct, if dramatic rehearsal were the only method of moral deliberation Dewey endorsed, then it might be correct to argue that Dewey's account of moral deliberation is Hobbesian. But from the foregoing, it should be clear that Stevenson was wrong. Dramatic rehearsal is *not* the only method of reasoning that has a place in ethics. Moreover, if it were, the lengthy construction of principles for the rational evaluation of prima facie goods that takes up the bulk of Part II would have been for naught. Since Dewey clearly believed that rational criteria of evaluation can and should play a role in moral life, he must have thought there was more to moral deliberation than dramatic rehearsal.[18]

18. Alternately, it is sometimes suggested that moral deliberation might be interpreted as a special case of aesthetic appreciation, as Dewey was later to describe it in his 1934 *Art as Experience* (*LW* 10). That is, the problematic situation is interpreted as a situation whose meaning is indeterminate. Dramatic rehearsal is interpreted as the process by which the beholder/agent constructs a series of alternative interpretations culminating in the construction of an interpretation that yields a 'consummatory experience' of the situation as unified, meaningful, and fulfilling. The objections to this approach scarcely need to be pointed out. If moral situations were structured so that they could end only in a happy or fulfilling manner, an immediate feeling of fulfillment or of unified meaning at the thought of some one option might be an adequate basis on which to prefer that one over other prima facie good options. But as Dewey defines them, moral situations do not necessarily end in any particular fashion. Moral situations may offer us nothing but a choice among evils, no one of which could conceivably be experienced as fulfilling. And it may remain the source of chaotic rather than unified thought and feeling, whatever choice we make. Thus immediate feelings of fulfillment or unified meaning at the thought of one of a set of competing options will not be a reliable guide to the resolution of problematic moral situations.

After accounting for the element of immediate appreciation in the identification of goods and evils, Dewey analyzes the nature of moral judgment. In our judgments, he holds, we aim not only at the discovery of valued ends of action but at the justification of a choice of a particular value or set of values as an end of action. So in judgment there is explicit appeal to and use of theoretical principles. Some of the principles to which an agent may appeal in the course of making a moral judgment will be the broad, intersubjectively valid, fundamental principles of ethics Dewey has just sought to construct. But these principles provide only a general framework for moral inquiry. Intermediate generalizations relating specific features of actual moral situations to the framework definitions and classifications must also be formulated. These include principles stating the special relations holding between certain types of dispositions and of consequences and/or of their special relations to certain conditions required for those dispositions or consequences to be realized.

What are typically referred to as 'moral principles' and 'moral rules,' Dewey holds, are intermediate generalizations inductively derived from past observation of human conduct and its consequences. Unfortunately for the scientific ethical theorist, the function and purpose of these intermediate generalizations have been poorly understood. Morals, being practical, have been often treated as analogous to 'crafts.' Thus the intermediate generalizations of morals have been thought to be analogous to a craftsman's rules of thumb. So moralists have tried to construct rules of thumb dictating the sorts of overt behavior appropriate to specific circumstances. Rules of thumb can be as useful in morals as they are in crafts. But it is important to note how they are useful. They do not facilitate moral judgment. They eliminate the need for judgment. Ideally, one simply recalls and applies the rule.

The idea that judgments about what our objectives should be could be eliminated, Dewey thought, was a product of wishful thinking. The rules human beings have formulated for themselves, as the student of history knows, have never been so consistent, harmonious, expedient, and socially beneficial as to justify unreflective reliance upon them. So rather than try to design intellectual tools for the impossible project of making moral judgments unnecessary, moralists should stick to the more manageable project of designing principles that could function as intermediate generalizations to facilitate moral judging, on analogy to the intermediate generalizations used in natural sciences.

In other words, moralists should devote themselves to reviewing critically the manifold moral rules that human beings have constructed to determine which are worth serious scientific consideration and testing. To be worth considering scientifically, of course, they must be consistent with the judgments and principles already scientifically constructed. Principles of virtue, Dewey argues, that is, principles defining social dispositions such as charity, justice, and sympathy, appear to meet the first test. All presumably need the check and correction of further experimental testing. Happily, this is something social scientists are independently working to provide. In the meantime, ethical scientists can hasten the process by theoretically reviewing our other prescientific, common-sense moral rules for experimental fruitfulness in the hopes that hypotheses can be identified that social scientists may be induced to see as worth their while to test.

SCIENTIFIC PRACTICAL JUDGMENT

Ethics, Part II, was devoted to the construction of fundamental principles for the special science of ethics. The process of construction was guided by Dewey's conception of the function such principles perform in any scientific inquiry: the provisional warranting of experimentally fruitful hypotheses, that is, hypotheses entailing predictions about what would be experienced under specified conditions. Consequently, Dewey accepted among his fundamental principles of ethics only those empirical definitions that seemed to him to capture the characteristics of moral phenomena without significant 'remainders.' The result, he presumes, is a theory or set of principles that is minimally adequate to perform the function for which his principles are designed.

But at the end of Part II, as we discussed above, this is only a presumption. To be warranted, it must be shown that the principles actually can function as scientific principles ought to do. This is the object of Tufts's contributions in Part III. In Part III, Tufts considers several sets of competing hypotheses about the methods of the design of life most likely to produce the sort of outcomes we think rationally desirable, starting with hypotheses about the design of political systems, passing on to hypotheses about the design of economic systems and then to hypotheses about the design of family life. Each discussion is in effect a thought experiment, meant to show that the principles adopted in Part II do permit us to discriminate rationally between competing members of each set of hypotheses. Along the way, Tufts occasionally develops, from the hypotheses he selects, predictions about the effects to be expected from social or legislative experiments contemplated or then under way in Europe and the United States. The implication of these references is not only that the Part II principles permit us to make rational selections among competing hypotheses, but that the hypotheses selected are in fact experimentally fruitful.

Above I argued that the fact that neither Tufts nor Dewey actually designed or ran experiments to confirm the hypotheses warranted by their theory did not by itself preclude the recognition of the theory or the hypotheses it warranted as scientific. It is not necessary that theoreticians of any science test their hypotheses, so long as the hypotheses they provisionally advance are experimentally fruitful and are in principle confirmable or disconfirmable by practitioners of the appropriate physical, life, or social sciences. This at least Dewey and Tufts can claim to have done by the conclusion of Part III. Be that as it may, it might be argued, cooperative inquiry of the sort Dewey envisions between moral theorists and social scientists is still a long way off in the future. If individuals are now to try to make scientific practical judgments, they must attempt to confirm their own hypotheses experimentally. Moreover, if and when ethical science gets truly under way, it will still be necessary for individuals to perform experiments themselves. It will not always be the case that moral decisions can be deferred until scientific advice or analysis can be obtained. How then are these experiments to be performed?

It is a question to which Dewey effectively committed himself to answering when in his Introduction to *Ethics* he urged:

> If we can discover [scientific] ethical principles, these ought to give some guidance for the unsolved problems of life which continually present themselves for decision. Whatever may be true for other sciences, it would seem that ethics at least ought to have some practical value. "In this theater of man's life it is reserved for God and Angels to be lookers on." Man must act. . . . If he has reflected, has considered his conduct in light of the general principles of human order and progress, he ought to be able to act more intelligently and freely, to achieve the satisfaction that always attends on scientific as compared with uncritical or rule-of-thumb practice. (*MW* 5:10)

Clearly, Dewey believed that individual moral agents can settle their dilemmas in moral situations by scientific methods of reasoning. That is, if they committed themselves to the rules of scientific inquiry, they would be able to discriminate reliably between hypotheses about the courses of action available to them and between the goods of expressing the dispositions urging those acts. Further, they would be able to decide rationally which course of action open to them it would be right to view as desirable. But to discriminate scientifically between hypotheses about the outcomes and values of various courses of action would involve experimentation. And about ethical experimentation Dewey said less than he might and a great less than he should. At the very least, he should have explained how individuals are to validate their hypotheses experimentally and whether or to what degree individuals would be at fault if they did not. Since Dewey did not take the trouble to spell out the procedures he thought individual moral agents ought to use, we shall have to try to spell them out for ourselves.

We might begin by considering a hypothetical situation and applying the decision procedures Dewey recommends. Imagine that Jane, the adult daughter of an increasingly infirm elderly woman, June, is wondering whether she should try to persuade her mother to give up the large, physically challenging home in which she now lives alone, in favor of some other arrangement that would be safer and more convenient. Jane knows that June will agree to whatever Jane thinks best. What should Jane do?

The first step Jane should take is to perform a dramatic rehearsal of the options open to her in this novel situation. She should try to imagine possible responses to this situation and their respective probable objective consequences. The options whose probable consequences she finds immediately attractive will be the prima facie good options that she has reason to believe potentially satisfactory. Let us further imagine that after she performs a dramatic rehearsal, three inconsistent options emerge as prima facie good: to accede June's request that Jane move back into the family home (a request Jane has hitherto resisted out of a desire to maintain her own privacy and independence); to hire a live-in companion; and to persuade June to sell her home and move into a bungalow or condominium in a retirement community, an environment in which she can continue to manage on her own for some time.

Each option is in some respect prima facie good, which is to say that each would give free play to some one or more of Jane's dispositions to act, the expression of which would contribute to her satisfaction. The next step is to try to determine (1) what are the dispositions each option would express and (2) which other dispositions to act might be thwarted were any one option adopted.

Here Jane should begin to make use of both scientific principles of moral reasoning and any intermediate generalizations antecedently formulated. Using those principles and generalizations, she should try to identify the dispositions urging her toward each course of conduct. Are they 'virtuous' or socially constructive dispositions? If she acts to satisfy any one disposition (or set of dispositions), what dispositions will be repressed or reinforced as a result? For example, would any one of her options repress or reinforce dispositions to be generous or just to others or to herself? Would any one tend to encourage expression of dispositions to anger, rejection, self-pity? Such assessments would have to be made of each one of her three options.

Once she has settled the questions of what dispositions her three options would express, reinforce, and/or repress, she can construct hypotheses about the sort of person she would be and the sort of life she would live if she were to commit herself to any one. She then has to decide which sort of person she has reason to think it desirable (or more desirable) to try to be. Using Dewey's standard for the evaluation of prima facie goods, she would ask herself whether each of these three sorts of personalities or characteristic ways of behaving will be flexible, stable, harmonious, social, and so on. Eventually, she should be able to decide which one of these options she is provisionally warranted in believing desirable (or the least undesirable of the three).

Here the problem of experimental confirmation arises. Since it is not feasible to appeal directly to social scientists in such a case, Jane will have to play the roles of theorist and experimentalist herself. Perhaps it would be possible for Jane to make an experiment of moving in with June without giving up her own (Jane's) current residence. Or perhaps June could be persuaded to visit local retirement communities or to hire a live-in companion on a trial basis. In that case, Jane could make up a detailed list of the expectations she has of the option she has judged most desirable and then carefully observe the effects she actually produces when she tries that option. If the results cohere with her expectations, she would have some experimental warrant for her provisionally warranted judgment. If not, she would have some experimental warrant for rejecting her beliefs about that particular option as incorrect. This presumably is the course of action Dewey would recommend.

It is not always possible to make trials of our options in moral situations, however. The effects of such trials cannot always be reversed. What should we do in such cases? Where experimental trials are not practical, another possibility is to search out historical trials of options relevantly similar to those we would wish to make and to compare the historical effects with the effects we expect in our own case. Rather than predicting future events, we would try to 'retrodict' past events, validating a hypothesis by demonstrating that the predictions it entails would have been successful predictions of what are now past events (a technique often used in such sciences as geology and astronomy). Case studies compiled by social workers or health care professionals might be able to provide Jane with empirical data relevant to her situation, which might tend to confirm or refute her hypotheses about the effect of her preferred option on June's welfare and happiness. Dewey would probably recommend that she try this procedure in addition to or, if necessary, as a substitute for an experimental trial of her hypothesis.

But even this will be impossible in many situations. We can readily imagine circumstances that would constrain the most conscientious agent to act upon merely provisionally warranted hypotheses. This being the case, would Dewey's decision procedure be inapplicable in such circumstances? And if so, how will such cases be rationally resolved? Assuming for the moment that we were to say that Dewey's procedure as a whole was inapplicable, we could still respond that the situation has been rationally resolved. If the hypothesis accepted as action-guiding is provisionally warranted by the framework and intermediate principles of morals and scientific principles of preliminary warranting, and if circumstances permit no further trial or test of the hypothesis, then it would be rational to pursue the option provisionally warranted rather than the alternatives.

Nevertheless, there is usually some scope for experimental confirmation. Imagine that Jane must make an immediate decision, because an injury has made it impossible for June to manage on her own any longer. To complicate matters further, Jane works as the live-in supervisor of a halfway house for juvenile delinquents. As supervisor, she must be on call in the building sixteen hours a day, six days a week, a condition she can meet only if she resides in the building. Thus moving home with June would cost Jane her job and her independence for some time to come. Suppose now that this is precisely the option she thinks she has most reason to believe desirable.

Dewey might remind us that although Jane is committing herself to a single option, no one option in this situation is a single act but rather an interconnected series of acts occurring over time. Provided Jane had researched her options as thoroughly as is possible under the circumstances and reasoned carefully before deciding in favor of any one of her options, her decision to pursue that option is justified. But whether she will be justified in persisting in her pursuit of that option once its concrete consequences begin to emerge has yet to be determined.

Dewey wrote: "A truly moral (or right) act is one which is intelligent in an emphatic and peculiar sense; it is a *reasonable* act. It is not merely one which is thought of, and thought of as good, at the moment of action, but one which will continue to be thought of as 'good' in the most alert and persistent reflection" (*MW* 5:278–79). An agent forced to act upon a merely provisionally warranted hypothesis must be especially attentive to the concrete effects produced when she begins to act. And she must be ready to abort that line of action or to undo it as far as possible should the effects be significantly different from those she anticipated.

If the actual consequences of Jane's decision confirm her predictions, Jane may treat that as empirical confirmation of her original judgment and may consider a judgment to continue as she has begun both provisionally and experimentally warranted. If, however, the consequences do not confirm her predictions, her original decision, though justifiable given the circumstances, must now be judged unreliable and a decision to continue as she has begun unjustified. Jane's deliberation must be resumed from scratch.

Assuming that the consequences of moving home with June are much worse than Jane had expected and that these consequences cannot be reversed for some time, ought Jane to blame herself for what has occurred? Ought we to blame her? We may presume that Dewey's reply would be negative. Surely, Jane need not hold herself responsible for bad effects of acting upon merely provisionally warranted hypotheses, if those effects could not have been predicted at the time the decision had to be made and if her failure to test the hypothesis before acting was not due to negligence. Only if on reflection it emerges that the consequences could have been foreseen or that experimental trials might after all have been made should Jane blame herself or be blamed by others. In his discussion of a similar problem in *Ethics*, Part III, Tufts writes: "The more conscientious a person is, the more occasions he finds to judge *himself* with respect to results which *happened because he did not think or deliberate or foresee at all*—provided he has reason to believe that he would have thought of the harmful results if he had been of a different character [or unconstrained by circumstances]" (*MW* 5:415). Only if on reflection Jane realized that the fault did not lie in the circumstances would she be obliged to hold herself liable for the poor outcome of her choice. He continues: "Because we were absorbed in something else we did not think, and while, in the abstract, this something else may have been all right, in the concrete it may be proof of an unworthy character. The very fact that we permitted ourselves to become so absorbed that the thought [of foreseeable bad consequences] did not occur to us, is evidence of a selfish, i.e., inconsiderate, character" (*MW* 5:415). But for unavoidable errors made through no fault of our own, we are not culpable. A decision, in constrained circumstances, to accept and act upon merely provisionally warranted hypotheses is justified even when the hypotheses accepted subsequently prove false. But a decision to persist once the error has been detected would be unjustifiable. It would suggest moreover that the dispositions from which the persisting agent acts are unworthy.

If the foregoing is correct, then Dewey's failure to spell out in detail what he took ethical experiments to be like is not fatal. Nor does the decision procedure he advocates seem likely to prove impracticable. Interestingly, to the early reviewers, the practicality of Dewey's decision procedures was among the chief merits of his theory.

Only one, W. Caldwell, questioned whether practicality was quite as central to ethical theory and conduct as Dewey imagined. Caldwell wrote:

> Analysis and experiment may be good practical politics, or good sociology, or they may indeed be the one need of the student of social questions, but they are hardly important results for ethical theory, or even for "Applied Ethics," for both of which . . . all mere "experimentation" and all "good living" even . . . are subservient to an ethical ideal. . . . I mean that many things might liberate and "set free" character and capacity, but they might not be ethical at all; and the fault alike of our Western (or American) civilization and the general Pragmatist outlook on life and morals is their eternal belief in "experimentation" and "setting free," instead of in the *legitimacy* or the *illegitimacy* of certain kinds of "experiments."[19]

Caldwell's was among the first of what was to become a chorus of voices calling for assurance that Dewey's minimally adequate set of fundamental principles for ethics really would be adequate to preserve individuals and communities from those unwilling to submit to reason or to the spirit of compromise. In the following chapter, I discuss how Dewey attempted to answer those calls in articles and books that followed the publication of *Ethics*. For the moment, we may note that Caldwell's very complaint is a testament to Dewey's success in at last resolving the problem that had driven his ethical thought since the later 1880s: the reconciliation of scientific and moral philosophical theorizing.

19. W. Caldwell, review of *Ethics*, *Philosophical Review* 18 (1909): 226.

⦃7⦄ Toward a Pragmatic Communitarianism

The time will come when it will be found passing strange that we of this age should take such pains to control by every means at command the formation of ideas of physical things, even those most remote from human concern, and yet are content with haphazard beliefs about the qualities of objects that regulate our deepest interests; that we are scrupulous as to methods of forming ideas of natural objects, and either dogmatic or else driven by immediate conditions in framing those about values.

The Quest for Certainty

D espite or perhaps because of its success as an academic textbook, the 1908 *Ethics* raised as many questions about Dewey's ethics as it answered. Dewey was undoubtedly to blame for at least some of the confusion. He operated throughout the text on an understanding of scientific and of moral judgment that he had worked out five years earlier, in "The Logical Conditions of a Scientific Treatment of Morality." This 1903 monograph had appeared in a relatively obscure University of Chicago publication and thus was neither widely available nor widely read. Since Dewey did not bother to restate his position in *Ethics*, few of its early readers would have been aware of precisely what he meant by urging that ethics adopt experimental techniques or how exactly *Ethics* contributed to the establishment of an experimental ethical science. Consequently, the significance of the text's structure must have been obscure to many of its readers.

As a result, *Ethics* lent itself to a variety of misinterpretations. The most common and probably the most frustrating to Dewey himself was the reduction of his pragmatic constructivism to a sort of Hobbesian ethic by the exaggeration of the 'instrumental' character of his moral principles, rules, and judgments. Readers unfamiliar with Dewey's conception of scientific judgment and the instrumental role fundamental principles play in warranting provisional hypotheses could hardly be expected to understand what Dewey actually meant the instrumental role of moral principles to be. Consequently, they not unreasonably supposed that Dewey's moral rules and judgments were merely means to the same sort of end Hobbesian agents pursue—the satisfaction of active dispositions. So read, Dewey's elaborately constructed ethical theory necessarily begins to unravel. If moral principles and rules are interpreted as merely instrumental to the satisfactory expression of private ends, rather than as instruments of collective scientific inquiry, Dewey's belief in moral agents' obligations to adopt or abide by particular moral principles or rules becomes incomprehensible. The fact that it is usually in one's interest to abide by the moral principles and rules current in one's society hardly constitutes an obligation to do so. As a result, Dewey began to seem to have a problem with his account of moral obligation.

Whether a pragmatic ethics could support a plausible social and political theory also came into question. Dewey argues in *Ethics* that a pragmatic moral community of individuals pursuing harmonious, stable, and social forms of conduct and character will necessarily be egalitarian in its attitudes to persons and democratic in its political organization. Democratic rule by an egalitarian community, he believed, would afford individuals greater opportunities to realize their goals than any other form of political association. But if we think of moral rules and principles as merely instrumental to the satisfaction of individual preferences, then to a pragmatic community, democracy might simply be one among many social and political instruments to be adopted or rejected as the inclinations of the majority warrant—rather than the one form of political organization a pragmatic moral agent would be justified in accepting. If one imagined that moral principles, intermediate generalizations, and rules are all about the best means to the satisfactory expression of private dispositions, one would not feel bound to reject any principle of social organization that served one's private ends. If tyranny would better serve one's private interests or those of one's family or class, so much the worse for egalitarian democracy.

It was such a view of pragmatism and its ethics that led Bertrand Russell to protest in 1909 that pragmatism was inimical to both morality and liberal democracy. He wrote:

> The hopes of international peace, like the achievement of internal peace, depend upon the creation of an effective force of public opinion formed upon an

estimate of the rights and wrongs of disputes. . . . But the possibility of such a
public opinion depends upon the possibility of a standard of justice which is a
cause, and not an effect, of the wishes of the community; and such a standard
of justice seems incompatible with the pragmatist philosophy. This philosophy, therefore, although it begins with liberty and toleration, develops, by
inherent necessity, into an appeal to force and the arbitrament of the big
battalions.[1]

Even friendly critics, better informed about Dewey's conceptions of
scientific and moral inquiry than Russell, not infrequently accused
Dewey of being overly optimistic about the practicality of his pragmatic
constructivism. These charges became more widespread in the two decades following publication of *Ethics* as Dewey argued for the application of pragmatic techniques to contemporary political and social problems. The charge came, broadly speaking, in two forms, both given
peculiarly bitter voice in Randolph Bourne's famous 1917 essay, "Twilight of Idols."[2] The first charge echoes an objection made many years
earlier by Josiah Royce that Dewey 'too gayly' ignores the possibility of
moral tragedies, situations having no satisfying resolution, whose evils
no amount of inquiry, reflection. or science can evade or control.[3] For
Bourne, Dewey's hope that the First World War would serve liberal
political forces was evidence that his philosophy had "no place for the
inexorable."[4] Wars, Bourne argued, are not natural forces to be controlled or directed for human betterment like fire, electricity, or water.
Wars are disasters to be avoided if possible, grimly endured if not, but
never welcomed as instruments of social change.

The second charge is related to the first. Just as pragmatism promises
too much, it demands too much of the ordinary person. As Bourne puts
it: "a rational nation would have chosen education as its national enterprise. Into this it would have thrown its energy though the heavens fell
and the earth rocked around it. But the nation did not use its isolation
from the conflict to educate itself. It fretted for three years and then let

1. Bertrand Russell, "Pragmatism" (1909), reprinted in *Philosophical Essays* (New York:
Simon & Schuster, 1966), p. 110.
2. Randolph S. Bourne, "Twilight of Idols" (1917), reprinted in Bourne, *War and the
Intellectuals: Collected Essays, 1915–1919*, ed. Carl Resek (New York: Harper & Row, 1964),
pp. 53–64.
3. The charge was made regarding Dewey's *Outlines of a Critical Ethics* and is discussed in
Chapter 3, above.
4. Bourne, "Twilight of Idols," p. 59.

war, not education, be chosen."[5] Societies do not function as impartial rational entities. So, Bourne insists, it is foolish to expect a modern political society to decide policy questions in accordance with the rational and impartial standards of inquiry Dewey has constructed for their use. Pragmatism's social philosophy is thoroughly impractical.

Bourne's second argument would later be taken a step further by critics and former allies, such as Walter Lippmann.[6] It is not only foolish to expect rational principles of inquiry to be overriding in the formation and implementation of public policy. It is foolish to expect them to be overriding in the average individual's formation and selection of long-term life plans and projects. Human beings are emotional and passionate beings first and rational second. Moreover, relatively few people are conversant with scientific principles of inquiry, and fewer still could put them to work. Education might gradually increase the number capable of making pragmatically justifiable moral decisions, but it could never undo differences in natural talents or abilities. Nor could education guarantee that one would always have adequate time to make rational, reflective decisions in particular cases. Thus a pragmatic moral community could function only if those with the ability, training, access to information, and time to pursue inquiries act as moral experts, guiding and advising the majority. Or in other words, a pragmatic ethics is an impractical basis for social philosophy, if by that we mean, as Bourne did, a *liberal* social philosophy. Pragmatism could in principle be workable, but only if democratic decision making is abandoned in favor of a benevolent dictatorship of technocrats, including experts in the techniques of inquiry, diagnosis, and treatment of moral problems.

In a letter of 1915, Dewey acknowledged that the 1908 *Ethics* had not provided clear solutions to these sorts of objections. He writes, "I have not given or tried to give any 'solutions.' But it doesnt [*sic*] seem to have occurred to the objectors that to say that the moral life is a sries [*sic*] of problems and that morality *is* their solution as they arise would naturally preclude me from proffering solutions."[7] But in the 1910s and

5. Ibid., p. 56.
6. See, for example, Walter Lippmann, *Public Opinion* (New York: Free Press, [1922] 1965), and *The Phantom Public* (New York: Macmillan, 1925). Others had evidently gotten a similar point across to Dewey even before Lippmann's books appeared. Dewey's 1922 *Human Nature and Conduct* replies to those, among others, who object to his ethics "as placing too much emphasis upon intelligence" (*Human Nature and Conduct, MW* 14:171).
7. The quotation is taken from a letter of May 6, 1915, to Scudder Klyce, Scudder Klyce Papers, Library of Congress, Washington, D.C., excerpt reprinted in Abraham Edel and Elizabeth Flower, introduction to *Ethics* (1932), *LW* 7:xxxiii.

1920s, Dewey did indicate how he thought solutions could be arrived at and what relation the methods of ethics bore to the methods of the natural sciences. In some instances, he even went so far as to proffer solutions: specifically, democracy and education, both of which he saw as integral to the moral resolution of the obstacles life presents to the development of satisfactory character and conduct. Increasingly, Dewey was concerned with trying to test the practical bearings of his solutions by getting them put into practice. He became heavily involved in promoting progressive educational and political reforms, through lectures, addresses, reviews, and popular essays, most notably perhaps his essays for the newly founded *New Republic* magazine.

As a result, much of Dewey's output in these two decades was popular and applied. Nevertheless, this period was philosophically fruitful as well. Dewey made use of his lectures, essays, and addresses to experiment with illustrations, refinements, and reformulations of his more controversial conceptions and their application to contemporary philosophical debates. Eventually, all these experiments resulted in the systematic naturalistic reinterpretations of human nature, metaphysics, art, and epistemology that constitute the major works of his mature pragmatic philosophy for which he remains best known: *Human Nature and Conduct* (1922), *Experience and Nature* (1925, 1929), *Art as Experience* (1934), and *Logic: The Theory of Inquiry* (1938). It was not until 1915, however, that Dewey began crystallizing the results of his tentative reformulations into systematic form. "The Logic of Judgments of Practice," a two-part article in the *Journal of Philosophy, Psychology, and Scientific Methods*, as the first significant fruit of his labor. The second was his 1916 text, *Democracy and Education*, to which Dewey referred in 1930 as "for many years that in which my philosophy, such as it is, was most fully expounded."[8]

FACTS AND VALUES: "THE LOGIC OF JUDGMENTS OF PRACTICE"

"The Logic of Judgments of Practice" might best be described as a revised and considerably expanded version of "The Logical Conditions of a Scientific Treatment of Morality." As its title implies, "The Logic of Judgments of Practice" discusses the nature and manner of confirmation of practical judgments generally, including but not limited to the overtly

8. See John Dewey "The Logic of Judgments of Practice," *MW* 8:14–82; and *Democracy and Education, MW* 9. The quotation is from Dewey's autobiographical essay, "Absolutism to Experimentalism," *LW* 5:156.

ethical. As in the earlier paper, Dewey opens by attempting to rebut the presumption that practical judgments about what is to be done differ in kind from nonpractical judgments of fact, in that the former are conditional or hypothetical in a way the latter are not. He argues that judgments of fact are all conditional upon the acceptance of various presuppositions, usually unstated, about the procedures appropriate for the assertion of an observation as 'fact' and for the confirmation of such assertions. Thus, he maintains, "all propositions which state discoveries or ascertainments, all categorical propositions, would be hypothetical, and their truth would coincide with their tested consequences" (*MW* 8:22). Here Dewey is careful to distinguish his notion of confirmation from that of his fellow pragmatist, William James. With Russell in mind, Dewey writes that his is "a type of pragmatism quite free from dependence upon a voluntaristic psychology. It is not complicated by reference to emotional satisfactions or the play of desires"[9] (*MW* 8:22). In other words, he will look to precisely the same sorts of consequences to confirm both practical hypotheses and predictions and their nonpractical, scientific counterparts.

Dewey then elaborates on a point, virtually taken for granted in the earlier paper, that 'values' are to be understood as analogous to 'facts.' He attributes misinterpretation of his position on value to a misunderstanding of the analogy intended. First, values, like facts, are to be viewed as constructs, not as items of immediate or direct 'knowledge by acquaintance.' Just as, in the past, observations had been confused with sensations, facts with unconfirmed anecdotes, so also, Dewey argues, values have been confused with immediate, unreflective instances of liking, prizing, or esteeming things, persons, or events. "As against all this," he writes, "the present paper takes its stand with the position stated by Hume in the following words: 'A passion is an original existence, or, if you will, modification of existence; and contains not any representative quality'" (*MW* 8:24). The experience of prizing, esteeming, liking, disdaining, or loathing is, relatively speaking, an immediate, direct subjective response to a situation or its constituents, on a par with the subjective experiences of feeling, hearing, smelling, and so forth. Such experiences, Dewey argues, never constitute knowledge. Attention to, that is, selection of, an immediate apprehension of warmth, for example, from the interpenetrating whole of one's immediate ongoing experience transforms the apprehension into an 'observation' or 'per-

9. Russell is referred to on the same page.

ception' of warmth. Such an observation is merely anecdotal until confirmed by another intellectual process, reading a thermometer, perhaps. Only after some such confirmation does the observation become a 'fact.' So although one may have felt warm before one actually checked a thermometer, it was not a fact (i.e., *known*) that one was warm before the thermometer was checked. Since facts are intellectual constructs, they obviously cannot exist before they have been constructed. Likewise, Dewey argues, a value—say, the goodness, beauty, efficiency, or rightness of a given act—comes into being only as a result of a series of intellectual processes.

Consider the following example. Walking along the pier at your favorite seaside resort, you approach a seafood stand and, on impulse, order a lobster roll. So far, an impulse has been transformed into a string of perceptions or observations—that you are hungry for something to eat and that what you are hungry for is a lobster roll. You do not yet know if your perceptions are correct. You cannot know this until you have found some way of verifying your perceptions. Now suppose you receive a lobster roll and consume it eagerly. It could then be said to be a fact that you had been hungry and that what you had been hungry for was a lobster roll. Could it also be said that the lobster roll was 'good' to you? Or more specifically, could it be said that the lobster roll had a value for you? Dewey's answer would be negative. Although you *enjoyed* the lobster roll, it has as yet been of no *value* to you. Before it can be said to have a value, the immediate experience of enjoyment must be in some manner tested and approved.

For example, suppose that in answer to your request for a lobster roll, you were told that you could have one if you were prepared to wait fifteen minutes. Faced with a dilemma, you pause to weigh the pros and cons of the alternate possible responses you might make. As you do so, you determine the relative worth of your options. If you opt for the lobster roll, then as far as you are concerned the lobster roll is both a good and a good superior to the rival possibilities of ordering something else or ordering nothing at all. Dewey writes: "In this process, things *get* values—something they did not possess before. . . . At the risk of whatever shock, this doctrine should be exposed in all its nakedness. To judge value is to engage in instituting a determinate value where none is given" (*MW* 8:35). Just as nothing is a fact for Dewey until it has been verified, nothing is or can have a value until it has been reflectively evaluated.

Further, values, like facts, are revisable. In situations where determinate values do present themselves as a result of previous considerations, those values may be revised, rejected, falsified, or confirmed in light of subsequent events. For example, suppose two hours after consuming a lobster roll, you feel the first stages of what is evidently going to be a serious bout of indigestion. You suddenly realize that this is not the first time that indigestion has followed your consumption of lobster rolls. What before you had put down to an unfortunate choice of lobster-roll vendors, you now recognize as the consequence of your eating lobster rolls. These reflections will probably lead you to revise your earlier assessment of the value of lobster rolls in general and the specific lobster roll you had eaten two hours before. What you had hitherto regarded as an unqualified good, you may now consider good only in moderation, if you continue to think of it as good at all.

To use the language of this 1915 paper, what we uncover or discover through a dramatic rehearsal of our options in a problematic situation are not 'values' or 'goods' or 'evils' (except or unless some of these options have been valued on previous occasions). What one uncovers or discovers is simply what one's specific subjective responses to one's situation are. We learn which options are attractive, repellent, or indifferent to us. But until our options have been rationally weighed or valued, they have no value. In the case of specifically moral situations and their options, the options we immediately like, prize, or enjoy will be evaluated in terms of their potential to serve as constituents of a good life and character, by means of pragmatically established theoretical moral principles and intermediate generalizations of the sort Dewey discussed in *Ethics*—and subject, of course, to subsequent confirmation.

Dewey's thesis that no option has a value until it has been 'valuated' was at least one source of the crude instrumentalist interpretation of his ethical theory. As Dewey notes, what he is calling 'valuation' has traditionally been characterized as "a process of applying some fixed or determinate value to the various competing goods of a situation; that valuation implies a prior standard" (*MW* 8:36). In other words, we can value our options in a problematic situation because we already know what is of value. All we have to do is determine whether our options possess the qualities we already know to be of value or how well or ill they would serve as means to what we know to be of value. Whatever our own particular theories of value, it will never be the case that reflection on the information gained from a dramatic rehearsal of our options will result in the discovery or justification of intrinsic value. Dramatic rehearsal can at most be a vehicle for determining which of our incompatible options is most valuable as a means to our intrinsically valued ends. If one approaches Dewey's theory of moral deliberation and judgment from such a perspective, one will naturally conclude that this theory selects between options solely for their instrumental value.

The crude instrumentalist interpretation of Dewey's theory of moral deliberation thus misses the central point of that theory: the rejection of the thesis that we can know in principle (at least) what we value intrinsically in advance of choices of action. Dewey rejects the presumption that it is in principle possible to ascertain, by a purely a priori analysis of human nature and its essential properties, what the ideal life or character would be, in terms of which particular courses of action could be assessed. This is, he insists, precisely the same sort of presumption that so long retarded the advance of physical science. Ancient theories of knowledge, for instance, explained one's ability to identify a tree as a member of a given species by virtue of one's possession of an ideal model or conception of that particular species of tree, with which the present specimen is compared. Likewise, it was by virtue of one's possession of an ideal model or conception of a given sort of tree that one could evaluate the quality of a given specimen in terms of its conformity or nonconformity to the ideal type. But as Dewey points out, these theories of knowledge have long since been abandoned by modern physical science. It is time moral science did the same. "Physical knowledge," he argues, "did not . . . advance till the dogma of models or forms as standards of knowledge had been ousted. Yet we hang tenaciously to a like doctrine in morals for fear of moral chaos" (MW 8:44).

Granted, it is often the case that the problematic situations one encounters can be resolved by reference to the judgments or standards of value agents bring with them into the situation. But it does not follow from this that there is never a time when agents have to construct their values deliberately. Nor does it follow that their constructions of values are different in kind from their constructions of facts about physical objects. On the contrary, Dewey insists, one and the same method is used in each case: "Only by a judgment of means—things having value in the carrying of an indeterminate situation to a completion—is the end determinately made out in judgment" (MW 8:37).

Recall that for Dewey, knowledge of a physical object is knowledge of the operations by which that object may be produced. By analogy, one's knowledge of values or valuable ends of action is knowledge of the operations by which those valued ends can be constructed. To believe, for example, that human beings evolved from lower animal species is not to *know* that they did so, unless one also knows of some mechanism that can have brought the change about. Similarly, for Dewey, to believe that a certain possible goal or objective is a value, a valuable end of action, is not to know this is the case, unless or until one also knows of means adequate to bring that end about. Not infrequently, he argues, our beliefs about what our ends or values are in problematic situations are radically altered when we consider what in practice is involved in their pursuit. Means are not simply instruments for the realization of ends. Means define and constitute ends, every bit as much as the natural selection of genetic traits defines and constitutes biological evolution.

For a modern scientific theory of ethics, as Dewey conceives of it, means and ends must be reciprocal. Moreover, ends not only are the means involved in their accomplishment; ends are themselves means to the completion of particular projects that then form the basis from which new projects spring. As a result, the decision to identify a particular act or event in a life as a 'means' or as an 'end' is like the decision to identify a particular event in a chain of events as a 'cause' or an 'effect'—appropriate for certain purposes and inappropriate for others. In reality, nothing is exclusively one or the other.

Reading back to the 1908 *Ethics*, we see that the putative end of human action, the good life, cannot be conceived of as a discrete thing, event, quality, or state. It must instead be conceived of as a series, a series of challenges overcome giving rise to new challenges. Each new end is a new construction, the outcome of a process of investigation and discovery of the materials and opportunities of one's circumstances, subject to eventual confirmation. Naturally, then, whatever our ends have been or are next to be, we will have reason to want them to be harmonious and stable, yet flexible and personally and socially enriching rather than the reverse.

PHILOSOPHY, DEMOCRACY, AND EDUCATION

"The Logic of Judgments of Practice" explained and expanded Dewey's conception of the relation of facts to values, of scientific and practical judgment. It was not particularly concerned with the philosopher's role in the construction of either. This topic is discussed in *Democracy and Education*, a book that might as well have been titled 'Democracy as Education' and subtitled 'The Vocation of Philosophy.' What is most fully expounded in this text is less Dewey's philosophy than his emerging conception of philosophy.

Before his break with idealism, Dewey had seen philosophy as the highest expression of the urge to know. Philosophy's vocation was the complete and ordered comprehension of the world, a comprehension to which the special sciences made their several, piecemeal contributions. Subsequent transformations in his conception of knowledge and science made it impossible for Dewey to continue to maintain this conception of philosophy or its relation to the special sciences. Since he no longer thought of the world as an eternally perfect creation of an eternally conscious mind, he no longer believed it possessed of an unchanging order that it could be the business of philosophy to transcribe. Philosophy would either have to find itself a new vocation or join the growing ranks of trades and crafts made redundant by modern technological and scientific development. *Ethics* points the way Dewey believed ethical philosophy must go if it was to survive in the modern world. Ethical theory, that is, ethical philosophy, must become the theoretical wing of a practical science largely conducted by professional experimental scientists. Anthropology, sociology, psychology, and physiology investigate the materials of human conduct and character. These sciences will formulate hypotheses about how particular objectives may be reached, under what circumstances, with what effects, and at what costs. And tests will be performed to confirm hypotheses. But knowledge of what can be done does not determine what should be done. Nor indeed is it philosophy's job to determine what should be done. The determination of what should be done is the fundamental project of society at large. Philosophy's contribution is the development of procedures and principles of assistance in the collective social construction and evaluation of ideals (ends) of human flourishing and the materials and means of their construction.

Ethical philosophy's job, one might say, is to teach us to think rationally and critically about conflicting and incommensurable values. In *Democracy and Education*, Dewey takes this approach a step further. As he depicts them, every branch of philosophy operates at the intersection of positive science and human culture. He writes:

> Positive science always implies *practically* the ends which the community is concerned to achieve. Isolated from such ends, it is a matter of indifference whether its disclosures are used to cure disease or to spread it; to increase the means of sustenance of life or . . . to wipe life out. If society is interested in one of these things rather than another, science shows the way of attainment. Philosophy thus has a double task: that of criticizing existing aims with re-

spect to the existing state of science, pointing out values which have become obsolete with the command of new resources, showing what values are merely sentimental because there are no means for their realization; and also that of interpreting the results of specialized science in their bearing on future social endeavor. (*MW* 9:339)

As the theoretical wing of the social sciences, philosophy has a twofold vocation: critical and constructive. First, philosophy, in all its branches, will analyze and critique human objectives (whatever these may be) and their relation to available resources and materials—in particular, pointing out what those objectives really mean by reference to the practical bearings of a social commitment to them. Second, because science and technology run ahead of our understanding of their use and significance, philosophy will assist in the design of new institutions and practices by which new ideas and powers can be put to humanly fruitful use.

Philosophy, as Dewey now conceives of it, is in a sense analogous to architecture: neither art nor science, but involving application to the design both of new constructions and of improvements to or replacements for old ones. The analogy, however, is not complete. Whereas architecture (at the practical level at least) is taken up with the design of particular constructions, philosophy is concerned with the design of designs, the general principles by which particular designs may be guided and evaluated. Thus Dewey argues, "The most penetrating definition of philosophy which can be given is, then, that it is the theory of education in its most general phase" (*MW* 9:341). From Dewey's pragmatic perspective, philosophy is general education in the principles of thought as a doubt-inquiry or problem-solving process. Ethical philosophy, specifically, is education in the principles of thought appropriate to the rational resolution of doubts or problems about values.

The apparently irreverent, 'engineering' approach to the problems of collective action and social organization of Dewey's pragmatic ethical philosophy has always been worrying to those who, like Russell, doubt that a pragmatic community would recognize or respect minority rights and interests whenever their sacrifice would permit a more efficient engineering of social harmony and prosperity for the majority. Would a pragmatic community respect individual autonomy in its design of social institutions, if a benevolent paternalism augured better? For the same reason, pragmatism's commitment to democratic political organization has been questioned.

The 1908 *Ethics* had not improved matters as far as Dewey's contemporaries were concerned. After his construction in Part II of the theoretical principles for the rational evaluation of hypothetical courses of action, individual and social, one would have expected Dewey to demonstrate the effectiveness of the principles in Part III by using them to select (among others) principles of social justice. One's expectations would most likely have been heightened by the thought that Dewey was politically liberal, of a camp to which, as John Rawls has put it, "justice is the first virtue of social institutions, as truth is of systems of thought."[10] But those expectations would have been disappointed. In his contributions to Part III, the chapters entitled "Social Organization and the Individual" and "Civil Society and the Political State," Dewey talks primarily about the dependence of individual personal development and flourishing on social institutions. Then he rather baldly proposes that we use this relationship to *test* the practical effectiveness of given social institutions and their particular practices: "The Test is whether a given custom or law sets free individual capacities in such a way as to make them available for the development of the general happiness or the common good. This formula states the test with the emphasis falling upon the side of the individual. It may be stated from the side of associated life as follows: The test is whether the general, the public, organization and order are promoted in such a way as to equalize opportunity for all" (*Ethics, MW* 5:431). For reasons he does not explain in *Ethics*, Dewey evidently thinks it is freedom, rather than justice, that is the first virtue of social institutions. More specifically, it is "effective freedom" meaning both freedom *from interference* by others as well as freedom *to command* resources essential for the realization of one's desires and aims, that is Dewey's first virtue of social organization.

Were he compelled to state what exactly his conception of justice was, Dewey would probably say that it was simply the rational choice of institutions or acts. Societies and their members are more or less just as their institutions and actions more or less contribute to effective freedom. That is, institutions and acts are just to the extent that it is rational for a group collectively to adopt them. If what we most fundamentally want (whatever else we want) is what we are due, then what we are most fundamentally due (whatever else we are due) is freedom. But someone might object that it is not yet clear that what we want (whatever else we want) *is* what we are due from others. If effective freedom is the freedom or liberty to contribute to the general happiness or the com-

10. John Rawls, *A Theory of Justice* (Cambridge: Harvard University Press, 1971), p. 3.

mon good, might it not seem just or reasonable to enhance individuals' effective freedom through compulsion? If, for example, children could be raised more efficiently if their mothers were prevented from holding jobs outside the home, would not these mothers be made more effectively free by these restrictions? And if equal opportunity for all is likewise an opportunity to contribute to the public good, might not a totalitarian social system assigning duties to each citizen as governmental experts see fit maximize equal opportunity and thus be more just than liberal, democratic alternatives? Dewey would certainly reject these suggestions. But it is not at all clear from the arguments of the 1908 *Ethics* why the reader should agree. *Democracy and Education* supplies the missing rationale. Nondemocratic, authoritarian social organizations are less rational, and therefore less just, because of the inferior education they provide their citizens.

The aim of education, Dewey holds, is to promote the growth and development of the individual. Too often the nature of this objective is misunderstood. People imagine that the object of education is to transform an immature, unfinished individual into a mature, finished individual, that is, "the fulfillment of growing is taken to mean an *accomplished* growth: that is to say, an Ungrowth, something which is no longer growing" (*Democracy and Education, MW* 9:47). Yet surely this is a contradiction in terms. All living things are continually growing: growing new structures or replacements, internal and external, and in the case of higher living things, growing in experience and in the range of adaptive responses to the challenges of the surrounding environment. The end of growth is the end of life. Dewey reasons: "When it is said that education is development, everything depends on *how* development is conceived. Our net conclusion is that life is development, and that developing, growing, is life. Translated into its educational equivalents, this means (*i*) that the educational process has no end beyond itself; it is its own end; and that (*ii*) the educational process is one of continual reorganizing, reconstructing, transforming" (*MW* 9:54). The goal of education is thus the goal of human life and conduct: the development of dispositions and habits of character that cooperate to afford stability, flexibility, harmony, and enrichment of one's character and activity over time and through the inevitable changes of circumstances.

Education, that is, guided or directed development and growth, is not a product of schools alone. On the contrary, all the social institutions with which anyone interacts are educative. A culture's law, art, religious traditions, etiquette, fraternal associations, sports, and political institutions each educate the society's members to view themselves and their futures in certain ways, from within that particular culture's world view. So whenever one evaluates an institution alone or the fundamental principles of organization underlying an entire society's social institutions, one must rationally consider what the effects of the education that institution or set of institutions is liable to have on the collective social enterprise of constructing the conditions of rewarding personal life. Dewey argues:

> The problem is to extract the desirable traits of forms of community life which actually exist, and employ them to criticize undesirable features and suggest improvement. Now in any social group whatever, even in a gang of thieves, we find some interest held in common, and we find a certain amount of interaction and cooperative intercourse with other groups. From these two traits we derive our standard. How numerous and varied are the interests which are consciously shared? How full and free is the interplay with other forms of association? (*MW* 9:89)

A gang of thieves, for example, has relatively few interests in common and must either live apart from its victims or hide its true interests and activities from the surrounding community. Opportunities for enriching interactions with one's fellow gang members will be relatively few, and opportunities for enriching associations with outsiders are liable to be fewer still. And when such opportunities do arise, the need to keep one's true interests hidden will necessarily inhibit deep or lasting involvements with outsiders. As Dewey puts it, "the education such a society gives is partial and distorted" (*MW* 9:89), in comparison to other, more open associations, institutions, and group practices. The effects of participation in gang culture are well known and well documented. Nevertheless, gangs typically operate within societies. Thus the gang's education of its members is counteracted in part by the educative effects of the surrounding culture. More pervasive and thus more profound in their effects on attitude and outlook are the fundamental principles of association of that surrounding culture. Thus to safeguard our own and others' educational interests, it makes sense to consider the educational opportunities different types of social organization afford their members.

When we do, Dewey believes, we will see that of all the forms of social organizations so far developed in the modern world, the alternative we are most warranted in accepting will be egalitarian democracy. Aristocracy, oligarchy, monarchy, and authoritarian dictatorships all invariably have the effect of dividing the interests of different classes within the society and turning them against one another. Association and interaction across class lines is thus curtailed and, with these, the opportunity to learn and benefit from free association with others' ideas and experience. Authoritarian regimes, he suggests, seem particularly prone to try to limit association and communication across their countries' borders and to cultivate in their citizens a feeling of having been set apart—superior to, or at least different in kind—from other peoples. The effect of the cultivation of such attitudes is that even those who are able to travel freely outside their own country will have their minds relatively closed to the ideas and the technical innovations they meet with elsewhere.

By contrast, mutual participation in the design of the principles of association typical of a democratic society, Dewey argues, increases educational opportunities for all by increasing contact, interactions, and shared interests between social classes and national borders. He states:

The devotion of democracy to education is a familiar fact. The superficial explanation is that a government resting upon popular suffrage cannot be successful unless those who elect and who obey their governors are educated. . . . But there is a deeper explanation. A democracy is more than a form of government; it is primarily a mode of associated living, of conjoint communicated experience. The extension in space of the number of individuals who participate in an interest so that each has to refer his own action to that of others, and to consider the action of others to give point and direction to his own, is equivalent to the breaking down of those barriers of class, race, and national territory which kept men from perceiving the full import of their activity. The . . . points of contact . . . secure a liberation of powers which remain suppressed as long as the incitations to action are partial, as they must be in a group which in its exclusiveness shuts out many interests. (*MW* 9:93)

If we are as a group to achieve our goal of a richly fulfilling personal and social life, our principles of association, whatever they may be, must be principles freeing us to grow and develop, to educate ourselves in our own and our society's possibilities. Democratic principles of association maximize our freedom and our opportunities to grow and develop. Thus liberal democracy is the one basis of social organization that

Dewey believes a pragmatist could rationally approve (consider justified) for himself and others.[11]

Intellectual growth requires experimentation. So what we must want whatever else we want is the freedom to experiment with our lives. And what we are due is whatever we must want everyone else to have whatever else they want. And that too is the freedom to experiment. The development of personal life, of personality itself, as Dewey often reminds us, is a social project. If we stunt the freedom of one to innovate and experiment (beyond the limits necessary to protect the freedom and safety of others), we stunt the growth and the development of the whole community.

So what we are each due is effective freedom, that is, the absence or removal of any legal or social obstacles to free access to social participation and command of resources adequate to allow us to participate in meaningful ways. Equal command of resources for meaningful participation, however, does not in Dewey's opinion entail equal command of the wealth or other benefits gained by a society or its members. Although his theory of social justice is communitarian, it is neither communist nor a variety of radical egalitarianism. Dewey believed the wealth or other benefits an individual gains through the development of his or her capacities should be his or her own. He only insists that the differences in social outcomes be determined by differences in individual capacities and tastes, not by such artificial differences as birth, class membership, race, and so forth. Inequalities of social outcome are only unjustifiable for Dewey if they are the results of inequalities in the ad-

---

11. Democracy as it existed in the United States in 1915 or as it exists today was not the sort of democracy Dewey had in mind here. The freedom that makes democratic principles of social design rationally desirable in Dewey's eyes is the *effective* freedom a society's members receive. And effective freedom means not only the absence of legal restraints to participation in all of a society's collective functions but also the *command of resources* at least minimally adequate for active participation. The United States, Dewey thought, promoted freedom primarily in the negative sense. Legal barriers privileging certain classes were nonexistent or being removed. But, the educational resources minimally adequate for active participation in public and private life were not (and are not now) being made available to each and every citizen. Consequently, individual freedom to pursue rewarding careers, influence public policy, and enjoy public amenities such as libraries and museums were effectively unequal. Before the United States could become truly democratic and just in its liberation of its members, the inequalities in individuals' opportunities to participate in social intercourse would have to be removed. Dewey says: "School facilities must be secured of such amplitude and efficiency as will in fact and not simply in name discount the effects of economic inequalities, and secure to all the wards of the nation equality of equipment for their future careers" (*Democracy and Education, MW* 9:104).

vantages (especially the education and training) society provided each individual at the outset of his or her career.

Contra Russell, then, Dewey's pragmatic constructivism can provide a theoretical foundation for liberal democratic institutions and for the protection of minority group freedoms against the tyranny of the majority. And if Dewey is correct, it secures a form of social democracy that seems no more likely to resort to gunboat diplomacy than any other—and possibly less. A pragmatic community will presumably see the maintenance of friendly relations with other communities as in its own long-term best interests. And since friendly relations of the sort most likely to contribute to social and personal growth are relations between equals, a pragmatic community would have particular reason to resist temptations to subjugate and make enemies of its neighbors. Or in other words, such conduct would be unreasonable and therefore unjustified in Dewey's conception of justice.

OPTIMISM, MELIORISM, AND HUMAN NATURE

The charge that Dewey's ethics was overly optimistic, as we noted above, really incorporated two charges. Dewey was said to have (1) underestimated or even ignored the existence of inexorable forces that give rise to moral tragedies and (2) overestimated the rationality of the average person so enormously that a pragmatic community could only save itself from democratically bringing about its own destruction if its affairs were taken out of the hands of the unreflective majority and left to the ministrations of a trained, rational or scientific elite. The first is ultimately a metaphysical objection on which Dewey offered occasional comments throughout his work, up to the publication of his 1925 *Experience and Nature*. The second was a more largely psychological or anthropological charge, to which Dewey replied in 1922 with *Human Nature and Conduct.*[12]

The issue of what exactly a pragmatic philosophy can make of what Dewey called 'the generic traits' of nature and our experience of it lies outside the scope of this book and has in any case received considerable and useful comment elsewhere.[13] For that matter, it lies outside the

12. Dewey's reply is continued in later works, most notably perhaps *The Public and Its Problems* (1927), *LW* 2.

13. For a text that specifically links Dewey's pragmatic metaphysics with his later theory of value and value judgments, see James Gouinlock, *John Dewey's Philosophy of Value* (New York: Humanities Press, 1972).

scope of the criticisms made by commentators such as Bourne who were more concerned with the inexorability of tragic consequences, given the initiation of certain chains of events (like war), than with the necessary existence or inexorability of particular forces in nature, human and non-human. As Bourne saw it, Dewey is committed to the thesis that reflective and rational intelligence can, by means of its grasp of any given situation, influence that situation or its outcome for the better. Bourne argues that this is surely false for the sort of situation war represents. Writing in 1917, he comments, "I find the contrast between the idea that creative intelligence has free functioning in wartime, and the facts of the inexorable situation, too glaring."[14] Intelligent foresight, in his view, is not sufficient to manage war or the effects that follow in its train: prejudice, hatred, and injustice. It is the irrevocability of these evils once the practice of warfare is allowed to flourish that Bourne argues Dewey's ethics and its followers too gaily ignore. As a result, pragmatic moral agents who optimistically act in the belief that situations can always be managed for the better will find themselves faced with tragic outcomes that a less optimistic, nonpragmatic philosophy could have helped them avoid. There are situations all of whose possible resolutions are disastrously bad. And if pragmatic ethical theory cannot cope with this fact, then pragmatic ethical theory had better be abandoned.

The charge is of course true—at least in part. As Dewey himself made clear in his 1920 *Reconstruction in Philosophy*, his philosophy allows no room for inexorable or irrevocable evils in human events.[15] He denies their existence. According to Dewey, desires to express given dispositions in given ways receive their valuations only when considered in light of an agent's long-term projects and the obstacles and materials the immediate situation provides. Consequently, the value of any given desire or any mode of its expression will be unique to the problematic situation at hand whether that value is positive or negative. He remarks: "*Moral* goods and ends exist only when something has to be done. The fact that something has to be done proves there are deficiencies, evils in the existent situation. This ill is just the specific ill that it is. It never is an exact duplicate of anything else. Consequently, the good of the situation has to be discovered, projected and attained on the basis of the exact defect and trouble to be rectified" (*MW* 12:176). No desire or contem-

---

14. Bourne, "Twilight of Idols," p. 55.
15. See John Dewey, *Reconstruction in Philosophy, MW* 12.

plated course of action has a value independent of all situations. And since the number and variety of problematic situations in which a desire or course of action may be an option are infinite (in principle), so also must be the values any desire or course of action can have. Nothing, then, not even war, is inexorably good or evil. But this does not mean that a pragmatic moral agent cannot or should not search for and act upon warranted generalizations about values where these can be constructed: for example, the generalization (if warranted) that the burdens of war usually outweigh the benefits. Denial of the inexorable does not entail denial of the probable. A moral agent who insists on choosing improbably successful options in problematic situations is stupid, not optimistic.

Does it follow, then, that there will always be a way out of every problematic situation that is acceptable to the agent involved, that there be no moral tragedies from a pragmatic perspective? Dewey's answer is that, on the contrary, a pragmatic ethical theory is the only theory that truly recognizes the possibility of moral tragedies. Dewey argues that it is a virtue of a pragmatic approach to value that it is not "under obligation to find ingenious methods for proving that evils are only apparent, not real, or to elaborate schemes for explaining them away or, worse yet, for justifying them. It assumes another obligation:—That of contributing in however humble a way to methods that will assist us in discovering the cause of humanity's ills" (*MW* 12:181). Pragmatic moral agents facing problematic situations are not assured, as their Kantian, utilitarian, or intuitionist counterparts are, that any 'right' course of action exists to be discovered. The pragmatic moral agent has no infallible way of determining which options open are certainly wrong or certainly right. It is entirely possible that lack of time for reflection or lack of the ability or resources to make use of the time available will make it impossible for an agent to reach a decision he or she will retrospectively approve as correct. In this respect, the pragmatic moral agent is in the same boat as the physical scientist. It is always possible that the project of inquiry will fail and that it will fail through no fault of the inquirer.

Yet the absence of a guarantee that each problematic situation can in principle be resolved successfully is no reason for pessimism. No matter how tragically a given situation may turn out, there is always the hope that *that* sort of tragedy may be avoided in future. If the evils of life, natural and artificial, cannot certainly be avoided, they can, as a rule, be ameliorated. For this reason, Dewey rejected both optimism and pessimism in favor of 'meliorism': "Meliorism is the belief that the specific conditions which exist at one moment, be they comparatively bad or comparatively good, in any event may be bettered. It encourages intelligence to study positive means of good and the obstructions to their realization, and to put forth endeavor for the improvement of conditions. It arouses confidence and a reasonable hopefulness as optimism does not" (MW 12:181–82). If we presume, as most people do presume, that further improvements to the quality of human life are possible above and beyond those already achieved, Dewey's ethical philosophy is not unduly optimistic. Or if it is, it must be for reasons other than his denial of the existence of inexorable goods and evils.

After his 1887 Psychology, Dewey had avoided writing metaphysical prolegomena to his ethics, preferring to appeal directly to experience in defense of his views. For those who desired them, Psychology existed, and Dewey regularly referred interested readers to the work throughout the 1890s. By 1908, when Ethics appeared, Psychology was badly out of date. The pressure of criticisms and of confusions about his pragmatic constructivism evidently convinced Dewey that a new text was needed. Or rather, two new texts were needed: Experience and Nature, his prolegomenon to philosophy in general, and Human Nature and Conduct, his prolegomenon to philosophical ethics.[16] Thus Human Nature and Conduct complements rather than supersedes Ethics. Unlike Ethics, Human Nature and Conduct does not seek to justify or defend Dewey's first principles of a theoretical science of ethics or the manner of their construction. Instead, it tries to establish that human beings are the kind of agents who could have a theoretical science of ethics and at the same time be its subjects. The text defends a conception of Homo sapiens as a product of evolution, an animal species whose behavior is susceptible to the same sort of ethological studies that are used to elucidate the behavior of lower forms of animal life. If and when human nature is approached as simply another naturally occurring phenomenon, Dewey was confident that it would become clear that human beings are capable of scientific management of their own social behavior by democratic and nonpaternalistic means.

This is not to say that Dewey expected the study of human nature to reveal each human being to be the sort of 'omnicompetent' individual of eighteenth- and early-twentieth-century liberal moral and political thought. To the contrary, he expected wide varieties of interests, skills,

16. See John Dewey, Experience and Nature (1925) LW 1 and Human Nature and Conduct (1922), MW 14.

and abilities, as well as accomplishments, to appear. From Dewey's perspective, variations in skills and abilities are not problematic per se, because they do not have any particular negative implications for the justification of social democracy. Given his view of society, we can readily understand why this would be. Social organizations offer their members a multitude of stations to be filled and, in addition, areas of social blank space where new stations can be created. Presumably, no two sets of stations constituting individual ways of life are ever exactly the same or employ exactly the same skills and interests. It is not therefore necessary that individuals be identically competent, since they will not be called upon to fulfill identical social duties. Inequalities in native talents—physical, intellectual, or emotional—do not entail inequalities in individuals' effective freedom, their ability to contribute to the overall social good or to construct for themselves fulfilling personal lives.

But this is hardly a controversial claim. Critics of the practicality of a pragmatic community did not imagine that possession of identical capacities and interests were required for a social democracy to work: only the possession of *comparable* rational faculties and skills. And that this condition was being met they thought they had excellent reason to doubt. Contemporary experimentation in intelligence testing performed on army recruits during the First World War seemed to show that as much as 70 percent of these average young American men were rationally or mentally deficient. To the reigning social Darwinism of the day, these results, albeit preliminary, pointed to basic and probably irremediable inequalities in intellectual ability too significant to be ignored.[17] The average man simply could not be relied upon to have that average intelligence or judgment necessary for constructive participation in the establishment of social policy and projects. Education might perhaps soften the sharp distinction between individuals, but it could hardly be expected to erase what social Darwinism considered native, inborn capacities.[18] Psychoanalytic theory indirectly reinforced the notion of in-

17. On intelligence testing in this period, see Daniel Kevles, "Testing the Army's Intelligence: Psychologists and the Military in World War I," *Journal of American History* 55 (1968): 565–81. On the relation of contemporary intelligence testing to the development of Dewey's social theory, see Westbrook, *John Dewey and American Democracy*, esp. chap. 9, "The Phantom Public."

18. It is not unusual to find the same point being made in more recent discussions of the probable effect of trying to institute Dewey's sort of egalitarian, democratic ideal. Antony Flew has argued that an ideally democratic society will not "thereby preclude 'stratification by classes'; for even the sort of group which sociologists would be prepared to admit as a social class can in its recruitment be wide open to the rising talents. It can be open

eradicable mental differences between individuals through its account of human psychology as determined by inborn, unchanging instincts and the traumas engendered by their clashes with the surrounding cultural environment. Psychoanalysis aimed to provide relief from dissatisfaction and frustration by helping clients understand how events and their instinctual drives had shaped their characters. In other words, the aim was to make one *feel* better about the character one had developed, but not necessarily to *be* better or to have a better character as a result. In this way, the idea that education and understanding were relatively ineffectual in altering or improving an individual's character or mental capacities was inadvertently bolstered by the latest scientific theory of psychological treatment.

If in fact significant differences in native human mental capacities exist which education cannot eradicate or substantially alter, it was argued, democratic rule by a fully and freely participating community is a pipe dream. Granted that democratic organization will foster cooperative interactions within and without the community that would further each member's growth, the growth being achieved by many if not the majority might well be negligible. And if the most is to be made of the opportunity to bring about even negligible growth, decisions about what and how to learn (that is, with whom and how individuals will interact inside and outside their own community) will have to be taken out of the hands of the mentally deficient to have any chance of success. For the most part, it is already and rightly out of their hands as a result of the inability of the relatively incompetent to collect or efficiently employ the resources and power necessary to participate meaningfully in republican American policy making. Thus, unless or until some way of equalizing human intellectual abilities and skills has been achieved, a benevolent paternalism is the only form of social organization on which a pragmatically minded community can reasonably rely.

Although the social Darwinism of the 1920s has long since fallen out of favor, the objection may yet seem pointed. Dewey expects his ideal community to conduct its deliberations about public policy on the same

---

downwards too, to the lack of talents. To the extent that actual social classes are in fact thus open, both upwards and downwards, and to the extent that any relevant natural endowments are heritable, the children of these open social classes are bound to become as such members of a group of people distinguishable from other groups of people by an average difference in respect of those particular endowments." (Antony Flew, "Democracy and Education," in *John Dewey Reconsidered*, ed. R. S. Peters (London: Routledge & Kegan Paul, 1977), p. 88.

sort of scientific basis he recommended to individuals. In effect, a democratic community is or ought to be a scientific community of inquiry,
investigating the obstacles to human flourishing with a view to their
amelioration. Now scientific communities of inquiry are meritocracies
in which those with the most significant abilities, skills, and accomplishments decide for the average practitioner what questions are worth
studying, whose techniques are worth using, which laboratories are
worth funding, and which individuals are worth cultivating as future
leaders of their fields. If science is not a participatory democracy, how
could a pragmatic society, modeling itself on the scientific community,
be a participatory democracy either?

Human Nature and Conduct functions as a prolegomenon to Dewey's
ethics by clearing the ground of such doubts about whether human nature as we find it is capable of sustaining liberal democratic social institutions in the collective pursuit of the progressive amelioration of the ills
of human life, without resort to eternal or immutable values, transcendental reasoning, or a moral 'sense.' Of these, Dewey evidently saw "the
tendency, especially among psychologists, to insist upon native human
nature untouchable by social influences and to explain social phenomena by reference to traits of original human nature called 'instincts'" as
the most serious obstacle to be overcome.[19] The bulk of the book is devoted to debunking the explanatory value of 'instincts' for the elucida-
tion of human behavior. Dewey argues that much of the behavior popularly attributed to instinct appears to have been acquired. Human nature
gives evidence of few biologically determined or instinctive activities.
Infants perform some acts instinctively, no doubt. They reach, suckle,
cry, and follow movements with their eyes without conscious thought
or direction. Unlike the instinctive behavior of lower animal species,
infants' instinctive behavior does not produce organized or purposeful
actions. A human infant, Dewey argues, is simply a mass of uncoordi-
nated impulses, each in itself nothing but "a physical spasm, a blind
dispersive burst of wasteful energy," which is for the infant "as meaningless as a gust of wind on a mudpuddle apart from a direction given it
by the presence of other persons, apart from the responses they make to
it" (*Human Nature and Conduct, MW* 14:65). For the infant gripped by an
impulse, any outlet will do. No particular act is dictated by any particular surge of energy. Parents' responses make impulses meaningful by

19. At least, that is how in retrospect he characterized his thinking. See Dewey's foreword to the 1930 Modern Library edition of *Human Nature and Conduct, MW* 14:230.

associating them with various forms of changes in the infant's circumstances. The results are habits, tendencies, or dispositions to act in specific ways under particular sets of environmental circumstances.

In themselves, impulses have no distinguishing features. They come to be distinguished by reference to the consequences to which they give rise in particular situations. So, Dewey argues, "any impulse may become organized into almost any disposition according to the way it interacts with surroundings" (*MW* 14:69). A surge of energy that allows one runner to pass a leader in the last moments of a footrace is 'courage.' An identical surge of energy experienced by an examinee on seeing another examinee finish her test and leave the room is 'anxiety.' Again, to experience a similar surge of energy at the sight of a stranger walking toward one on a dark and lonely road is 'fear.' The impulsive surge is in itself the same in each case. It is the situation that determines what character we assign it and what value we assign to the character of the person who gives the impulse free reign in the situation at hand. So Dewey holds that there are few if any separate, discriminable 'instincts' determining human nature or behavior. What instinctive behavior we manifest after earliest infancy is a matter of our socialization. Dewey concludes that our instincts are themselves social products.

Moreover, Dewey does not consider our instincts, our settled dispositions to act in regular ways in recurring situations, to be the only contributions our socialization makes to the formation of our characters. Intelligence is itself in large part a social product, according to Dewey, and like our instincts, as readily modifiable. Intelligence is just a name for all those habits or dispositions to act in ways that inform us about the qualities of objects we meet with in the world. In Dewey's words: "Concrete habits do all the perceiving, recognizing, imagining, recalling, judging, conceiving and reasoning that is done" (*MW* 14:124). Reason, he holds, is an activity, rather than a property, of persons. More precisely, reason is a settled or habitual tendency to respond with disciplined curiosity and reflection to situations disrupted by novel or mysterious things or events and with which our other dispositions to act are inadequate to deal. Rationality or reason, on this view, is a set of strategies for coping with sources of doubt and uncertainty, whether mundane or abstruse: "The elaborate systems of science are born not of reason but . . . of impulses to handle, move about, to hunt, to uncover, to mix things separated and divide things combined, to talk and to listen. Method is their effectual organization into continuous dispositions of inquiry, development and testing. . . . Reason, the rational attitude, is the resulting disposition, not a ready-made antecedent which can be invoked at will and set into movement" (*MW* 14:136).

Variations in intelligence or rationality among individuals may reflect variations in native endowments, at least in part. But it is likely that the more significant contributing factor is variation in the educational influences to which society exposes its younger members. Some are born and mature in circumstances that foster the development of a rational attitude to problems; others are not. Some are introduced to formal tools and techniques of logical and scientific analysis with a view to making their application habitual; others are not. If much of the variation in intellectual competence is a product of educational and social practices, it should not be beyond the scope of these same institutions to address them. Although we do not yet fully understand how to go about rectifying or ameliorating the imbalances our current educational and social practices create, it is neither impossible nor unlikely that the advancing social sciences could construct significantly better and more successful methods of cultivating rationality in all.

Dewey recognized that "it sounds academic to say that the substantial bettering of social relations waits upon the growth of scientific social psychology" (*MW* 14:221), that is, the science of the social construction of personality and its constituents. But if by the bettering of social relations we mean the realization of liberal values, especially effective freedom to participate in and contribute to social action, then Dewey was prepared to concede that true participatory democracy could not be established until the social and human sciences had evolved into practical sciences whose research into the material of human nature could be fruitfully applied to the education and training of an intelligent, cooperative community. In the meantime, presumably, paternalistic social institutions will continue to exist. But though the sorts of improvements needed will not occur immediately, there is no reason in principle why they should not occur. And thus there is no reason in principle why a pragmatic community's normally endowed adult members should not each be capable of sufficient rationality to be fit to participate in the direction of public policy as well as their own private affairs. Certainly, experts in the nature and administration of social institutions will be necessary for the endeavor to succeed. But it will be their analyses and advice that will be necessary, not their rule. The charge that Dewey's social philosophy rests on overoptimistic estimates of average human intelligence or rationality may be rejected as unfounded.

There remains the question of whether the means and ends Dewey is recommending may not turn out to be self-contradictory. Or if means define ends, we may wonder whether the ideal social state can truly be the sort of robust participatory democracy he imagines. Dewey sees the pragmatic community as essentially a community of scientific inquiry into human flourishing. Yet scientific communities of inquiry do not appear to operate democratically. For example, the question of whether a given disease is caused by a virus or a bacterium is not a matter to be settled by majority vote. Further, opinions simply are not equally valued within scientific circles. So if a pragmatic community were to organize itself as, broadly speaking, a scientific community of inquiry, its internal organization would be hierarchical and paternalistic, rather than egalitarian and democratic.

Dewey did not specifically deal with this sort of objection in *Human Nature and Conduct*, but from the material supplied by this and earlier texts an answer can readily be constructed. First, we must remember not to confuse 'science' with 'basic research,' basic research being only one form scientific inquiry takes. Physicists, analytical chemists, clinical psychologists are all practitioners of science. But so also are physiologists, pharmacists, civil engineers, and psychiatric social workers. The amateur astronomer who carefully searches the heavens and records her observations may not be among the upper echelon of her field of interests, but to the extent that she follows scientific procedures and subjects her results to scientific methods of confirmation, she is a practitioner of science. What is more, her observations are of precisely the same value as any other astronomer's observations in and of themselves. All observations are in and of themselves equally valuable (or valueless) as potential facts. Credentials do not make an observation better or worse, more or less significant. In this respect, then, science is egalitarian. All and any data, so long as they are properly obtained, must receive equal consideration, whatever the source. And if an interpretation of any given phenomenon does not recognize a given observation as factual, the rationale must in principle be adequate to persuade even those who supplied the rejected observation to agree to its rejection. Certainly, greater respect, esteem, and funding go to those whose abilities set them apart from run-of-the-mill scientific workers. But this does not in itself entail that science is or must be inherently nonegalitarian in its operations.

Similarly, the outcome of each individual's dramatic rehearsals about the future directions in which his or her society may go yield 'observations' of the desired traits of each option. Provided those moral observations are made with reasonable care and in accordance with objective standards of investigation, each individual's observations are of equal significance in themselves. And if any given valuation of those options does not recognize any particular observation as reporting a value, the rationale for the refusal must in principle be adequate to persuade even those who supplied the rejected observation to agree to its rejection. In themselves, a pederast's observations are no less potential values than are a Mother Teresa's. Only consideration of the role to be played by desired options and the dispositions they express, in light of the social good of enhancing the effective freedom of all, determines the relative desirability of or value of what is desired. As in the physical sciences, greater respect, esteem, and even funding would probably go to those whose abilities to value options rationally and objectively set them apart from run-of-the-mill moral inquirers. Nevertheless, it does not follow from this that the average moral inquirer's input counts any less than the input of individuals of more pronounced ability or achievement. Nor does it follow that a pragmatic community organized as a community of inquiry into human flourishing must inherently descend into paternalistic rule by a hierarchy of moral specialists.

Take, for example, an issue from contemporary public debate in the United States: whether equality of public funding for public schools at the primary and secondary levels should be ensured by governmental redistribution of resources from richer to poorer school districts (on the presumption that the money involved is sufficient to ensure more than adequate funding for all). How would a pragmatic community decide the justice of equalizing public funding for public education? It would begin by collecting the relevant data: say, by polling public opinion, holding public hearings, and so forth. The views of all as to the attractiveness (or the reverse) of making accidents of birth irrelevant to the quality of the education one receives and the attractiveness (or the reverse) of the means by which this outcome might be achieved would be collected. Next, the data collected would have to be interpreted; the options people found attractive would have to be valued in terms of their relations to other existing and projected social commitments and values. In favor of the equalization of public funding would be the increase in the effective freedom of those who would otherwise attend ill-funded and inferior schools. Against the plan would be the fact that fewer decisions about the allocation of school tax money would be in local hands—a decrease in the negative liberty, or liberty from interference, of individuals contributing to public education. And so it would go, point by point. Finally, a hypothesis would be formed about the best way to enhance the effective equality of education at the least possible cost to individual negative freedoms. This hypothesis, whatever exactly it might be, would then have to be tested—say, by demonstration projects around the country—and the results carefully studied. If the results actually obtained are in line with the outcomes predicted, then the hypothesis would be warranted. If not, the hypothesis would have to be reconsidered and revised or rejected. What reason endorses is from Dewey's standpoint what justice demands. And if reason endorses some form of pooling and redistribution of funding for public education, then this is what justice demands.

To make this scheme work, one must have in place (1) developed social sciences adequate to formulate and perform tests of hypotheses about social institutions, existing and proposed, and (2) a public committed to and sufficiently educated in scientific procedures to understand and apply the results of those tests. These conditions certainly had not been met in the America of 1922. But Dewey believed that "through the development of physical science, and especially of chemistry, biology, physiology, medicine, and anthropology we now have the basis for . . . a science of man" (*MW* 14:222) capable of meeting the first condition. Commitment of educational resources to bettering public understanding of scientific principles and procedures of inquiry, evidence, and explanation would make it possible to satisfy the second. So to Dewey, it was by no means impossible that in the relatively near future a genuinely liberal democratic and pragmatic moral community could come into being, nor was it an unrealistic goal toward which to work. Although the accomplishment of such a community would not, Dewey warned, bring about the millennium: "It would enable us to state problems in such forms that action could be courageously and intelligently directed to their solution. It would not assure us against failure, but it would render failure a source of instruction. It would not protect us against the future emergence of equally serious moral difficulties, but it would enable us to approach the always recurring troubles with a fund of growing knowledge which would add significant values to our conduct even when we overtly failed—as we should continue to do" (*MW* 14:11).

Although Dewey's acknowledgment of the possibility (even the probability) that a pragmatic moral agent's most conscientious efforts to resolve moral situations will result in failures, that tried and tested principles of action will have to be revised over time, and the policies built upon them reversed or abandoned, should be sufficient to remove the charge that his ethics is over-optimistic, it has at the same time been grounds for complaint that his ethics is not optimistic enough. To the "anti-empirical school in morals," as Dewey called it (*MW* 14:222), the conception of ends as an endless series, a means-end continuum, would have been profoundly dispiriting. If every end once attained simply turns out to be a means to yet another end, surely progress is an illusion. Unless human beings are measurably advancing toward a final goal, how can they be said to be progressing? Or as Dewey put it, if life is nothing but a series of problematic situations, whose solutions only give rise to new problems, "does not this reduce moral life to the futile toil of a Sisyphus who is forever rolling a stone uphill only to have it roll back so that he has to repeat his old task?" (*MW* 14:144).

From the seriousness with which this objection is addressed in *Human Nature and Conduct*, Dewey evidently believed it to be widely held. Nevertheless, he had relatively little patience for it. The question of the relation of means to ends he considered one of fact, not to be decided by reference to personal tastes. And the idea that moral life and action can be effectively 'guided' or given purpose by fixed, final ends was simply sentimental nonsense. First, as in "The Logic of Judgments of Practice," Dewey argues that ends and means are reciprocal, because means define ends. Moreover, every means is an end, and vice versa. For example, to a real-estate developer, building a house is a means to the end of making a profit. But the house will never get built if the developer views the house as merely a means to an end, not as an end in itself. Before getting a profit can be the end of the developer's activity, building the house must become his end. Laying a foundation, framing the walls, raising the roof must each in their turn be his end if the house is to be completed. Only after it is finished and ready to be turned over to a buyer can the building of the house be merely a means to a further end. So also, Dewey argues, to a mariner at sea, getting to harbor is an end. But it is an end because it is a means to some other activity: selling goods, meeting a contract, picking up freight, taking a vacation. When we consider the practical bearings of our ends, he argues, we should see that it is a mistake to think of our aims or objectives as 'ends of action.' We do not cease to act upon obtaining our ends. Dewey suggests we instead think of our ends as 'ends of deliberation,' on the grounds that what the selection of an end ends is deliberation about what our next course of action should be.

One might argue that the sorts of ends discussed above are not truly ends of action precisely because they are reciprocal with means. These so-called ends, getting to a harbor, making a profit, building a house, are all instrumental to the achievement of our ultimate ends, ends that are never a means to anything beyond themselves. Dewey replies that the notion of an end that is not also a means is vacuous. It may once have seemed meaningful; "when men believed that fixed ends existed for all normal changes in nature, the conception of similar ends for men was but a special case of a general belief" (MW 14:154). But we do not now believe in a world furnished with occult qualities, attracting objects to their proper place in the great chain of being. Nor can we doubt that for living things like ourselves, an end to struggle and exertion represents the end of life. Our understanding of the world no longer supports the idea that human life has an end, a unique function to fulfill, by reference to which individual lives can be graded.

But although there is no universal a priori meaning or end to human life and action, Dewey argues, there is no lack of motivation to carry on living and struggling to improve our lives. He states:

> We content ourselves with remarking that we find in this conception of a fixed antecedent standard another manifestation of the desire to escape the strain of the actual moral situation, its genuine uncertainty of possibilities and consequences. We are confronted with another case of the all too human love of certainty, a case of the wish for an intellectual patent issued by authority. The issue after all is one of fact. The critic is not entitled to enforce against the facts his private wish for a ready-made standard which will relieve him from the burden of examination, observation, and continuing generalization and test. (MW 14:166)

Moralists had been claiming for centuries that human life has a purpose, end, or value in itself with which precise and certain evaluation of particular acts and dispositions can be made. So Dewey expected that a sense of anticlimax would attend an ethical theory that did not. But a feeling of anticlimax is hardly grounds for pessimism or despair. Because life has no intrinsic value from a pragmatic perspective does not entail that it is valueless. It simply means that life has no value until it is valued. And to say that life has no intrinsic meaning does not entail that it is meaningless, only that its meaning has still to be constructed. "In the largest sense of the word," Dewey writes, "morals is education. It is learning the meaning of what we are about and employing that meaning in action" (MW 14:194). As a result, our lives and their meaning for us grow continually deeper and more complex. Dewey dismissed the suggestion that the belief that the meaning and value of our lives is up to us will give rise to general despair of life and morality. He remarks:

> Men have constructed a strange dream-world when they have supposed that without a fixed ideal of a remote good to inspire them, they would have no inducement to get relief from present troubles, no desires for liberation from what oppresses and for clearing-up what confuses present action. . . . Sufficient unto the day is the evil thereof. Sufficient it is to stimulate us to remedial action, to endeavor in order to convert strife into harmony . . . and limitation into expansion. The converting is progress, the only progress conceivable or attainable by man. (*MW* 14:195)

If progress means the eradication of evil or unhappiness, then a pragmatic community will not in fact progress. But then, it could be argued, neither will the nonpragmatic community that looks to the realization of a priori values or categorical imperatives for moral progress. No moral theory will eradicate suffering or wickedness. But if progress means "increase of present meaning" through increased understanding of the structure of present experience and increased capacity to influence or control the meaning of future experience, then a pragmatic community will progress. As for the question of whether the pragmatic moral agent is a sort of modern Sisyphus, Dewey's answer is both yes and no. The agent is a modern Sisyphus if we define progress as significant movement toward the realization of some ideal of moral perfection. The agent is not if we recognize that each new endeavor or project is colored and enriched by the meaning and value created by the projects that went before. Unlike Sisyphus, Dewey argues, pragmatic moral agents "are not caught in a circle; we traverse a spiral" (*MW* 14:225). Whether and how we take advantage of this relationship is up to us to decide.

Philosophers are rarely allowed to have the last word on their own work. Dewey has not proved an exception. In his foreword to the 1930 Modern Library edition of *Human Nature and Conduct*, he wrote that "were it not for one consideration, the volume might be said to be an essay in continuing the tradition of David Hume" (*MW* 14:228). In my introduction, I noted that Dewey's critics had one view of what his one divergence from Hume was, Dewey another. Among his admirers, there is a third. Although this third group has generally agreed with Dewey that the one consideration is *not* a violation of Hume's dictum with regard to deriving an 'ought' from an 'is,' they have their own view about what the one consideration is. Dewey identifies it as Hume's atomistic individualism, which Dewey rejects in favor of a more Hegelian, organic conception of personality or selfhood as a social construct. To many of his admirers, such a departure looms so large as to dwarf the significance of any similarities that may remain between Hume's and Dewey's moral and social theories. In which case, the one significant difference between Hume's and Dewey's projects is—everything. For this reason, presumably, Dewey's conceptions of virtue and vice, of social institutions as educative, and of the community as the ground of the realization of virtue is frequently characterized as Aristotelian. It might fairly be said that Dewey encouraged this identification. Such was his lifelong antipathy for British empiricism that he was rarely able to find a good word for any one of its representatives. Thus when Dewey looked to the history of moral philosophy for earlier examples of naturalistic ethics with which to illustrate his own, he gravitated toward ancient rather than modern moralists, in particular to Aristotle.

Indeed, one might well imagine that Dewey would find more to his taste in Aristotle's than in Hume's conceptions of human nature and conduct. Aristotle considered human beings naturally and inherently social. The realization of distinctly human character in isolation from social contacts he considered impossible. Hume, by contrast, operated in a tradition that sought to explain the existence of human societies as the creations of individual human beings, whose humanity predates any form of social cooperation. Furthermore, Aristotle sees moral character as a social construct. Individuals are habituated to good and virtuous conduct by the laws and the customs of their societies. Indeed, Aristotle goes so far as to hold that one cannot become virtuous unless one is already possessed of involuntarily developed virtuous dispositions. Only the man who is already good will be a reliable judge of what is good or of why it is good. Whereas, as Dewey points out: "[Hume] saw the part played by the structure and operations of our common nature in shaping social life . . . [but] failed to see with equal clearness the reflex influence of the latter upon the shape which a plastic human nature takes because of its social environment."[20]

But it does not do to exaggerate the differences. Hume was as fully persuaded as Aristotle that humanity's "very first state and situation may justly be esteem'd social." Hume dismisses "the suppos'd *state of*

20. Foreword to the Modern Library edition, *Human Nature and Conduct*, MW 14:229.

nature" as "a mere philosophical fiction, which never had, and never cou'd have any reality."[21] And although the social sciences of his day, as Dewey points out, provided Hume with little scientific justification for believing that society shaped human nature as profoundly as human nature shapes society's, nevertheless he recognized that the relationship was reciprocal. His rejection of the possibility that individuals created a social contract in a presocial state of nature was based in part upon his appreciation of the effect of socialization on human nature. For example, Hume believed: "In order to form society, 'tis requisite not only that it be advantageous, but also that men be sensible of its advantages; and 'tis impossible, in their wild uncultivated state, that by study and reflection alone, they should ever be able to attain this knowledge."[22] To enter into social life, in other words, human beings must already have been socialized. Thus there can never have been a time when human beings were not naturally social. And their socialization must begin before they attain an age at which the question whether to ally themselves with a particular community can ever be entertained. Hume explains: "Custom and habit operating on the tender minds of the children, makes them sensible of the advantages which they may reap from society, as well as fashions them by degrees for it, by rubbing off those rough corners and untoward affections, which prevent their coalition."[23] Equally, it will not do to exaggerate the similarities between Dewey's and Hume's conceptions of human nature and the role and function of morality in human life, but significant similarities exist. There is, for example, considerable common ground between Dewey's and Hume's respective accounts of moral decisions and choices. Hume anticipates Dewey's depiction of human acts and projects as the outcomes of human passions and dispositions to act rather than from the agency of a will governed by a faculty of reason.[24] Moreover, Hume's theory that many, if not all, virtues and vices are artificially constructed is nearer to Dewey's view than is Aristotle's. For Dewey, the expression of any particular disposition to action is desirable (thus virtuous) if it enhances an individual's freedom

21. David Hume, *A Treatise of Human Nature*, 2d ed., ed. L. A. Selby-Bigge and P. H. Nidditch (Oxford: Clarendon Press, 1978), p. 493.

22. Ibid., p. 486.

23. Ibid.

24. For example, Hume holds that "society is absolutely necessary for the well-being of men; and [moral conventions] are as necessary to the support of society. Whatever restraint they impose on the passions of men, they are the real offspring of those passions, and are only a more artful and refin'd way of satisfying them. Nothing is more vigilant and inventive than our passions" (*Treatise of Human Nature*, p. 526).

to construct harmonious, flexible, stable life projects that further enhance the individual's capacity to participate in his or her community's life. Dispositions to action are undesirable (vicious) if they tend to promote the reverse. The virtuousness or viciousness of, say, a disposition to recycle one's used aluminum cans and glass bottles is always largely determined by the context in which one operates. Thus such a disposition may be virtuous in one context and yet lack any moral significance in another. Dewey does not identify virtuous dispositions by their essential characteristics. Nor is there any internal structure, as in Aristotle's ethics, by which a Deweyan agent can evaluate a disposition independent of a specific social context. Hume's artificial virtues, dispositions to behave justly, truthfully, and modestly, and the like, notoriously depend for their value on the social context of action.

Hume could take this view of the vices and virtues in part because, like Dewey, he had rejected the belief that success in the search for mankind's summum bonum depends upon the achievement of success in the search for man's essential self. Hume was notoriously skeptical about the existence of an unchanging, essential self.[25] But even if such a self existed, it would be ultimately unknowable on Hume's empiricist methodology. Since we cannot know what the essential self of man is, we cannot hope to discover the one, true 'good life for man.' Morality for Hume, as for Dewey after him, is melioristic. Morality ameliorates the ills of human life by removing or reducing obstacles to social cooperation. And since every success clears the way for further improvements, at no point will the challenges to moral ingenuity ever be complete or completely solved.

Hume's rejection of 'natural law' as instantiated in human nature or the natural world is a third important point of comparison. Human beings, Hume insists, "*invented* the . . . fundamental laws of nature, when they observ'd the necessity of society to their mutual subsistance."[26] Morality is an adaptive response to a precarious, sometimes hostile environment. And the fact that some fundamental conventions are so ubiquitous as to seem 'natural' to all mankind, Hume argued, is readily explained. It is simply a matter of objective fact that some conventions work better than others. Moreover, some are simply indispensable to any sort of cooperative living. As Dewey notes, for Hume, morality is for the most part a project of social engineering, incorporating "all of the

25. See Hume, "Of Personal Identity," in *Treatise of Human Nature*, pp. 251–63.
26. Hume, *Treatise of Human Nature*, p. 543.

social disciplines as far as they are intimately connected with the life of man and as they bear upon the interests of humanity."[27]

This is not to suggest that Hume is a proto-pragmatist. He is no more a proto-pragmatist than he is a proto-utilitarian. Dewey and the utilitarians each made their own use of Hume's ideas. Neither usage gives more insight into Hume's own intentions than the other. What I am suggesting is that Hume's communitarian social philosophy may give us insights into Dewey's pragmatic ethics that Aristotle's does not. To read Dewey's ethics and moral psychology as a sort of pragmatic Aristotelianism is to highlight the lasting effects of Dewey's early involvement with teleological metaphysics, idealist theories of self-realization, and the neo-Hegelian conception of science and philosophy as methods of uncovering categories inherent in our common-sense experience of the world. Traces of all these early beliefs are indeed to be found more or less transformed in Dewey's mature ethical theory.

On the other hand, to read Dewey as a pragmatic Humean is to highlight the nonteleological, antimetaphysical aspects of Dewey's thought, including the temporality and fragility of the values we cherish and pursue, their origin and dependence on the character of our transactions with our physical and social environments, and finally, the possibility of enhancing those values through the creative application of the latest insights and techniques of modern experimental science. It is, in addition, to highlight the centrality of education in Dewey's social philosophy. Whereas the Aristotelian agent can in principle complete his or her education—that is, know once and for all what the good and the right and the virtuous are—the Deweyan agent cannot. Life, as Dewey sees it, is a process of continual change, the context of action ever varying. Completion of one's moral education is thus unthinkable. The Deweyan agent can have no such aspiration. Since the social and physical environments in which human communities operate are not static, communal strategies for ameliorating the ills of the situations to which they fall heir will require continual reconstruction, renovation, and replacement. Commitment to an ideal of lifelong education and personal and social growth must be the hallmark of any viable pragmatic community and of the role of the moral philosophers within it.

For these sorts of reasons, I believe that Dewey's own assessment of the relation of his work to Hume's is fundamentally correct. Dewey's moral philosophy does continue the tradition of Hume, as much as, if

27. Foreword to the Modern Library edition, *Human Nature and Conduct*, MW 14:228.

not more than, the tradition of Aristotle. At the same time, we need not reject Dewey's more famous remark about his general philosophical development: "I should never think of ignoring, much less denying, what an astute critic occasionally refers to as a novel discovery—that acquaintance with Hegel has left a permanent deposit in my thinking."[28] Dewey's pragmatic ethics is a synthesis of antithetical elements drawn from both British empiricism and nineteenth-century idealism, from William James and F. H. Bradley, J. S. Mill and G. S. Morris, David Hume and G. W. Hegel.

28. "From Absolutism to Experimentalism," *LW* 5:154.

Bibliography

Adler, Felix. "The Freedom of Ethical Fellowship." *International Journal of Ethics* 1 (1890–91), 16–30.

Alexander, Thomas M. *John Dewey's Theory of Art, Experience, and Nature: The Horizons of Feeling*. Albany: State University of New York Press, 1987.

Allard, James. "Bradley's Principle of Sufficient Reason." In *The Philosophy of F. H. Bradley*, ed. Anthony Manser and Guy Stock, pp. 173–89. Oxford: Clarendon Press, 1984.

Angell, James R. "James Rowland Angell." In *A History of Psychology in Autobiography*, ed. Carl Murchison, vol. 3, pp. 1–38. Worcester, Mass.: Clark University Press, 1936.

Aristotle. *Nicomachean Ethics*, trans. Terence Irwin. Indianapolis: Hackett, 1985.

Bentham, Jeremy. *An Introduction to the Principles of Morals and Legislation*, rev. ed. 2 vols. London: W. Pickering, 1823.

Bosanquet, Bernard. "The Communication of Moral Ideas as a Function of an Ethical Society." *International Journal of Ethics* 1 (1890–91), 79–97.

———. *Logic, or the Morphology of Knowledge*. 2 vols. Oxford: Clarendon Press, [1888] 1911.

Bourne, Randolph S. "Twilight of Idols." In Bourne, *War and the Intellectuals: Collected Essays, 1915–1919*, ed. Carl Resek, pp. 53–64. New York: Harper & Row, 1964.

Boydston, Jo Ann, ed. *Guide to the Works of John Dewey*. Carbondale: Southern Illinois University Press, 1970.

Bradley, F. H. *Ethical Studies*, 2d ed. Oxford: Clarendon Press, 1927.

———. *The Principles of Logic*, 1st ed. London: Kegan Paul, Trench, 1883. 2d ed. London: Oxford University Press, 1922.

Brehier, Emile. *History of Philosophy*, vol. 7: *Contemporary Philosophy since 1850*, trans. Wade Baskin. Chicago: University of Chicago Press, 1979.

Brodsky, Garry M. "Absolute Idealism and John Dewey's Instrumentalism." *Transactions of the Charles S. Peirce Society* 5 (1968): 44–62.

Buxton, Michael. "The Influence of William James on John Dewey's Early Work." *Journal of the History of Ideas* 45 (1984): 451–64.

Cahn, Steven, ed. *New Studies in the Philosophy of John Dewey*. Hanover: University Press of New England, 1977.

Caird, Edward. *The Critical Philosophy of Immanuel Kant*. 2 vols. Glasgow: James Maclehose & Sons, 1889.

———. *The Social Philosophy and Religion of Comte*. New York: Macmillan, 1885.

Cambell, James. "William James and the Ethics of Fulfillment." *Transactions of the Charles S. Peirce Society* 17 (1981): 224–40.

Candlish, Stewart. "The Truth about F. H. Bradley." *Mind* 98 (1989): 331–48.

Cannon, Susan Faye. *Science in Culture: The Early Victorian Period*. New York: Science History Publications, 1978.

Cooke, Gary A. *George Herbert Mead: The Making of a Social Pragmatist*. Urbana: University of Illinois Press, 1993.

Coughlan, Neil. *Young John Dewey*. Chicago: University of Chicago Press, 1975.

Daniels, George, ed. *Darwinism Comes to America*. Waltham, Mass.: Blaisdell, 1968.

Davidson, Thomas. Review of *Outlines of a Critical Theory of Ethics*. *Philosophical Review* 1 (1892): 95–99.

Dewey, Jane M. "Biography of John Dewey." In *The Philosophy of John Dewey*, ed. Paul A. Schlipp, pp. 3–45. Evanston: Northwestern University Press, 1939.

Dewey, John. *The Early Works: 1882–1898*, ed. Jo Ann Boydston. 5 vols. Carbondale: Southern Illinois University Press, 1967–72.

———. *The Later Works: 1925–1953*, ed. Jo Ann Boydston. 17 vols. Carbondale: Southern Illinios University Press, 1981–90.

———. *The Middle Works: 1899–1924*, ed. Jo Ann Boydston. 15 vols. Carbondale: Southern Illinois University Press, 1976–83.

Dykhuizen, George. *The Life and Mind of John Dewey*. Carbondale: Southern Illinois University Press, 1973.

Eames, S. Morris. "The Cognitive and the Non-cognitive in Dewey's Theory of Value." *Journal of Philosophy* 58 (1961): 179–94.

Flower, Elizabeth, and Murray G. Murphey. *A History of Philosophy in America*. 2 vols. New York: G. P. Putnam's Sons, 1976–77.

Friess, Horace L. *Felix Adler and Ethical Culture: Memories and Studies*, ed. Fannia Weingartner. New York: Columbia University Press, 1981.

Gallie, W. B. *Peirce and Pragmatism*. New York: Dover, 1966.

Gouinlock, James. "Dewey's Theory of Moral Deliberation." *Ethics* 88 (1977–78): 218–28.

———. *John Dewey's Philosophy of Value*. New York: Humanities Press, 1972.

———. "What Is the Legacy of Instrumentalism? Rorty's Interpretation of Dewey." *Journal of the History of Philosophy* 28 (1990): 251–59.

Green, T. H. General Introduction to *The Philosophical Works of David Hume*, ed. T. H. Green and T. H. Grose, vol. 1, pp. 1–299. London: Longmans, Green, 1879.

———. *Prolegomena to Ethics*, 3d ed., ed. A. C. Bradley. Oxford: Clarendon Press, 1890.

Hall, G. Stanley. "Critical Notice of *Psychology*, by James McCosh, *Introduction to Psychology*, by Borden P. Bowne, and *Psychology*, by John Dewey." *American Journal of Psychology* 1 (1888): 146–59.

———. "Philosophy in the United States." *Mind* 4 (1879): 89–105.

Hawkins, Hugh. *Pioneer: A History of the Johns Hopkins University, 1874–1889*. Ithaca: Cornell University Press, 1960.

Hegel, G. W. F. *Phenomenology of Spirit*, trans. A. V. Miller. Oxford: Clarendon Press, 1977.

Hendel, Charles W., ed. *John Dewey and the Experimental Spirit in Philosophy*. New York: Liberal Arts Press, 1959.

Hobbes, Thomas. *Leviathan*, ed. C. B MacPherson. London: Penguin, 1968.

Hofstadter, Richard. *Social Darwinism in American Thought, 1860–1915*. Philadelphia: University of Pennsylvania Press, 1944.

Holmes, Robert L. "The Development of John Dewey's Ethical Thought." *Monist* 48 (1964): 392–406.

——. "John Dewey's Moral Philosophy in Contemporary Perspective." *Review of Metaphysics* 20 (1966): 42–70.

Hull, David L. *Darwin and His Critics: The Reception of Darwin's Theory of Evolution by the Scientific Community*. Chicago: University of Chicago Press, 1973.

Hume, David. *A Treatise of Human Nature*, 2d ed., ed. L. A. Selby-Bigge and P. H. Nidditch. Oxford: Clarendon Press, 1978.

Hyslop, James H. Review of *Outlines of a Critical Theory of Ethics*. *Educational Review* 2 (1891): 297–98.

——. Review of *Outlines of a Critical Theory of Ethics*. *Andover Review* 16 (1891): 95.

Inwood, M. J. *Hegel*. London: Routledge & Kegan Paul, 1983.

Isenberg, Arnold. Foreword to *Theory of the Moral Life*, by John Dewey, ed. Arnold Isenberg, pp. iii–vi. New York: Holt, Rinehart & Winston, 1960.

James, William. *Pragmatism and the Meaning of Truth*. Cambridge: Harvard University Press, 1978.

——. *Principles of Psychology*. 3 vols. Cambridge: Harvard University Press, 1981.

Johnson, Roger B. Review of *The Study of Ethics: a Syllabus*. *Psychological Review* 2 (1895): 2.

Kant, Immanuel. *Kant's Critique of Practical Reason and Other Works on the Theory of Ethics*, 3d ed., trans. Thomas Kingsmill Abbot. London: Longmans, Green, & Dyer, 1883.

Kliebard, Herbert M. *The Struggle for the American Curriculum, 1893–1958*. New York: Routledge & Kegan Paul, 1987.

Kuklick, Bruce. *Churchmen and Philosophers: From Jonathan Edwards to John Dewey*. New Haven: Yale University Press, 1985.

——. *Josiah Royce: An Intellectual Biography*. Indianapolis: Bobbs-Merrill, 1972.

——. *The Rise of American Philosophy*. New Haven: Yale University Press, 1977.

Lippmann, Walter. *The Phantom Public*. New York: Macmillan, 1925.

——. *Public Opinion*. New York: Free Press, [1922] 1965.

Locke, John. *An Essay Concerning Human Understanding*, ed. P. H. Nidditch. Oxford: Clarendon Press, 1975.

Lovejoy, Arthur O. Review of *Ethics*. *American Journal of Theology* 13 (1909): 140–143.

McCosh, James. *Realistic Philosophy*. 2 vols. New York: Charles Scribner's Sons, 1882.

McGilvary, Evander B. Review of *Ethics*. *Psychological Bulletin* 6 (1909): 14–22.

Manser, Anthony. *Bradley's Logic*. Totowa, N.J.: Barnes & Noble, 1983.

Manser, Anthony, and Guy Stock, eds. *The Philosophy of F. H. Bradley*. Oxford: Clarendon Press, 1984.

Martineau, James. *Types of Ethical Theory*. 2 vols. Oxford: Clarendon Press, 1885.

Mill, John Stuart. *Autobiography*. London: Longmans, Green, Reader, & Dyer, 1869.

——. *A System of Logic.* In *Collected Works of John Stuart Mill,* ed. J. M. Robson, vol. 8. Toronto: University of Toronto Press, 1974.

——. *Utilitarianism.* In *Collected Works of John Stuart Mill,* ed. J. M. Robson, vol. 10, pp. 203–59. Toronto: University of Toronto Press, 1969.

Morgenbesser, Sidney, ed. *Dewey and His Critics.* New York: Journal of Philosophy, 1977.

Morris, George S. *British Thought and Thinkers.* Chicago: S. C. Griggs, 1880.

——. "Philosophy and Its Specific Problems." *Princeton Review* N.S. 9 (1882): 208–32.

Murchison, Carl, ed. *A History of Psychology in Autobiography,* vol. 3. Worcester, Mass.: Clark University Press, 1930.

Noble, Cheryl. "A Common Misunderstanding of Dewey on the Nature of Value Judgments." *Journal of Value Inquiry* 12 (1978): 53–63.

O'Donnell, John M. *The Origins of Behaviorism: American Psychology, 1870–1920.* New York: New York University Press, 1985.

Peirce, Charles S. *Philosophical Writings of Peirce,* ed. Justus Buchler. New York: Dover, 1955.

Perry, Ralph B. "Dewey and Urban on Value Judgments." In *Dewey and His Critics,* ed. Sidney Morgenbesser, pp. 586–98. New York: Journal of Philosophy, 1977.

——. *The Thought and Character of William James.* 2 vols. Boston: Little, Brown, 1936.

Persons, Stow, ed. *Evolutionary Thought in America.* New York: George Braziller, 1956.

Peters, R. S., ed. *John Dewey Reconsidered.* London: Routledge & Kegan Paul, 1977.

Pilon, Francois. Review of *The Study of Ethics: A Syllabus. Revue Philosophique* 43 (1897): 328–32.

Putnam, Hilary, and Ruth Anna Putnam. "Epistemology as Hypothesis." *Transactions of the Charles S. Peirce Society* 26 (1990): 407–33.

Randall, John H., Jr. "The Future of John Dewey's Philosophy." *Journal of Philosophy* 56 (1959): 1005–10.

——. *Philosophy after Darwin: Chapters for the Career of Philosophy, Volume 3, and Other Essays.* New York: Columbia University Press, 1977.

Ratner, Sidney, and Jules Altman, eds. *John Dewey and Arthur F. Bentley: A Philosophical Correspondence, 1932–1951.* New Brunswick: Rutgers University Press, 1964.

Rawls, John. *A Theory of Justice.* Cambridge: Harvard University Press, 1971.

Reck, Andrew J. "The Influence of William James on John Dewey in Psychology." *Transactions of the Charles S. Peirce Society* 20 (1984): 87–118.

Review of *Outlines of a Critical Theory of Ethics. Mind* 16 (1891): 424.

Review of *Outlines of a Critical Theory of Ethics. Monist* 1 (1891): 600–601.

Review of *Outlines of a Critical Theory of Ethics. New Englander and Yale Review* 55 (1891): 275.

Review of *The Study of Ethics: A Syllabus. Revue de Metaphysique et de Morale* 3 (March 1895, Supp.): 5.

Rodier, G. Review of *Outlines of a Critical Theory of Ethics. Revue Philosophique* 33 (1892): 97.

Rorty, Richard. *Consequences of Pragmatism.* Minneapolis: University of Minnesota Press, 1982.

———. *Philosophy and the Mirror of Nature.* Princeton: Princeton University Press, 1979.

Ross, Dorothy. *G. Stanley Hall: The Psychologist as Prophet.* Chicago: University of Chicago Press, 1972.

Royce, Josiah. Review of *Outlines of a Critical Theory of Ethics. International Journal of Ethics* 1 (1891): 503–5.

———. Review of *The Study of Ethics: A Syllabus. International Journal of Ethics* 6 (1895–96), 110–13.

Rucker, Darnell. *The Chicago Pragmatists.* Minneapolis: University of Minnesota Press, 1969.

Russell, Bertrand. *Philosophical Essays.* New York: Simon & Schuster, 1966.

Salter, William M. "A Service of Ethics to Philosophy." *International Journal of Ethics* 1 (1890–91): 114–19.

Scheffler, Israel. *Four Pragmatists: A Critical Introduction to Peirce, James, Mead, and Dewey.* New York: Humanities Press, 1974.

Schiller, F. C. S. "Empiricism and the Absolute." *Mind* N.S. 14 (1905): 348–70.

———. "The New Developments of Mr. Bradley's Philosophy." *Mind* 24 (1915): 345–66.

Schlipp, Paul A., ed. *The Philosophy of John Dewey.* Evanston: Northwestern University Press, 1939.

Schneider, Herbert W. *A History of American Philosophy,* 2d ed. New York: Columbia University Press, 1963.

Sidgwick, Henry. "The Morality of Strife." *International Journal of Ethics* 1 (1890–91): 1–15.

Singer, Marcus G., ed. *American Philosophy.* London: Cambridge University Press, 1988.

Sleeper, Ralph W. *The Necessity of Pragmatism: John Dewey's Conception of Philosophy.* New Haven: Yale University Press, 1986.

Spencer, Herbert. *The Data of Ethics.* New York: D. Appleton, 1879.

Stagner, Ross. *A History of Psychological Theories.* New York: Macmillan, 1988.

Stephen, Leslie. *The Science of Ethics.* London: Smith, Elder, 1882.

Stevenson, Charles L. *Facts and Values.* New Haven: Yale University Press, 1963.

———. Introduction to *The Middle Works: 1899–1924,* by John Dewey, ed. Jo Ann Boydston, vol 5., pp. ix–xxxiv. Carbondale: Southern Illinois University Press, 1978.

Stroh, Guy W. *American Ethical Thought.* Chicago: Nelson-Hall, 1979.

Tawney, G. A. Review of *Ethics. American Journal of Sociology* 14 (1908–9): 687–90.

Thilly, Frank S. Review of *Ethics. Science* N.S. 30 (1909): 89–92.

Tiles, J. E. *Dewey.* London: Routledge, 1988.

Titchener, E. B. "The Postulates of a Structural Psychology." *Philosophical Review* 7 (1898): 449–65.

———. "Structural and Functional Psychology." *Philosophical Review* 8 (1899): 290–99.

Warnock, Mary. *Ethics since 1900,* 2d ed. Oxford: Oxford University Press, 1978.

Welchman, Jennifer. "From Absolute Idealism to Instrumentalism: The Problem of Dewey's Early Philosophy." *Transactions of the Charles S. Peirce Society* 25 (1989): 407–19.

Westbrook, Robert B. *John Dewey and American Democracy.* Ithaca: Cornell University Press, 1991.

White, Morton G. *The Origin of Dewey's Instrumentalism.* New York: Octagon, 1964.

———. *Science and Sentiment in America: Philosophical Thought from Jonathan Edwards to John Dewey.* New York: Oxford University Press, 1972.

———. *Social Thought in America: The Revolt against Formalism.* New York: Viking Press, 1949.

———. "Value and Obligation in Dewey and Lewis." *Philosophical Review* 58 (1949): 321–30.

Wilde, Norman. Review of *Ethics. Journal of Philosophy, Psychology, and Scientific Methods* 5 (1908): 636–39.

Wilson, Daniel J. *Science, Community, and the Transformation of American Philosophy, 1860–1930.* Chicago: University of Chicago Press, 1990.

Wollheim, Richard. *F. H. Bradley.* London: Pelican, 1959.

Woodbridge, Riley I. *American Philosophy and American Thought from Puritanism to Pragmatism and Beyond.* New York: Henry Holt, 1915.

Index